Yosemite—My Heart and Home

Yosemite—

My Heart and Home

a memoir of growth and change

Marian Woessner

2002 · FITHIAN PRESS, SANTA BARBARA, CALIFORNIA

Published by Fithian Press
A division of Daniel and Daniel, Publishers, Inc.
Post Office Box 1525
Santa Barbara, CA 93102
www.danielpublishing.com

LIBRARY OF CONGRESS CATALOGING-IN-PUBLICATION DATA
Woessner, Marian, (date)
  Yosemite, my heart and home : a memoir of growth and change / by Marian
Woessner.
    p. cm.
  ISBN 1-56474-396-9 (pbk. : alk. paper)
1. Yosemite National Park (Calif.)—Social life and customs—20th century.
2. Yosemite National Park (Calif.)—Biography. 3. Wawona (Calif.)—Biography.
4. Woessner, Marian, (date) 5. Woessner, Marian, (date)—Family. 6. Woessner,
Marian, (date)—Friends and associates. 7. Yosemite National Park (Calif.)—
History—20th century. I. Title.
  F868.Y6 W75 2002
  979.4'47—dc21
                        2002002878

To my Charlie,

and to Chuck, Anne,
Rob, and Betsy,
who added so much to our
adventure

I wish to give heartfelt thanks to Jim Snyder, Yosemite National Park Historian, for factual aid and ongoing supportive encouragement; to Linda Eade, Yosemite National Park Research Librarian for unstinting help in procuring background material and for graciously sharing her domain; to Catherine Hayden, faithful proofreader and encouragement personified; to Charlie and Chuck Woessner, Ken Ashley, and Suzanne Munson—all loyal proofreaders, fact checkers, questioners, and moral supports; and to Marilyn Harper, editor, whose professional expertise aided so much in putting it all together. Thank you.

Contents

A section of photographs begins on page 171

Preface

Had a cartoonist, sketchbook in hand, popped into our Wawona home that quiet morning in January of 1997, his drawing would undoubtedly have shown the proverbial light bulb exploding over my head.

We were experiencing the calm that followed the New Year's Day flood. Yosemite National Park, our Park, was still closed to the outside world, and a time to reflect was at hand. Like the floodwaters of the Merced River, a great sense of appreciation for the life I had been given in this glorious Yosemite National Park swept over me— and I felt an urgent need to add *my* history to the volumes already written about the Park. Mine is the story of having lived nearly five decades in a small but vital community, one often spotlighted by the very nature of its being a sacred crown jewel in the National Park System. It is the story of the friendly, self-contained community into which I came in 1951, and of raising our family there. It is the story of the special women I came to know, who were so rarely in the limelight, and of the gradually changed role of women in the Park. It is the story of the forceful tides of change that crept, often swept, in from the outside world, and how the community as a whole reacted and became so changed by them. Millions care about the fate of Yosemite National Park. At its heart is its community. This is the chronicle of Yosemite and the Yosemite community, of their history and their glory as I lived it.

Yosemite—My Heart and Home

1. In the Beginning

Life is what happens to you when you're making other plans.
—Betty Talmadge

In the spring of 1950 I met Charlie. He was a senior dental student at the University of California San Francisco, set for graduation, the State Dental Boards, and a practice of his own. I had graduated from the University of California at Berkeley in medical technology two years earlier, had completed my apprenticeship at Children's Hospital in San Francisco, and was now working at the UCSF Medical Center on a research project for the Division of Dental Medicine, happily adapting to the life of a city girl. April, which brought an end to the winter ski season, found Charlie Woessner no longer rushing off toward Tahoe and his Echo Lake Ski Area job each Friday after class. We met—and were engaged by the end of June.

By the end of summer word came that Charlie had passed the boards. He was now qualified to pursue the opportunity of a lifetime: He was to practice dentistry in Yosemite National Park, under the auspices of Dr. Avery Sturm, director of the medical/dental concession. Charlie and Avery had hit it off well at their first meeting. The position was offered and accepted. Charlie was elated—and I was swept along. We said goodbye to a tentative practice plan in Palo Alto, California, set a January wedding date, and off Charlie went to Yosemite that September.

LEADING THE WAY

Charlie's first Valley home was the Ranger Club, at that time a haven for single employees. Assistant Park Superintendent John Wosky soon chided him, however, saying that he had been assigned the traditional dentist's house, was to start paying rent on it, and had better move in and "start filling it up." Move in Charlie did, with his meager collection of furniture, consisting of a damp, rolled-up carpet,[1] a makeshift sawhorse and plywood table, two chairs, and a bed. On the plus side, this sparsely furnished living room provided an ideal place for local ski buffs to gather for the messy job of sanding and waxing their then-wooden skis. Nic Fiore and the Gallison brothers, Glenn and Bob, were a part of this activity and lifelong friendships were cemented. Gradually more furnishings arrived, thanks to parents' attic emptying and forthcoming wedding presents.

Charlie's earliest Yosemite flood swept through the Valley that November of 1950. We were to be married in the Episcopal Church tradition, with its requirement that he be baptized. He'd arranged with minister Al Glass to drop by the Valley Chapel one afternoon for an informal private baptism, before joining us in the Bay Area for Thanksgiving. By the time the brief ceremony was to begin, floodwaters were rising in the meadow. Al dipped up some of this water to use in the rite. It wasn't quite a baptism-by-submersion but very close. After helping Al move everything that could be moved to higher locations in the chapel, Charlie made a dash in his trusty Ford V8 down Highway 140 and through the Merced canyon. His was one of the last cars to get out of the Park before the road was closed by rising water. Our Yosemite adventures had begun.

FOLLOWING ALONG

Charlie and I were married in Walnut Creek, California, in the small chapel of St. Paul's Church in January 1951, and I came to Yosemite with my two suitcases, my love, and my curiosity. My love affair with Yosemite took root when the magic of spring appeared that year. The river-edge and lake ice began to disappear. The ice cone at the base of upper Yosemite Fall, whose growth we had watched over the winter, began to crack, crumble and melt, to be swept to the waiting pools below. The falls themselves worked up to the window-rattling roar of springtime and sent a far-reaching mist into the air. Pearly-white dogwood blossoms appeared, first in the west end of the Valley, then on the occasional dogwood tree in the neighborhoods. The greening began. Our Chuckie later dubbed this vibrant spring color "fresh green." It was everywhere: the shoots of the sprouting grasses, the newly-opened creek maple and black oak leaves, the just-awakening wild flower shoots, leaves, then buds, and the uncurling fern fronds. As a coastal native Californian, this was my first experience of living with seasons. The rebirth of nature that spring was breathtaking. I was hooked.

I soon learned that the main entities of the Yosemite Valley community were the National Park Service (NPS, "the Park Service") and the Yosemite Park and Curry Company (the YPCC, "the Company"). The next lesson was easy to absorb: the NPS ran the national park, while the YPCC ran the concession that provided lodging, food, merchandise, certain activities, and other conveniences for the Park visitors and residents. Other much smaller concessions included Best's Studio, Degnan's Restaurant and Bakery and the medical/dental group. The U.S. Post Office was a separate government entity. The U.S. Commissioner (Judge) was under the jurisdiction of the U.S. Department of Justice. The resident minister was, at that time, appointed by the National Council of Churches of Christ, and later by its offshoot the Christian Ministry in the National Parks. The Yosemite Elementary School by then was affiliated with the Mariposa School District.

The Yosemite NPS was under the guidance of Superintendent Carl Russell—and his gracious wife, Betty. John Wosky was his Assistant Superintendent; Oscar Sedergren, Chief Ranger; Donald Edward McHenry, Chief of Interpretation; Emil Ernst, Chief Forester; Charlie Hill, Chief Administrative Officer[2]; and Carlton Smith, Chief Engineer. Each had a staff.

The YPCC, in 1948, three years prior to our arrival in the Park, suffered the loss of Dr. Donald Tresidder, husband of Mary Curry

Tresidder. He served as President of Stanford University as well as Chairman of the Board of YPCC. On his death, Mrs. Tresidder took over as YPCC President, with Hilmer Oehlmann continuing as Vice-President. In 1951, Mr. Oehlmann's staff consisted of Harold Ouimet, Personnel Division; George Goldsworthy, Hotel Division; Charley Proctor, Sales Division; and Sterling Cramer, Comptroller, each with his own operational staff.

Drs. Avery Sturm and Robert Murphy held down the Valley medical practice with Clare Phillips as the head nurse. Alfred Glass was our minister, Fred Alexander the postmaster, Gene Ottonello the U.S. Commissioner, and Pauline Shorb the school principal. Virginia Adams, with manager Ernie Johanson, ran Best's Studio, and Frank Donohoe managed Degnan's Restaurant and Bakery for the Degnan/Donohoe family.

THE LAY OF THE LAND

In the early weeks, before the joy of spring burst forth, an occasional pall of loneliness swept over me. True, the Sturms had welcomed us with open arms and a rousing community introduction, and Mary Murphy, whose doctor-husband was Avery's assistant, was very much in the forefront of welcoming faces. But there was so much new: home, husband, area, climate, everyday experiences, acquaintances. I found it quite overwhelming at times. One afternoon I was in the kitchen when the wonderful sound of laughing children poured in from next door. Quickly I was drawn to the dining room window for a sneak-peek out over the yard. There it was: a party in progress. Children were bouncing around and laughing while a couple of mothers good-naturedly organized the games. It was neighbor Anita Holmes' birthday party. I was lonely, twenty-three years old, and wanted to be next door at that party. Never mind that they were all eight-year-olds: they were having fun and I wasn't. I peeked around the edge of the curtain, feeling quite sad and sorry for myself. Although each day was a welcome new page in my introduction to Yosemite Valley, I missed the family and friends I'd left in the Bay Area. The telephone and the U.S. Postal Service were my lifelines in the beginning. The loneliness dissipated as I settled in, got busy, got out and got into things. I had quite a community to figure out and needed to get on with it.

The dentist's house to which we had been assigned lay on the upper loop of the Lost Arrow residential area, the large, main NPS residential area to the west and north of the NPS administration area. It was a "Wosky Brown"[3] National Park Service house, two stories, with slate front steps built smack up against a wonderfully large granite rock with several authentic Indian mortar holes on its flat top. This rock was to be the scene of much kid fun in the coming years. The Valley's north side hiking/horse trail lay just a short distance uphill from the rear of our house. From our back yard, we could look up to Sunnyside Bench, on up to the fabled Lost Arrow, and then over to the highest portion of Upper Yosemite Fall as it came rushing over the edge of the high cliff. From the front yard, we looked across the Valley to Glacier Point, scene of the world-famous firefall. There were houses on just two sides of us—south and west—with government-maintained lawns between. We had several lovely black oaks in our yard, perfect for swings, and there were many more in the open space across the street from us. Fences in or around yards were not permitted, and Fred Quist of the NPS maintenance/grounds division made certain that yards were kept to a very high standard. The neighborhood looked trim and park-like. There was even a little-used, weed-infested tennis court across the loop, later to be replaced by the Mission 66 houses. The Yosemite Elementary School was conveniently just around the corner on the next lower loop.

The Sturm and Murphy homes were a mile to the east on the hillside behind the hospital, as was the nurse's dorm. The YPCC residential areas included the Ahwahnee Meadow/Indian Creek corridor and the hillside across Indian Creek from the hospital. At the three guest lodgings—the Ahwahnee Hotel, the Yosemite Lodge, and Camp Curry—the Company provided on-the-spot housing for many of its employees. A few NPS ranger families lived in the old "Soapsuds," or Army Row, northwest of the lodge. Some YPCC families lived in the area that later became the Lower Yosemite Falls parking lot, a dank, tree-shaded group of houses where we had some fine bridge and poker sessions. Indian Village, further west, was home to the Indian population.

The postal employees lived in apartments above the post office, while Best's Studio maintained three or four apartments behind the Studio. Minister Al Glass lived with his family in the Chris Jorgenson cabin,[4] one of two interesting old houses on the bank of the Merced River north of Sentinel Bridge. The Degnan/Donohoe families lived in Old Village behind their business establishment. Most of the teachers were women who had housing by nature of their husbands' jobs, but the school also maintained two houses for employee needs in the school area.

Gene Ottonello, the part time U.S. Commissioner, and wife Adrienne had an NPS house very close to ours. Their daughters, Sue and Carol, ages three and five, were my first callers after I moved in. My second set was Maynard Moe and Buddy Young, sixish, who came knocking at the door one day to see if "my dad could come out to play." Gradually I got to know some people my own age, but those four have always kept their special spots in my heart.

Superintendent and Mrs. Russell lived in the charming home in the meadow between Yosemite Creek, to the west, and the Merced River, to the south. The history of this house, Residence 1, came to reflect much of the change in the Yosemite Valley community over the next five decades.

Like many other small towns in the country, jobs for women were pretty much the usuals: teacher, nurse, secretary, shop clerk, telephone operator, waitress, and homemaker, with a strong emphasis on the latter among the year-round residents. There were no single-parent families at that time, no working mothers, other than the occasional teacher. It was a typical father/breadwinner-mother/caregiver community, as it would remain for many more years. Socio-economically it was a community in which housing was predicated by employment, either with the NPS or with one of the concessions. Since there were no privately owned homes, retirement or death of the provider meant a move from the Valley. It was basically a community with no senior citizens, as we know them today. I felt this lack after we had children when I often thought how lovely it would be to have a grandmotherly type down the street, one who would eagerly offer to care for a little one on an occasional afternoon.

MY YOSEMITE LIFE BEGINS

I had entered a warm, close community where there was time to nurture close friendships and to explore the beauty around me. I soon jumped into both activities with gusto. There is such a world of difference between the interpretations of "time to grow" and "boredom," and the crux seems to be in one's own approach. Later on, our four grew up with the quickly learned lesson that Mom did not like—or accept—what came to be known as the "b-word." To be bored in a place like Yosemite, to this mom, denoted a great lack of imagination and ingenuity. They did not fail me: The message stuck. As I read over the input from each of them, requested when I began this saga, I was amazed—sometimes aghast—at the antics, projects, and "entertainments" they took on in their quest to grow. In the case of the more dangerous, I'm just thankful for their survival.

Many of the activities were self- or group-created. There was no television but there was the movie pavilion across the river in Old Village. Features were shown two or three nights a week, always with two showings. Later on, when that scarce commodity *babysitter* was rarely available, we found it very possible for one of us to go to the early showing, then scoot home across the Valley to let the other get to the second run. There was always someone to sit with, as many others were doing the same thing. It was a true date when parents went to the movies together. We also enjoyed some excellent amateur theatricals put on in the summertime by the Yosemite Centennial Theater group.

There were public swimming pools at both Camp Curry (renamed Curry Village in the sixties) and Yosemite Lodge, but we much preferred the river—and soon had our own secret beaches. In the off-seasons eating out was done at the old lodge cafeteria, with only very special occasions taking us to the Ahwahnee. In the summer, the favorite places to go were the charming Camp Curry dining room, with its friendly, attractive group of college student waiters and waitresses, and the Mountain House at Glacier Point. Later we would discover the Wawona Hotel. Our best man, Stanford student Dave McKean, worked in the Curry dining room the first two summers we were in the Park. During his college summers, my brother Rob held a variety of jobs at Curry—including the calling of the firefall—and later in Wawona. We loved having some of the "old ties" come our way. For an unlimited supply of orange juice and a home-cooked dinner, Rob would even baby-sit occasionally.

The Valley was a self-contained community. In those early days, people didn't drive down the river road to Merced or go over the hill to Fresno at the drop of a hat. Our own Old Village Store, with Bill Brown the congenial manager and Jack Ring his able assistant, was the meeting place for housewives. Andy Koller and Charlie Bond held forth over the butcher counter: no prepackaging here. Bill kept a stack of comic books in an out-of-the-way corner to keep the kids occupied while the mothers shopped. Tacked on to the west end of the store was John Schweifler's barbershop, which sported a small barber pole identifying his trade. There was also a shoemaker's facility somewhere in all this. At the other end of the store was the "Greasy Spoon" with Nat Bredeman in charge. The movie pavilion was just a few yards to the east, approached over a wooden plank walkway covering some often very damp ground. Although removed before we came on the scene, the Sentinel Hotel had stood in the area between the pavilion and Sentinel Bridge.

Across the street from the Old Village Store was Degnan's, the bakery/restaurant and the family home. On the small spur road behind Degnan's stood the jail (later moved to the Pioneer Village), the Masonic Hall and, of course, the Village Chapel, still on this spot these many years later. For the care and feeding of cars, there were three gas stations, at Camp Curry, in the Tecoya area,[5] and near the Yosemite Lodge, and garages at both Curry and the Tecoya area, which were able to handle most repairs on the simpler cars of those days. The Valley even sported a taxi service.

Medical and dental concerns were dealt with at Lewis Memorial Hospital, as were pharmaceutical needs. The post office gave space at the west end of the building to the Western Union office, with Kenny English at the teletype. The Yosemite Credit Union, our resident bank, Gene Ottonello in charge, was located in the rear of the old Lost Arrow Studio building, with community social activities occupying the front. Our laundry and cleaning could be taken to the YPCC facility housed at the Yosemite Lodge in what is now the dressing/locker room area of the swimming pool.

As well as being the site of our special occasion social life, the Ahwahnee Hotel provided a small barbershop on the main floor, a beauty salon on the mezzanine, a high quality gift shop, and a small Lanz clothing store. The YPCC dispensed "privilege cards" to Valley residents, including its employee families and those of the NPS and other concessioners. This card entitled one to a ten percent discount on purchases at stores and gift shops, a thirty percent reduction on meals at the lodge cafeteria, and the right to purchase a discounted thirty-ride ski lift ticket at Badger Pass. With these helpful discounts, most of our groceries were purchased locally. Thanks to the then well-equipped ski shop at Badger, and the welcome discount, ski paraphernalia and clothing could also be purchased at home. Grocery store purchases were made with scrip, $18 buying a $20 scrip book. Privilege cards were also the magic ticket to the ice rink, swimming pools, and other events that required some local identification. It became a rite of passage when the children reached the age of twelve and were issued their own privilege cards.

During the summer tourist season, there were active, smaller grocery stores at both Camp Curry and Camp 16 (later Housekeeping Camp). There was a seasonal post office branch at Curry and the "Kiddee Kamp" where a tot could, for a price, be parked for an hour or so.

About the only family need lacking in the community for full-containment was a high school. The Yosemite Elementary School graduated its students out into the world after grade eight. Local families handled the high school situation in different ways. Some youngsters rode the bus daily over the forty-five mile route to Mariposa County High School, some went away to various boarding schools, and others boarded with friends or relations in school-accessible areas. The choice involved difficult decisions.

This, then, was the friendly community into which I stepped that January of 1951. Its names and places would become etched into our early Valley history. It was a community we were anxious to know, in the Park we were eager to explore. Little did we know, as our Yosemite life took shape, that we would spend the next five decades on that journey of acquaintance and exploration.

2. Two Practices

In youth we learn; in age we understand.
                              —Marie Ebner-Eschenback

OUR PRACTICE

As I was learning my way around this unique community, Charlie was establishing a dental practice that would remain his calling for the next thirty-seven years. Who would have then envisioned that his whole practicing career would be in Yosemite, or that his mother would finally have to give up hope of our ever "returning to civilization."

Charlie became the fourth resident Park dentist since the inception of the dental program in the late twenties. The first of these was Raleigh Davies, a man of great charm, who practiced in Yosemite for seventeen years before moving his practice to San Mateo when the U.S. Navy took over the Ahwahnee Hotel and Lewis Memorial Hospital in 1942. For the remainder of the war years these facilities were used in a rest and rehabilitation program for battle-weary navy personnel.

After WWII, with the navy's exit, Dr. Roy Starr practiced dentistry in the Park for three years, followed by Jack Wilhelm's two-year stint before he headed off to a full-time practice in Merced. I wondered about the so-few years these men had spent in the Park and was told that the wives had not been particularly happy with the Yosemite lifestyle. Was this a warning—or a challenge? I chose it to be the latter.

Lewis Memorial Hospital was situated on the north side of the Valley in close proximity to the area later referred to as the Yosemite Village. The majority of the building's space was devoted to medical purposes: examining rooms, offices, patient rooms, the surgery, and a small lab facility/dispensary. From the front, one entered directly into a large, shared waiting room. The medical reception area was to the right; the dental office to the left. This dental office was a one-room everything. The dental unit, a remnant of the navy's occupancy, stood at one end of the office, a desk and reception area at the other. Often, as I patiently awaited my turn to see Dr. Sturm, I would have to listen to strangers bemoaning their upcoming dental ordeal—as people are prone to do. I just buried my nose further into a magazine! When, in 1953, Charlie's office moved into the newly constructed area at the west end of the hospital building, he was overjoyed by the addition of more facilities, space, and privacy. I was overjoyed to no longer share the medical waiting room with dental patients.

Throughout his Park career, Charlie was a combination family/emergency dentist, the now-rare breed of general dentist. He developed a practice encompassing all phases of dentistry, even simple orthodontics. When our children needed uncomplicated orthodontic work, he took a short post-graduate course at his alma mater in San Francisco. If knowledge of a developing procedure was needed, he found a short course to cover the subject. Only the most unusual cases of periodontics and oral surgery were referred to Merced or Fresno. He did much of his own lab work. The remainder was sent out on the mail truck to Merced or on to Fresno. Since he could not send the fragile dental impressions, he poured all of his own models and cast most of his own inlays.

Holding down a practice many miles from equipment repair services—with costly mileage charges—required Charlie to master basic repair skills and a working knowledge of plumbing, wiring, and carpentry. These skills proved boons to home maintenance as well.

A fine working relationship with the medical team evolved.

Charlie helped them with jaw fractures on occasion and in turn borrowed their expertise when it was needed. A prime example of the latter occurred one winter afternoon in the late fifties. On returning from lunch, Charlie found a ski clothes-clad man lying unconscious on the waiting room floor, blood oozing from his mouth. Avery Sturm was hastily summoned from his office down the hall. Together he and Charlie revived the man and moved him into the dental chair. The story slowly unfolded that the man had taken a hard fall while skiing, which slammed the pointed end of his ski pole into his mouth and shattered his upper acrylic denture. Splinters had been driven into the flesh. It took the two doctors quite a while to pick the razor-sharp pieces of acrylic out of the skier's soft and hard palate. Charlie has always contended that the accident easily could have been fatal had the denture not been in place to soften the blow. And we've always wondered about that friend who simply dropped the man off in the waiting room to await the dentist's return from lunch.

For the first couple of years after our arrival, Charlie was his own receptionist. The phone rang, the dental procedure stopped, instruments were put down, said telephone was answered, the needed appointment was made, hands were washed—and back to the chair! This was tedious and time consuming. Efficiency soon demanded that he hire someone to answer phones, make appointments, and eventually assist chairside. His first employees were hired for the summers only and were usually local high school seniors. Pat Phillips[1], daughter of head nurse Clare and Frank Phillips, was the first assistant in the office. She was an adept worker, quick learner, and fortunately returned for two additional summers while pursuing a nursing program at UCSF.

Charlie operated under an employee contract with Avery Sturm for the first two years. Time and mutual agreement proved the practicability of the dental practice having its own contract with the National Park Service—and in 1953 Charlie became an official "concessioner-of-one." This honor brought with it a forty-page annual report to be compiled. A one-man concession and a multimillion-dollar concession each required the same annual report. Tense times prevailed at our house when it was due. In the early sixties, when the NPS placed the dental concession in a more reasonable special use permit category, much paper work—and mental anguish—went out of our lives.

When the dental office expanded into the new hospital wing in 1953, a degree of separateness was established. The new office had its own entrance, waiting room, and two operatories. One operatory had a magnificent view of Glacier Point. The other looked out on a lovely dogwood tree planted by Pat Sturm in earlier years. This too was a sight for all seasons, from the pearly white blossoms of spring to the vibrant red leaves of fall. Completing the dental suite were a small private office, a reception area, a compact lab, and a closet. This collection of rooms was to be a second home to Charlie for thirty-three years.

Home and office circumscribed much of our lives. Our house was a mere fifteen-minute walk from the office so foot power was the mode of transportation on good days. Some days Charlie strode home on the back trail below the cliffs and I would meet him, child on back. A few years later the bicycle took precedence. In the wintertime, Charlie drove to the office, getting home well after dark. His average workday was 8:00 A.M. to 6:30 P.M., last patient seated at 4:30. Then came the lab work and write-ups. Our usual dinner hour was close to 7:00—much to the consternation of our offspring, whose early-eating buddies were often banging on the door with "come out and play" urgings just as we were sitting down.

There were so many wonderful small-town touches in our community then. An important one was the telephone with a real voice that said, "number please" when one lifted the receiver. Our favorite operator, Donna Donielson, kept a discreet track of comings and goings in the community. If I needed to call Charlie at the office to see when he might be home, she very often would cut in to say, "He just rounded the corner, will be right home." Her telephone office was in the southwest corner of the government administration building—a perfect viewing spot. If one were trying to reach Dr. Sturm, she might offer, "He's not home, said he'd be at the Warrens' tonight." She was the original answering service. Avery always checked out with her when he was on call.

In the summer of 1956, our good friend Clark Burton arrived to be an aide. He was a third-year dental student at UCSF, having gone back to dental school after working several years as a chemical engineer for Shell Oil. The organization wanted an engineer in the east, and Clark had no desire to move east. He liked what he had seen of Charlie's lifestyle—living exactly where he wanted to live and being his own boss—so back to school Clark went. The Burtons, with their two little girls, lived in our rustic cabin in Wawona that summer while Clark assisted Charlie in the dental office.

Clark started a trend, and for several summers thereafter a third-year dental student assisted in the office. It was mutually beneficial in that it provided good, knowledgeable help for Charlie and practical on-the-job training for the student. After Clark's stint, the students were usually single or left a working wife in the Bay Area. Charlie worked through the YPCC to get tent accommodations for his employee in Camp 6. We thoroughly enjoyed having the students in and out during those summers. If they liked little kids, whom we were collecting by then, they often became a part of the family.

In the late fifties, Marlene Meeker became Charlie's first full-time, already-trained assistant. We were more than sorry to see her leave when her husband Joe's session with the newly established NPS Training Center[2] was over. Soon her sister, Gayle Sleznick, came to take Marlene's place in the office when husband Jim was assigned to the Yosemite. After 1957, Charlie no longer worked solo.

Jeannette Daugherty came into the office and into our lives in 1964—and remains a special entity in each. She stayed on with Dale Soria, Charlie's replacement upon retirement, and soon her tenure in the dental office will be longer than our thirty-seven years. All of our offspring worked summers in their father's office before moving on to the YPCC and it was always patient Jeannette who trained them, put up with them, and sometimes served as buffer.

The children did yard work (the boys), developed X-rays,

cleaned instruments, poured the plaster animal models given to small patients, occasionally answered the phone, were post office runners, learned to help with simple chair-side procedures and—remembers Chuck—when there was a no-show, filled in as patient! They were only expected to put in a half day. The afternoons—and part of their earnings—were theirs. The rest of the earnings went into the college fund. If our children learned only one lasting thing from that venture, it was to be on time for work. Their dad was a fair, but demanding, employer. That training proved invaluable.

A family practice in those days meant doing something for every need that came through the door. As Charlie's practice developed, and people learned we were here to stay, he began to draw patients from the surrounding communities as well as the Valley and El Portal. There was at the time no dentist in either Groveland or Oakhurst and only a sometimes dentist in Mariposa. Each summer saw the return of a growing, loyal-patient contingent of NPS seasonals. They and their families became a long-lasting component of the practice.

Summers brought an influx of tourists, with all the problems that so often develop when one comes to a higher elevation and is away from home. These were the years prior to the onset of preventive dentistry, the years before dental insurance programs made it possible for people to have yearly check-ups to catch problems at a much earlier, less traumatic stage. Fluoride programs for children were also just beginning. People were much more inclined to put off dental treatment until the situation became painful. This resulted in much work done on an emergency basis, without appointment. A typical day, aside from scheduled appointments, might involve a denture repair or two, as well as the treatment of toothaches by palliative measures or even extraction. It could include the attempted repair of a broken tooth that had resulted from a fall, a dive into too-shallow water, or the occasional bicycle or auto accident. Charlie also regularly re-cemented jackets, crowns, and bridges and made adjustments on dentures and orthodontic wires. All ages came to the Park, and all ages came to the Park dentist.

It is a fact of life that if something hurts that hurt is going to be greatly magnified as night falls and sleep fails to come. We had many night calls in the summertime. Since the arrival of our first baby, I had mastered the art of sleeping with one ear out, and so I was a natural for the job of answering the night telephone rings. But I had to cultivate the ability to grope my way to the hall phone and then make sense of the conversation. Only once did I blow it, but that was years later and not a professional call. Chuck called very late one night to say "Happy Mother's Day," waking me from that first hard sleep. Upon answering, I crumpled to the hall floor in a dead faint. On regaining consciousness a few seconds later, rather than sensibly acknowledging his voice, I just quietly hung-up the receiver. Of course he called back immediately to see if I was still alive.

Charlie was quite literally on call at all times—if he could be reached. We were not required to stay home by the telephone twenty-four hours a day, but if he was available, he was "on." The corollary to this was that family time together came to mean time out of range of a telephone on weekends and, later, in the evenings. Perhaps this is why our family developed such a love of beach supper picnics and Sunday trips to the high country. We appreciated the early ministers who accepted with grace our philosophy of communing with God by a beautiful alpine lake. Later, when the kids became active Sunday school goers, our wings were somewhat clipped, but only slightly.

My task evolved into—be it a beach supper, a day's outing or an extended vacation trip—having the car packed and the kids "at the ready." When Charlie finished with his last patient and write-up, we were off and away before the phone could ring.

How Charlie rued the lack of a back door to his office! One early afternoon's Park exodus required a quick detour by the office to pick up forgotten funds. As we waited in the car for Dad's return a tourist-in-pain ducked into the waiting room. The children and I waited forty-five hot minutes in the loaded car. Charlie learned to shelter our family times. On another occasion, as he passed the newly entered, would-be patient in the waiting room, he explained that he was the janitor and no, Dr. Woessner was not in.

One of the very few times we considered leaving the Park came in the mid-sixties when we spotted an intriguing placement ad in a dental journal. It was for a position in American Samoa. The adventure blood was set pulsating! We actually sent an application. Back came a swift, albeit terse, reply: "Oh my, no, not for you. We have no housing for a family of six, and you would not find our schools satisfactory for your children." Back to the daily routine we went— but a new adventure had been fun to contemplate. As it turned out, we went on to enjoy many more new adventures right in our own Park.

THE OTHER PRACTICE

Avery Sturm, M.D., conducted another all-encompassing practice at the other end of Lewis Memorial Hospital. In 1935, Avery interrupted a surgical residency at Southern Pacific General Hospital in San Francisco to answer a call to Yosemite to help with the summer emergency surgery.[3] The upshot was that Ave and Pat came for a summer—and stayed for thirty-six years (with a brief time away during the war).

Ave and Pat first lived in an apartment at one end of the nurses' quarters, then became the first occupants of the house in which we would later live our thirty-seven years in the Valley. From there they moved to another newly built house, this one behind the hospital. Upon returning to the Park after the war, they moved into yet another, larger hospital-area house. There they would remain until retirement in 1970.

Medicine arrived in the Valley with the army in the twenties, and a medical facility was established in the lodge/army row area. In 1928, at the behest of Superintendent W. E. Lewis, construction began on a hospital for the Park. The hospital opened in 1930, with Dr. Madison Dewey as medical director. Upon Lewis's death soon thereafter, the hospital was named Lewis Memorial Hospital in his honor.

Until he left in 1942 to serve in the Army Air Corps, Avery Sturm worked under Madison Dewey. When Ave came home, in 1946, he became the sole medical concessioner with a five-year contract from the NPS to provide medical, dental, and hospital service to the community. For the first two years he was the sole medicine dispenser as doctors were hard to find. He subcontracted for a dentist, Dr. Starr, hired a staff of nurses, cooks, and cleaners, and assumed the responsibility of running a twelve-bed hospital. As soon as he was able, Ave hired a second doctor, Dr. Baysinger. By the time we came, Bob Murphy was Ave's assistant. When Bob went off to the Korean War, Dana Howe replaced him. Terry Tennant was the next to come and go. This type of medical practice did not appeal to everyone.

In the spring of 1953, Bob and Carolynn Riechers came to look over both the practice and the Yosemite community. This time Pat and Ave asked Charlie and me to be in on the interview. Rather than have us join them at their house, Pat and Ave had daughter Mary Lou lead the Riechers over to our house on her bicycle. Through the government center, past the NPS stables and on to our Lost Arrow residential area she pedaled, the Riechers' station wagon close behind. She deposited them at our house, made the introductions and went on her way. The Riechers immediately appealed to Charlie and me. We eagerly entered into our sale's pitch for the job and for our community. We were successful and Bob and Carolynn soon moved into a house behind the hospital with their four children, Bobby, Peggy, Sal and Billy. They all jumped into Yosemite life, later added Susie to the family, and stayed in the Park five years. In the late fifties, they reluctantly left for a practice in Medford, Oregon, taking a big chunk of Yosemite with them in their hearts. They have returned to the Valley and to the high country many times, and have remained our lifelong friends.[4]

Avery came to feel the need of a third doctor in the summer as the number of patients continued to grow. He began hiring a medical student, recent graduate, or between-jobs doctor for the busy season. The gender complication hadn't appeared on the scene yet, so the summer helper could be lodged in the "pest house," a separate cabin by the hospital's rear entrance, and share the facilities in the basement of the hospital with the janitor, also male. The pest house doubled as the morgue at other times of the year. Where a body waited for pick-up in the summer months was anyone's guess.

Keeping a full-time assistant doctor for more than a year or two proved difficult. As a salaried employee, the assistant's remuneration was not great. The needs of a growing family and the lure of having one's own practice were often reasons for moving on. Between the Riechers' leave-taking in 1958 and Roger Hendrickson's return from the Army in 1963, there were numerous comings and goings.

One year, Ave hired two full-time assistants. One of the families was housed across the circle from us in an older Park Service house. After their settling-in, I went over to visit. I was stopped in my tracks at the doorway by the stunning sight of a newly painted black living room with gold stars affixed to the ceiling! It was quite a transformation of those sacrosanct white NPS walls. That lady had spirit but, unfortunately, both the stars and the family suffered short duration in the Valley.

Roger Hendrickson came as summer doctor in 1960, went off to Germany to do a stint as an army physician, and then returned in 1963 to become Avery's first partner. This arrangement proved more workable for all concerned. A partner has equity and standing in a practice. The change of status brought a greater degree of permanence to the position. The Hendricksons stayed for fifteen years, and Jim and Jody Wurgler joined the partnership in the late sixties.

Just as Charlie's practice proved to be, so too was Avery's: treat whatever walked through the door. To the locals, he was the dispenser of general medicine. He was our internist, obstetrician, pediatrician, surgeon (both general and orthopedic), sometimes-counselor, and always friend. He delivered our four babies, removed several sets of tonsils, casted a limb or two, sewed up bunches of things, treated a myriad of colds and sore throats, and kept us all ticking. We loved him. He was that very special breed of no-nonsense country doctor, one ready to go to a patient or accident wherever and whenever the need arose.

We had been in the Park only a few months when I had my first glimpse of just how far this small, vital man would go. A radio mes-

sage had come with the urgent news that a couple had lost their foot-
ing on wet granite and slid into the Tuolumne River as it made its
tumbling descent over Waterwheel Falls. They were still alive and out
of the water but in extreme need of a doctor. Avery, with NPS help
along, took the ambulance as far as Tuolumne Meadows then
mounted a horse for the twelve-mile ride down to Waterwheel. He
was relieved to find the man shaken but okay. His wife, on the other
hand, was quite banged up. She was stabilized enough to be loaded
onto a Park Service litter for the twelve-mile carryout on foot to the
Meadows, where the ambulance waited. Then came the long drive
to the Valley hospital, where she eventually recovered. In his own
retelling, shaded by his great love of the high country, Avery would
add how much he had enjoyed the beauty of that day's ride down the
spectacular Tuolumne Canyon.

A more serious call from the backcountry came in the early
fifties. A young boy camped at Benson Lake in the northern section
of the Park had suffered a head injury. He was thirty-four miles from
the nearest roadhead. In rode Avery with the rangers. They found the
boy unconscious, unresponsive, but alive. Stabilization procedures
were finally successful, and trail crew and other personnel were enlisted for the long litter carryout. Then word was radioed in that the
Hiller (helicopter) Company in Palo Alto had a new higher-altitude
model they wanted to try in a rescue attempt. The necessary paren-
tal and Park Service permissions were quickly granted and soon the
helicopter successfully reached the scene. The patient was gently
loaded aboard. As the machine lifted skyward, Avery and the others
mounted their horses for the long ride out to civilization. The overall
result was a triumphant mission and eventual patient recovery.

Thus began the career of the helicopter in the Park. It became
a vital tool in future search and rescue operations, fire fighting, and
medical evacuation. The sight of a helicopter in the skies over the
Park came to mean that something was amiss somewhere. Once,
while in the Bay Area with one of our youngsters, a helicopter flew
overhead and he commented, "I wonder who's lost, Mom."

Until the NPS brought in a sanitarian in the mid-fifties, Avery served as Park health officer. This job entailed yearly inspection of all tourist facility kitchens in the Valley and in Wawona and all facilities serving NPS employees. There were some much-enjoyed saddle trips into the backcountry to check the trail camps each summer. Avery was at home astride a good horse and came to know the backcountry of Yosemite like the back of his hand. When the official NPS Sanitarian took over, Ave and his family continued to mount their own traditional summer saddle trips into the beloved high country.

In the tourist branch of his practice, Avery and staff had to deal with the inevitable falls that brought broken bones, cuts, and abrasions. There was the rare snakebite to treat, fishhook to dig out, even bear scratches to handle. Ski season brought its own set of problems to the hospital: breaks, sprains, and the like. It was said that the coming of skiing to Yosemite in the post-depression years of the mid-thirties brought a much-needed source of income to the hospital. The going rate was $100 per broken leg. I was in Lewis Memorial Hospital having my first-born in December 1951 when the first ski injury of the season came in. Out of patient hearing the cheers went up, ski season was underway and the nurses' lives would become far more interesting. In those early years 6.6% of each 1,000 skiers sustained some manner of injury. By the seventies, the figures lessened to 2.2% per 1,000. Better boot support and safety bindings decreased injuries. The types of injuries changed as boots grew taller, from predominantly ankle injuries to leg injuries to present-day knee injuries. After the fifties, skiers hobbling around in good old plaster casts were not as prevalent.

THE SUPPORT SYSTEM

In December of 1951, when Chuckie was about to join the family, I was introduced to the waiting room, the nurses, and the caring, slightly gruff, professional side of Ave Sturm. Perhaps one remembers best the people and events surrounding the birth of a first child. Avery gathered a fine support system for his hospital and it spilled over into our dental office and our lives. We found a capable, affable group of nurses—and they became our friends. Among them were Helen Fisher, with her flaming red hair; bustly Lois Cummings, who could make a patient feel better just by entering the room, but could also get the laziest of the ski-injured up and moving when the time came to give it a try; unflappable, kind, head nurse Clare Phillips; and dear, grandmotherly Amy Bowman, who held my hand tightly as Chuckie came into the world. To be surrounded by a staff of caring friends, in a hospital radiating concerned efficiency, to be allowed to be awake for the birthing and that first cry—it was a wonderful introduction to motherhood.

Lewis Memorial Hospital did a good obstetrics business in the fifties and sixties, with twenty to thirty cases per year. Except for the occasional tourist birthing, these were Park and El Portal babies. The infrequent premature baby was snuggled into a heated crib in the nursery, as there were no incubators. The crib was placed in a surrounding box in which electric lights would maintain the desired temperature. Chuckie shared the nursery with two other hardy, boy-babies. All were far from being preemies!

Several other nurse friends came into our lives in the fifties: Mary Beth Smith Dart, Jean Bradburn Galli, Jane Gillingham Vella, and Opal Roessler, my hand-holder when Anne arrived in 1953. Avery was often accused of running a matrimonial agency for nurses, as well as a hospital. Over the years there were many marriages between nurses and Park rangers, ski instructors, or YPCC employees, always preceded by a bridal shower in Pat Sturm's home. The staff was a wonderfully wide, extended family that suffered, occasionally, the same ruffled feelings and tempers of any family. Confronting personnel bickerings was not Ave's forte. He avoided it like the plague, but sometimes had to step in.

Two other special additions to the staff in those early years, two who came to stay awhile, were Ingrid "Inky" Petersen and Al Evans. Al arrived to fill the janitor spot in the mid-fifties and stayed until the Sturm's retirement in 1970, retiring with them to their ranch in Midpines and his own small caretaker's house. Al was jack-of-all-trades around Lewis Memorial Hospital, for both the medical and the dental offices. He was the janitor, the fixer, and the mail and laundry go-fer. He kept the facility running. When he was a little guy, Chuckie always called him "typer-Al," so he must have come upon Al doing even some deskwork on occasion. Al was devoted to Lewis Memorial Hospital—and to the Sturm family.

Inky arrived on the scene from Solvang, a Danish community north of Santa Barbara, in December of 1959. She came to fill the scrub (surgical nurse) position and stayed on into the seventies, adding X-ray technician and routine lab work to her nursing duties. She was an avid golfer in her off-duty hours. In 1967, Inky married NPS mechanic Bob Ringrose and became an even more active community contributor. On Bob's retirement, they moved to their present home in Mariposa. She still remains active in the Mariposa County Health Department, where she gives painless flu shots, and pursues her golf and bicycling hobbies. Inky is my remembered "Betsy's-delivery" nurse.

As with the dental practice, there were occasionally major surgeries and other medical perplexities that needed to be referred to the outside world, where the "specialist" mind-set had begun to take hold. When our first tonsillectomy loomed on the horizon, my parents were aghast that we were not going to Fresno to a proper ENT man for the operation. Avery operated and merited our faith. On the occasions when Ave felt the expertise of a specialist was called for, out we were sent.

When Avery retired to his beloved ranch in Midpines at the end of 1970, he left the practice in the capable hands of Roger Hendrickson and Jim Wurgler. Ave's had been the best of years for an independent, all-encompassing medical practice in the Park. So many changes came to the practice in the decade after his retirement. We were often thankful that Avery and Pat were spared this confrontation.

It had been a perfect symbiosis between the two practices centered in Lewis Memorial Hospital for those two decades. The medical and dental personnel had great respect for, and cooperation with, one another. Theirs was a working team and the Yosemite community reaped the rewards. Just as a healthy community oiled the wheels of a functioning Park, so the expertise emanating from Lewis Memorial Hospital kept that community healthy.

3. The Roots Sink In:
Our Life in the Early Fifties

*The trouble with life is that you're halfway through it before
you realize it's a "do-it-yourself" thing.*
                                                    —*Author Unknown*
                              P. S. We found out earlier. —MPW

Looking back on the fifties, after the traumas of the sixties and seventies, the international uncertainties of the eighties, and the hi-tech
freneticism of the nineties, one finds the epitome of kinder, gentler
days. It was the best of times to be starting a family, and Yosemite
proved the best of settings. Charlie and I brought our individual ingenuity and creativity to our shared life in the Valley, and these traits
were invaluable along the way. In the fifties, Yosemite was an active
community of active people. It encouraged do-it-yourself living and
create-it-yourself fun. Satisfaction and enjoyment of life were in direct proportion to the amount of energy and imagination expended.

GETTING A LIFE

There were many activities out there waiting to be discovered and
joined, both actively and vicariously. The first year, of course, I took
up skiing. It did not come easily for me, as I have never been a natural in any sport, but I gave my all to skiing over the years. The sport
became, and remains, a major element in our family life, and we'll
explore its influence in "Ski Trails."

Vicarious enjoyment in our first year came from the Yosemite Centennial Theater productions. Over the years there was usually some form of theater in the Valley, but the offerings by the Centennialites that first summer were by far the most professional. It was true summer theater with excellent presentations. The setting was outdoors, an open area behind the Ahwahnee bungalows with an improvised stage and seating. Peter Tewksbury was the director, with Anne B. Davis and Richard Deacon starring. Locals and summer employees filled out the cast. Later, when Anne and Richard each had made a name in television, we loved to say we knew them when, and we always felt a special kinship with Alice on *The Brady Bunch*.

Finding our place in the community proved a bit daunting at first. We didn't belong to anyone—although Pat and Avery took us under their wing. We were not National Park Service, we were not Yosemite Park and Curry Company. Eventually this gave us the chance to draw friends from the entire community without politics becoming involved. Over the years the freedom to have all kinds of friends, no matter who their bosses, or whom they bossed, more than made up for those earlier alone times.

We had moved into a friendly neighborhood of people ready to welcome someone who really wanted to be there. Ours was a Park Service residential area, Ruth and Art Gallison on one side, Art and Dot Holmes on the other, and Will and Margaret Ellis just down the street. I didn't think of these people as being that much older, and yet the Gallisons retired three years after our arrival, the Ellises in six. Margaret Ellis was a super cook, and it was a treat to be invited to dinner in their home. Home entertaining was the name of the game in those days. Coming from a non-gourmet household, I quickly had to hone a few skills. *The Joy of Cooking* became my daily read. My first dinner guests were, of course, Pat and Ave Sturm. Feeling brave I tried my first black-bottom pie. Imagine my chagrin when I served perfect wedges of custard that left my slaved-over crust in the pie plate!

We soon got acquainted with Jane and Leroy "Rusty" Rust and

their pals Bill and Verne Ellis, the Martischangs, and the Sharps. Rusty and Bill worked in the post office. Marti Martischang and Bob Sharp were buck rangers stationed at the Arch Rock entrance station. This group introduced us to the Curry Dances that first summer. My memory can still bring forth the hall-like room, where Sid Hoff's band held forth at one end, where Fred and Earl Pierson alternated as bouncer at the door, and I hear the strains of good dance music. Fun while it lasted, but in just a couple of years this Curry building was rehabilitated into lodging units for additional guests.

We also formed strong ties with Jan and Art Robinson, Sue and Karl Munson, Ash and Ethel Ashley, and, after they arrived in 1953, Dr. Bob and Carolyn Riechers. These were the friendships that would last a lifetime. With the Bevingtons, Overtons, Rusty and Jane, and Pat Hansen, we formed the infamous "young men's" poker club and "young mothers'" bridge club. There were other bridge and poker clubs in the Valley, hence the designation "young," but this appellation lasted long into our middle age. We met on alternate Tuesday nights in members' homes. The men offered beer and pretzel fare, until John Curry joined and added a gourmet touch. The ladies concocted a fancy dessert with all the trimmings. Bridge cloths and napkins, the fanciest of dishes were brought out for the occasion: it was quite a production. The dads covered the home front and it was our night out. On many occasions there was far more talk than bridge playing. I cringe to remember the filled cigarette containers and assorted ashtrays on each bridge table, and at dinner parties as well.

Once a year the clubs joined forces for a Ski-dinner outing. The dinners were held in the Indian Room at the Ahwahnee two or three nights a week during ski season. In our early years this was to be the best bargain in the world: $2.75 for an elegant Indian Room buffet and an evening of live dance music. This was a great way to entertain—or to be entertained—and we took full advantage of the bounty. A group would be invited to someone's home for drinks, and then we'd move to the Ahwahnee for a no-host evening of good fun. The buffet was a work of art—in presentation and in cuisine. The most memorable offerings were generous bowls of lobster or crab salad, standing prime rib roast (with Fred Pierson wielding the carving knife, chef's hat atilt), and crème-filled swan pastries. The music was festive, the dancing lively, tables emptying as the beat began. Who could ever forget Dory and George Goldsworthy jitterbugging around the dance floor, a quick break, and there they were leading the hokey-pokey. Bob Seach's bunny-hop usually followed. In later years, a limbo contest was added to the evening's agenda, Jake Metherell being a natural for that. And no Ski-dinner was complete without Skimiester Nic Fiore's rendition of *Alouette* and the mice-in-the-rice-in-the-Village Store song.

The ski instructors were complimented for their dinners—and they were expected to be there. Many of the hotel and lodge guests turned up for the apres-ski festivities, and they liked to mingle with their instructor-of-the-day. We did too: they were becoming our friends. We were much interested each winter to see which seasonal instructors returned and what the new romances might be. There were always two or three intriguing foreign accents. A great rapport developed between ski school director Luggi Foeger's (later Nic Fiore's) instructors and the community.

PARENTING BEGINS

In late December 1951, we went to the traditional "Christmas Music by Candlelight" at the chapel. The wall-sconce and altar candles glowed warmly, casting reflections on the faces of the singers, and the fragrance of the pine wreaths wafted through the lovely chapel. There was snow on the ground and crispness in the air. It was Christmas in Yosemite, our first, and quite lovely. We came home in a peaceful, mellow mood—which, for me, lasted one hour. I had asked Avery a few days earlier how I would know when I went into labor. He got the wry, little half-grin on his face and said, "Marian, it's just like when you hear your first rattlesnake, you'll know." Well, it was, and I did, and off to the hospital we went. Amidst the love and moral support shown me by my new friends at Lewis Memorial Hospital, Charles Addison Woessner, Jr. was born at noon the next day. He timed his appearance well, allowing his dad, in his office down the hall, to finish some bridgework for Harold Ouimet. He seemed to already know "we don't bother Dad when he's working."

On my "maternity leave" I was introduced to Jack Curran, a patient in the room across the hall. Jack had worked in the Park since 1916 in various capacities at the Ahwahnee. He had striking white hair and a tanned handsome face, showing, perhaps, some of the ravages of more than just time. Together we watched as groups of Christmas-bedecked guests came and went from the Sturm's annual Open House. With this new friend I vicariously enjoyed my first Sturm Christmas gala. So typical of Park encounters over the years was this unique-to-Yosemite being who crossed my path and brought his own history to share. Jack Curran retired from the Ahwahnee in 1953 and died within the year.

Somewhere along the line I had picked up the idea that when one has a baby the outside world goes on hold. "Good-bye, world, I'll get back into you when my baby's older." I was a wreck-of-nerves for the first couple of weeks. Mom, Dad, and brother Rob came to be with us for Christmas, and Mom blessedly stayed on to help. With her encouragement, great moral support from Pat Sturm, and an understanding husband and doctor, we were soon back on track and Chuckie began to flourish. Then I realized it wasn't "good-bye world" at all, it was "hello from the three of us."

There was a heavy snowfall that winter of 1952. We have pictures of me standing in our shoveled walkway, baby bundle in arms, in a good two and a half feet of snow—at our 4000-foot elevation. By March I was back on skis. The slopes were not groomed in those days, just packed by those skiing them. This often left ridges and troughs to be got through or around. One afternoon I didn't make it through the unpacked snow and took a good tumble. I couldn't even fill my sitzmark—the depression left in the snow when one fell—before I was loaded onto the toboggan for a ride down the slope. It was into the First Aid room for a check, then into the station wagon and off to Lewis Memorial Hospital. The upshot was a chipped bone in my right ankle and an Avery walking cast for six weeks. (A year later I came to appreciate how much easier it was to take care of a three-month old baby, albeit a heavy one, when sporting a cast, than it would have been to cope with a toddler.) New friends rallied round during this misadventure. There came Ash to the door, in from Wawona, with a much-welcomed Ethel casserole and pie. Neighbors turned up with offers of all kinds of help. Soon the cast was off and life was in gear again.

In November of 1952 two things became happily apparent to me. First, I was again pregnant, and second, I could therefore put off my ski lessons for another year. It was a given, even when I was a more adept skier and pregnant with Betsy, that I did not ski when I was pregnant. So I settled in for a snug winter, with only a break at Christmas to join Charlie's parents in Oakland for the holiday, and a stop along the way to see my Danville family. That Christmas proved to be the only one we would celebrate away from the Valley until thirty-six years later when we moved to Wawona.

By late May, I was tired of waiting for the baby's overdue appearance. My mother was already in place to cover Chuckie, so Avery and I decided to stir things along. In those days that meant taking the castor oil and orange juice "sandwich." Didn't work—and ruined my taste for orange juice for years. A shot of something, I've forgotten what, did finally work, and our Anne Trevor arrived at half after midnight on May 26. Girl babies had been at a premium recently in the Park so I felt quite blessed and spent the remainder of that night dreaming girl stuff and carrying her along in my mind to a glorious wedding (pre-feminist thinking, to be sure). I felt quite smug, because I now wouldn't need the magic of "the pink dress." There had been a run of boy babies in Valley families, the first-born boy followed by a second. The legend was that if this magic dress were worn to the hospital for a third delivery, a girl child would appear. In the first two years we were in the Park it worked for the Murphys and for the Munsons. But the pink dress did not need to stop at our house.

While still in the hospital, I received a congratulatory telegram from my mother's English cousin Trevor Bent. In it he said, "Three great events: the coronation of Elizabeth II, Hillary's conquest of Everest—and the advent of Anne Trevor!" In light of Anne's later Everest attempt, was this prophetic?

During this stay in the hospital, my new friends were the Walquists. He, the dam-keeper at Lake Eleanor, had persevered against some tricky odds in bringing his ailing wife out to civilization on the primitive road from the lake, over the ridge, down to the dam at Hetch-Hetchy, then in to the hospital. She was settled in the adjoining room and we became well acquainted during my week's stay. Yes, we stayed a week in those days and I enjoyed every being-taken-care-of moment of it.

Mom's help was a godsend. A new baby, a seventeen-month-old toddler, and the onset of Charlie's busy summer season kept us hopping. We didn't get very far afield that summer, just enjoying our favorite Valley beaches as often as we could get to them. We had a great, strong baby buggy, the top of which could be lifted off the wheels and used as a bassinet. This was Anne's nest when we went to the beach. She adapted well to sleeping out at an early age. We would tuck her off under a tree to sleep while we swam with Chuckie. One afternoon I came out of the river just in time to hear one passing older lady lament to another, "Oh look at that poor little baby—way out here in the wilderness."

The biggest adjustment in handling babies came with the second child. Time and attention had to be divided. As with all mothers, I had to learn the art of tuning in to more than one wavelength at a time, a useful skill that has never left me. When Robert David came along two years later it was a breeze. It didn't hurt, too, that he was an easy baby who napped behind a log anywhere. He was an adapter from the outset.

GOD'S TERRITORY

There were several enduring organizations in the Valley. By the time we arrived, the church was well established. Alfred Glass came in 1945 to be the resident Protestant minister. During our earliest years, a Catholic priest came up from Mariposa to conduct weekly services.

Our little chapel was built in the late 1870s with contributions (twenty-five cents for one certificate) from Sunday school children all over the country.[1] In 1901 it was moved to its present location in the middle of a lovely meadow, surrounded by breathtaking views. Several times in our history, the chapel was a victim of floods. In 1966, the whole structure was painstakingly raised five feet, but the water still has swirled in on occasion.

The Yosemite Community Church was established in its own entity in 1955 with a membership of one hundred and fifteen persons. Although still under the umbrella of the Christian Ministry in the National Parks, a local board was set up to work with Al Glass, the guiding force behind the movement, to take over some of the growing responsibilities. By the time he retired from the Valley in the late fifties, Al had baptized three of our youngsters—and had me serving on the church board.

Many varied activities evolved under the auspices of the church: study groups, choral groups, and youth activities, which included the Sunday school, Vacation Bible School and, at one point, an active Junior High Youth Group. The various resident ministers had leeway to use their expertise to develop church programs. Don Baldwin, in the sixties, even took a church service to the skiers, holding a short service each Sunday near the top of the main lift at Badger Pass. Postmaster/ski coach Rusty Rust saw to it that the ski team got to church that winter—and on time.

IN SUPPORT OF THE COMMUNITY

One of the most active groups in the Park was the Yosemite Lions Club. When the Centennialites moved on to stardom, the Lions Club filled the gap with its "Mighty Mountain Art Players," under the direction of Sterling Cramer, later aided by Peggy Baldwin. Talent was solicited from the Lions membership and productions presented during the off-season (not summer). They were first staged in the Camp Curry dining room, later in the new school auditorium. Dana Morgenson, a true thespian at heart, always had a starring role. If the production was a melodrama, as it often was, Dana was the leering villain, just asking to be hissed and booed. Charlie was in several of the plays, perhaps a throwback to his great-grandfather Mart Taylor, who had drama ties to the early days of Nevada City, or to his uncle Ross Himes, who was a vaudeville song and dance man in the twenties and thirties. Also trodding the boards in the yearly productions were Wes Conner, Norm Herkenham, Harry During, Doug Hubbard, Roland Johnson and others as they came and went from the Valley. One year saw an excellent production of *Harvey*, another a bang-up *Mr. Roberts*. With all the parts played by men in those early days, it could be hilarious.

The Lions Club also generously supported youth activities in the community. It contributed money and manpower to the Scouts, to the ski and football teams, and to the annual school track meet. It sponsored the yearly Red Cross Blood Drive, bringing the mobile unit from Fresno, and later the eye-mobile.

In the fall the Lions' Giant Bargain Sale was as much a successful social event as it was a successful fundraiser. It was a great place to catch the local gossip while browsing through clothing racks, either to buy or to see if one's own contributions had sold. In addition to these racks of clothes, there were collections of books, records, and toys, as well as ski and camping equipment. A locked display case contained jewelry baubles and small appliances. With the help of wives, the Lions Club members ran the sale and retained 10% for their treasury. One year we even sold a car—the 10% from *that* sale helped swell the coffers considerably.

Each year before the summer crowds arrived, but after the days lengthened, the Lions threw their famous Mosquito Festival—a barbecue and fixings—at Rocky Point beach. This event was purely in the pursuit of fun, and it was—if one remembered to bring the mosquito repellent!

The Community Council was made up of a diverse group of appointed community members. Individuals and local businesses were solicited yearly to raise funds for community activities, various charities, and emergency needs. One of the supported activities was the Charles Goff Thompson Scholarship (later the Yosemite Scholarship). A nine-member Yosemite Scholarship Commission selected the scholarship recipient. The first scholarship was awarded in 1935 and, except for two years during WWII, a scholarship has been given annually. I was elected to the board in 1972, and served until we left the Park in 1998. I consider it to be one of the most worthwhile endeavors with which I became involved. It gave a number of local youngsters the support, be it moral or financial, needed to get on to college. When the Community Council died of apathy in the late eighties, the Yosemite Scholarship Commission took on its own biennial solicitation campaign.

Two other groups active in the Valley when we arrived were the Conversation Club and the Yosemite Women's Group. The former was a men's dinner/discussion gathering. The meetings were monthly, with dinner at one of the local restaurants, then adjournment to Hil Oehlmann's YPCC office for the discussion. In later years both the dinner and meeting took place in one of the Ahwahnee Hotel private dining rooms. Each member took his turn preparing and delivering a paper to the group. The goal was to produce some lively conversation and to keep everyone awake. Three subjects were taboo: politics, religion, and job. Sadly, in the eighties, with the advent in the Park of Monday night football and perhaps creeping apathy, interest began to fade. The Conversation Club had been a mixing pot of the diverse facets of the local government and business interests, and its later demise was a loss to community cohesiveness.

The Women's Group I found in 1951 met monthly, usually for a no-hostess luncheon at the Ahwahnee, followed by a program. This program might be a musical presentation, cooking demonstration, wreath-making session, a discussion on make-up secrets, a fashion show, or a travelogue. It was open to all the women in the Park, and there were no dues. Every so often the group would sponsor a benefit dance, luau, or other gala to raise funds to cover program costs. A sign of the times in the seventies was a program, "Investing in the Stock Market"—for women! In the eighties the group took on the yearly Christmas craft and soup-lunch project. This was a great fundraiser, a lot of fun, and a win/win situation for the community. The monthly meetings became a thing of the past by the eighties. Too many former participants entered the work force.

The school Parent Group has always been an active organization, sponsoring track meets, the early football games, ski-day, and much more. Money raisers to cover otherwise unfunded school needs were the ongoing project. After the new school was built and dedicated in February of 1956, the multi-purpose room was the scene of many lively meetings and activities. Later on the Parent Group was at the forefront of the drive for funds to create the school's library—and a fine one it became.

With the above-and-beyond support of the YPCC in early years, some great times were afforded the community. During this era the Ahwahnee Hotel closed at the end of October and reopened the week before Christmas. For several years, the Parent Group sponsored a Halloween Costume fundraiser in the Ahwahnee's Indian Room the night it closed. There was live music, a costume contest (first prize being an overnight at the hotel), and a scrumptious midnight supper. The supper was supposedly to use up the leftovers in the pantry and refrigerators, but it actually quite resembled the fine Ski-dinner fare. It was a "donation" from the YPCC. A nominal fee for the evening was charged, and all of the proceeds went into the Parent Group's school activities fund.

OUT INTO THE PARK

In these early years, Park rangers made snow survey trips into the backcountry on skis. Thanks to our ranger friend Ken Ashley, Charlie was invited along on a couple of these trips as a working member of the party. This was in the days of skins and waxing—no fishscale bases here. There were lots of pre-trip discussions about the proper waxes and when to use klister and where the climbing-skins had been stored.[2]

The route began at Mirror Lake. In normal years, the first of the infamous Tenaya zigzags could be handled on foot, with skis left strapped on the packs. One particularly heavy snow year, however, they had to put the skis on right at Mirror Lake, then slog the whole of the steep, five-mile zigzag trail to the Snow Creek cabin. It was exhausting work. Beyond this cabin, the route took them by the Snow Flat cabin, the May Lake trailhead, down the grade to skirt Tenaya Lake, and on to the Tuolumne ranger cabin. The cabins were stocked in the summertime, so they could always count on a hot dinner.

There were survey stations along the route and several at the Meadows and on up Rafferty Creek. At each station, the depth of the snow and the water content were measured. The statistics from these reports were used to predict spring and summer run-off and to adjust reservoir controls.

Charlie loved these trips and brought home glowing tales of Tuolumne Meadow's winter beauty. He also brought home amusing stories of the group's interactions. There was one member who had to be the first to reach each destination. Charlie questioned whether he ever stopped to take in the glorious scenery. After 1955, mechanized over-snow vehicles were used for transportation, the process was speeded up—and much of the fun was gone. In the seventies, the Tuolumne winter resident-ranger program was put into effect and these rangers took over the survey program. This was later one of daughter Anne and husband Chas's duties in their five winters at the meadows.

A second survey operation with which Charlie became involved was the yearly glacier surveys. These were done under the auspices of the Park Naturalist Division, Doug Hubbard in charge. Once again, because he was interested, willing to work and available, Charlie was invited to join several of the surveys into the Tuolumne/Lyell area to measure the growth or recession of the various glaciers. These trips took place in the fall, before the snow fell. He had some great high country trips as a result, with fellow mountain lovers Doug, Dana Morgenson, and Glenn Gallison, as well as Norm Herkenham, Wayne Bryant and Nic Fiore (in his summer role).

THE RIVER RISES

In late December of 1955, we went through my first Yosemite flood. The pattern was one that we would see several times during our years in the Valley and later in the flood of 1997. There was abundant snow at the higher elevations, less at the lower. The rains in the Valley had been heavy at times earlier in the week. By December 22, they were torrential, and warmer. In the high country, too, the snow had turned to rain. Eventually the rain-saturated snow above could hold no more water. The community rallied forces (NPS, concessioners, and individuals), the gauging stations were monitored, the alert sounded. In the Old Village Store Jack Ring, the manager, organized his crew of employees and volunteers to move the merchandise to the just-completed shell of the new Yosemite Lodge across the Valley. A makeshift store was set up and he later could pride himself on having missed not a day of merchandising.

Charlie and I were at the Sturms that evening for their traditional staff Christmas party when the call came for help. The water was rising at the Superintendent's house over in the meadow. The room abruptly emptied of men. Strong backs were needed to lift the Preston's furniture to the second story. The water from the river slowly invaded the lower floor, reaching a depth of thirty-one inches. Some days later the Prestons reported no personal damage but noted in a letter to Horace Albright, "It was not the kind of Christmas any of us in Yosemite had planned for!"[3]

At the chapel, more forces were gathered to raise or remove furnishings, books, and other paraphernalia. This prevented serious damage. With the clean-up help of church members and others, church services were back on schedule by January 8.

Much the same type of action was going on at the lodge. When the river finally receded, and damage could be assessed, there was not one cabin-with-bath or WOB (without bath) undamaged. The first floor of Pine cottage, closest to thundering Yosemite Creek, had been awash. The YPCC housekeeping department pitched in immediately, and with amazing effort had things pulled together and the lodge soon back in the hotel business. Over in the Old Village the movie pavilion had shifted a few feet on its foundations. The washed-out bridge leading to the pavilion was simply rebuilt a bit further west to match the pavilion's new location, and the movies, too, were back in business.

Because of the Park closure, most of the scheduled Bracebridge guests could not get to the Ahwahnee Hotel. That year Santa, too, considerately changed his destination, meeting the Yosemite children in the warmth and elegance of the Ahwahnee's Great Lounge rather than in his usual Curry Village gathering place. A simpler but lovely Bracebridge Dinner was offered to locals and to guests who had arrived in the Valley before the flood. Our chapel choir, with the accompaniment of Fran Hubbard, church organist, joined the two Bracebridge singers who had made it to the Valley to present some joyous, impromptu music.[4]

A great sense of pride and camaraderie prevailed in the Valley that holiday season. Everyone had pitched in and our Park was soon up and running, open and welcoming. Spirits lifted with the coming of the New Year. As for Charlie and me, we had been part of the operation and were establishing our place in the life of the Park.

4. Special Ladies

One is not born a woman, one becomes one.
—Simone de Beauvoir

Feminism, per se, had not yet surfaced in the Park when I arrived in the early fifties. Typically much had been made of the various outstanding men of the community. But as I settled into our Valley life I began to meet and know women who gained my lasting admiration in their own right. The story of the Yosemite community as it was then is in many ways the story of these ladies. And ladies they were, in the 1950's sense of the word.

THE DOCTOR'S WIFE

At the top of my list stands Pat Sturm. From the time she welcomed me to the Park as a bride, until her death of cancer in 1986, Pat was my mentor and my beloved friend. I knew her for more years than I knew my own mother—and when my mother died quite unexpectedly in 1962 Pat was there to pick up the pieces. She was the older sister I never had, and became my role model in so many ways. Pat loved Yosemite, with its close-knit community, and it was she who provided much of the glue that held the community together.

Pat and Avery Sturm came to Yosemite in 1935, married just eight months. Pat had graduated from nursing school on the same day Avery received his M.D. degree, both at the University of California San Francisco Medical Center. They came for just the summer, but soon returned—and stayed for over thirty-six years. From the small apartment in the nurses' quarters, to the house that would later be ours, to a newly constructed house behind the hospital, they progressed. The latter's floor plan had a very narrow stairway to the second floor, with a 90-degree turn in the middle of the ascent. When the construction timing was right, Avery had a double bed mattress hoisted through the upstairs window before the window was framed-in. That mattress remained upstairs for many a year and through many an occupancy: no one could get it down the stairwell!

During the WWII years, Ave was a flight surgeon with the Army Air Corps. Pat often amused us with stories of doggedly following him around the country, small daughters Ginnie Ann and Mary Lou in tow. Some glass apple-shaped bowls always went with her, and wherever those dishes were unpacked became home.

Pat and Ave returned to Yosemite from war duty in 1945. Avery became the Medical Director, the family settled into the bigger house behind the hospital—and son Danny arrived. Wildflowers proliferated in Pat's hillside garden and hospitality exuded from her home. She loved to entertain, and Ave must have happily gone along with the idea. Once or twice a week dinner gatherings were held, guests often arriving about the time that "Daddy" came up the hill from the hospital. Pat had the gift of mixing all kinds and ages of people. She seemed to entertain effortlessly; everyone was welcomed with warmth. Whether it was a cozy dinner in their home, a Christmas party for hundreds, a cocktail gathering before moving on to a ski dinner at the hotel, a grape stomp at their Mariposa ranch, or a picnic at Tamarack Creek or Peregoy Meadow, it always meant a good time—invitations were coveted.

In those fifties and sixties days, the hospital and the patients were Pat's domain as well as Avery's. For them, the medical practice was in many ways a joint endeavor. One mended the body. The other mended the spirit. As the age of medical privacy came more to the forefront, this joint venture was a hard act for some of the other doctors' wives to follow. These ladies were often not made privy to who was even *in* the hospital. But Pat and Ave together respected patient privacy. The dual attention was a wonderful combination to those on the receiving end. When our Chuckie was just a new baby Pat gave me such moral support: she was not about to let me drop out of the world. It was she who lined up our first babysitter, a lovely older woman, so that Charlie and I could join Pat and Ave for dinner on our first anniversary.

Pat was first and foremost a wife and mother, a homemaker par excellence, and she was a person to whom anyone could pour out a heart. This entailed making time to be of help to others and in this she gave unstintingly. Not without heartbreak in her own life, including the loss of a brother to WW II, Pat's faith and guts brought her through the lot. She seldom spoke of her own concerns, but the fact that on rare occasions she let me into that corner of her being was a closeness I cherished.

Throughout the sixties, many of Ave's off-hours were spent at their ranch near Mariposa. A wonderfully cozy, old white house on the property became "the little house." Pat furnished this with white wicker and a hodgepodge of old-timey artifacts, and it was delightful. They put in a small vineyard on the side hill and each year would host a wine stomp in October—a real wine stomp, no mechanical grape crushers used here! Into the halved wine kegs were piled the grapes, stems and all, and into the kegs climbed the stompers, bare feet and all. Johnny Murphy was always there to play the accordion, his Ima in tow. When the containers-full were stomped to Ave's standard of perfection, Pat laid out a gala repast on trestle tables nearby. Ave later added the necessary sugar, bottled the grape juice, sealed the bottles, and tucked them away to age. One year the germ-conscious side of Avery's nature came forth. He decided we should all walk our bare feet through a disinfectant bath before hopping into the vats. The proper fermentation did not take place in that batch of juice. And the idea was never mentioned again.

As retirement approached, Pat and Ave had a new home built at the ranch on a knoll beyond the little house. They used the floor plan from their Valley home, omitting the second story and making minor changes in the first floor plan. For the first few years after their move, it was most disconcerting to leave the warm hospitality of the familiar Sturm home, then step outside to the realization that one was *not* in Yosemite—and the long canyon drive still lay ahead.

Avery retired at the end of 1970, and we had the great pleasure of working on the retirement party held early in January. It was a smash! The lovely Ahwahnee dining room was filled to capacity with friends who came from near and far. A champagne party in the Great Lounge preceded dinner, then into the festive dining room we went. A myriad of speeches and toasts ensued. Never have I felt, before or since, such an effusion of warmth, admiration and love for a couple as was felt that night. So typical of Avery's getting on with the important things of life: the alerted community's gift to him that evening was the wherewithal to acquire the bull needed to become a full-fledged rancher. The purchase was soon made. The animal was christened "Tenaya."

Off moved Pat and Ave to their ranch on Whitlock Road in Mariposa. They became integral parts of the Mariposa community but for many years remained a part of numerous Yosemite activities—they just had a little farther to drive. They continued the tradition they had established, and each year, on our January anniversary, invited us to join them at the Ahwahnee for lunch. If it was a workday, Charlie unfortunately didn't get to join in on the martini toast. And for many years Pat continued to come to the Christmas Coffee at our house, usually bearing a Sturm-made yule log.

After the Sturm's retirement, I had sixteen more years of Pat's loving friendship, sharing with her the joys, frustrations, and sorrows of mutual friends and of our own loved ones. Pat's answer to feeling down-in-the-dumps was to get out and whitewash the fence that surrounded a glorious display of daffodils each year. It is so fitting that springtime daffodils continue to burst forth on the Sturm cemetery plot behind St. Joseph's Church in Mariposa. How much this dear lady enriched my life. I knew exactly what Avery felt when he said, the year following her death, "Life isn't fun anymore." She had made it fun for so many people.

THE INNKEEPER'S DAUGHTER

Charlie and I arrived in Yosemite about three years after the 1948 death of Dr. Donald Tresidder. At the time of his death, he was not only the President of The Yosemite Park and Curry Company Board of Directors, but also the President of Stanford University. On his death, Mary Curry Tresidder became the president of YPCC. Although she divided her time between Yosemite, her home on the Stanford campus, and extensive travel, "Mrs. T," as she was affectionately known, was very much a presence in the Park when I came on the scene. She was a striking, gray-haired woman with a soft-spoken, almost retiring manner. She was often the one woman among many men at board meetings and business gatherings. I've often wondered how easy this could have been for her. I suspect she was glad to have her great friend, Hilmer Oehlmann, Vice-President and General Manager of the Yosemite Park and Curry Company, at her side.

Mary Curry Tresidder's history is much the history of the Curry Camping Company, which merged with the Yosemite National Park Company in 1925 to form the Yosemite Park and Curry Company.[1] She first came to Yosemite in 1899 when Camp Curry was established by her parents David and Jenny Curry. The family summered in the Park, and spent the rest of the year in Palo Alto.

Mary Curry and Donald Tresidder both graduated from Stanford. They were married in the Valley's LeConte Memorial Lodge in 1920. Dr. Tresidder received his medical degree in 1927 but never practiced medicine, becoming instead assistant manager of YPCC and later president—and then the President of Stanford University. The Tresidders had no children, but the offspring of Mary's brother Foster Curry (David, John, and Jeanette) all worked for the Company at some point.[2] John Curry and his wife Mickey were our Tenaya Lake sailing buddies for many years.

Mrs. T's great interests were the flora and fauna of the Park and she became quite an authority. Her book *The Trees of Yosemite, A Popular Account* was published in 1932 and has been reprinted and revised several times over the years.[3] Longtime friend Della Hoss illustrated the book. Mrs. T spent much time in the Yosemite backcountry collecting information about the myriad of wildflowers along the trails. One of the legacies left when she died in 1970 was the financial means enabling Dana Morgenson to write *Yosemite Wildflower Trail*, a slim, white, hardback volume that I have carried with me for miles in the backcountry. My dog-eared, loved copy shows evidence of the pressing of an occasional bloom to bring home for further identification. But I am still searching for the elusive Steer's Head mentioned therein!

Mary Tresidder loved her trips in the backcountry and surely must have explored most of the quieter parts of the high country wilderness. She had good pals with whom she rode the trails, Lucy Butler and Mrs. Parmer Fuller among them. By the time we were aware of her travels, Bob Barnett was handling the YPCC stables and arranging her trips. I have a feeling that no possible comfort was spared.

It was not uncommon to run across Mrs. T.'s party in the backcountry. One September, Charlie and Ken Ashley were out in the wilderness, hiking along in—or out of—their usual comfortable attire, when they heard sounds of an approaching party of some size. They still laugh about how quickly they were able to pull themselves into presentable order, and there she was: Mrs. T.

Another legacy of Mary Tresidder, one appreciated by many a hiker in later years, was her personal financing of the construction of the Sunrise High Sierra Camp in 1961. It was built on a particularly favorite site of hers and was a great addition to the High Sierra Loop. I've enjoyed some very special stays at this camp where the sunsets can be incredible. Judging from the name of the camp, the sunrises must be pretty spectacular too, but I never seemed to be up and out in time to see one.

A favorite avocation of Mrs. Tresidder's was skiing, both downhill and cross-country. She and Don Tresidder skied in Europe often in the twenties and brought home to Yosemite many ideas and hopes for skiing in the Park. The couple was the force that brought enthusiasm, instructors, and, eventually, Badger Pass to Yosemite.

Mary Tresidder was the first woman to climb Mt. Hoffmann on

skis. Hoffmann rises above May Lake and this Snow Flat/May Lake area was one explored by the Tresidders and their friends on skis. Mrs. T skied well into the 1960s. Certain strong skiers were often asked to keep an eye on her on the ski slopes those last few years. They were to be available to "appear" and graciously help her to an upright stance should the need arise. (Now, when skiing, I often hope for just such a helpful presence nearby!) Often, Mrs. T would ski a few runs, have lunch in her quiet, private room next to the Snowflake Room on the second floor of the Badger Ski Lodge, and then cross the street to the Badger ranger cabin for a lively game of scrabble with ranger-wife Kathy Betts.

In March of 1964, Kathy Betts, Pat Brown (also a ranger-wife), Anne Hendrickson, and I had the great pleasure of being invited to join Mrs. T, Mrs. Butler, and Mrs. Fuller on a cross-country trip into Ostrander Lake. What a treat for this mother of four, ages four to thirteen! Charlie helped plan the logistics at home, and off I went for several days. Ski instructor Marcel Burrel came along, and Dean Conway drove the Sno-kat. On the way in, the older ladies rode and we younger women ski-jored behind the machine, riding only when it got rough. Ski-joring resembles water skiing on snow, with the towrope attached to the Sno-kat rather than to a speedboat. Following the custom of the times, we "youngers" religiously called each of these ladies by her Mrs. name, whereas we were first names to them. Age differences were respected.

We had a chance to test our cross-country skiing techniques around the lake and on a climb up Horse Ridge on the far shore. I was very much a beginner but had a lot of fun and Marcel proved an able instructor. The evenings of conversation were delightful, and the trip a great success. The four of us felt very honored to be included.

Well do I remember awakening to heavily falling snow on our leave-taking day and commenting that I was feeling quite far from home and very much a mother again. Weeks later, when Anne Hendrickson announced that she was expecting their first baby, she told me that she too had been feeling *very much* like a mother that morning!

In 1963, Mary Tresidder became chairman of the Yosemite Park and Curry Company Board. Hil Oehlmann took over the presidency of YPCC and Stuart Cross became vice president. Her last few years were divided between the home on the Stanford campus to which the university had given her life-tenancy and her suite at the top of the Ahwahnee. We saw her less frequently as the decade progressed. Mary Curry Tresidder died in October of 1970, about the time the Yosemite Park and Curry Company began to undergo many changes. Mrs. T was a great lady and a true caretaker of Yosemite. It was a pleasure to have known and admired her.

THE ARTIST'S DAUGHTER

Virginia Best, like Mary Curry, spent many of her early growing-up years in Yosemite.[4] Her father, Harry Best, was an artist, with his own Best's Studio in the Valley. Virginia and Ansel Adams met in the Park when he came with friends to hike and photograph. He was a pianist, the Bests had one of the few pianos in the Valley in those early days, and so they met. After an extended courtship, Virginia and Ansel were married in her father's studio in 1928. They lived most of the year in San Francisco, but when Harry Best died in 1936, Virginia and children, Mike and Anne, moved to the Valley. Virginia took over the management of Best's Studio while Ansel divided his time between the Valley and the Bay Area.

Since this is about women and their capabilities, I find it impressive that in 1931, Virginia was elected to the Board of the Sierra Club—a first for women! She retired in 1933 to devote time to a growing family, ran again two years later but was defeated by Ansel, for whom she had campaigned.

As youngsters, Mike and Anne attended the local grammar school. By the time we came upon the scene, they were away at boarding schools. Ansel was in and out, but Virginia was very much in residence. We would know Ansel was "in" when we glimpsed his trademark vehicle: a white station wagon with a wide platform on the roof for his photographic work. By the mid-sixties Virginia began to spend more of her time in their Carmel home, but in our fifties and early sixties she was often seen in Best's Studio and around and about the community. To say that Virginia was "old shoe" is, from my standpoint, a great compliment. She was married to an accomplished artist, one used to being in the limelight. Virginia graciously kept the common touch and was much appreciated for so doing. Although I did not know her intimately, I admired her and enjoyed her company immensely.

Charlie served a year on the Grand Jury panel with Virginia, and the association was one he, too, enjoyed. My connections involved the Yosemite Scholarship Commission and the cocktail gatherings at their home when Ansel was in residence presenting his workshops. For years after she left the Park, Virginia came back to vote, Yosemite being her voting residence in the years she managed Best's Studio. I served on the election board and always looked forward to her coming. She would cast her ballot, and then we would have a few minutes to catch up on local and individual news. She never lost her interest in the community and people of Yosemite.

In 1971 Bill Turnage was hired to manage the Studio and things began to change. All avenues to increase profits were explored. The name Best's Studio was changed to The Ansel Adams Gallery, something that was difficult for many locals to accept as the Studio had been in the Best family for decades. Soon Virginia turned the Gallery's general managership over to son Mike Adams's wife Jeanne and retired to Carmel. We saw her less frequently—and she was missed.

Our daughters, Anne and Betsy, both worked in the Studio/Gallery in the summers of their sixteenth and seventeenth years. Anne worked there in 1969 and 1970 for Virginia and then manager Ernie Johansen, Betsy in 1977 and 1978 when Jeanne Adams was president and Bill Scoble manager. Much of the warm, family atmosphere remained when Anne worked there. Virginia was often in and out, and there was a party for the Studio staff in the Adams's home each summer. The feeling was such that, when Anne applied for admission to the University of California at Santa Cruz, she had no qualms about asking Ansel to write a letter of recommendation for her.

Ansel died in 1984. By the next summer, Mt. Ansel Adams had become the official name of a peak lying near the headwaters of the Merced River. The name had been chosen in the thirties by a group of friends as they camped in the peak's shadow, but place names in the Sierra can be officially given only after death. Fifty years later, the name became official. It was dedicated at a very fine gathering near Parson's Lodge in Tuolumne Meadows. Among the many dignitaries, friends and acquaintances in attendance were Secretary of the Interior Walter Hodel, Senator Alan Cranston, Robert Redford, and author Wallace Stegner. I considered meeting the latter to be the high point of my day, in addition to again seeing Virginia Adams. I think that gala occasion was the last time I saw her. Virginia Best Adams lived many more years in her gracious Carmel Highlands home, dying peacefully on January 29, 2000 at the age of ninety-six.

In retrospect, I feel Mary Curry Tresidder and Virginia Best Adams had much in common. Each spent a great deal of her youth in the Park, with a family or father who had established a successful, ongoing business. Each stayed involved in that business venture for most of a lifetime, while adding commitment to family and other necessary obligations along the way. Each met her mate in Yosemite and brought him into the business. Each was married to an extremely dominant personality, hence "lived in the shadow," so to speak. Each in her own quiet, capable manner gained wide respect and admiration in her own right. Great ladies, both.

GREETER, PAR EXCELLENCE

Kit Whitman was elegance incarnate! She was holding forth as social director at the Ahwahnee when we arrived in the Valley. She personified the epitome of all that could be hoped for in a hotel greeter, and then some. She was a tall, handsome, gray-haired woman, straight-of-back with a regal bearing. That she had a distinct British accent and exuded an air of competence only added to her aura.

Kit's past was as fascinating as her "presence." She was born in

Victoria, B.C., educated in England, and married for fourteen years to a monied, much-traveled Englishman.[5] That marriage ended in a divorce obtained in Nevada. Kit spent the then-required year's pre-divorce residency on a working cattle ranch near Pyramid Lake, north of Reno, Nevada. Here, she came to feel very much at home around horses. From Nevada, she moved to Carmel to make her own living for the first time. At the Carmel Valley Ranch School, she became housemother/music teacher/riding companion to the sixteen eastern boys in attendance. In 1934 she married Colden Whitman, an old friend, gave up the school duties, and played golf while he dealt in real estate. Sometime later they bought property in the Coarsegold/Raymond area, and Colden became a rancher and homebuilder, with Kit's help. In 1948, Kit took the job of hostess at the Ahwahnee, and the days-off commute to the ranch began.

Kit drew on her background of international travel and association with money—and with people in general—to carve her niche at the Ahwahnee. She, in her trim jeans and plaid shirt to hostess the morning breakfast ride, in a fresh shirtwaist dress to greet guests at lunch, perhaps in a frilly white blouse and broomstick skirt for the pouring of afternoon tea, followed by an elegant outfit for the evening activities, must have been quite an act for style-conscious lady guests to follow. Under this mantle of elegance, however, lay an extremely capable, hard-working, friendly, problem-solving being. Kit literally led two lives and merged them gracefully. Each day off, she made the commute from the quiet elegance of the Ahwahnee Hotel to the coziness of her tiny cottage-room-studio hideaway at the ranch.

Kit told a wonderful story of occasionally picking up a local character, Gabby, by the side of the road near Coarsegold. She would give him a ride to his roadside shack, a "home" made from of a collection of this and that and surrounded by piles of more collected this and that. She did admit that the car needed a certain amount of airing-out after she had deposited him at his digs, but they'd certainly had a lovely chat! Our kids had always been fascinated by Gabby, each hoping to be the one to spot that flowing white beard amongst all the junk as we whizzed by his near-Coarsegold corner. Now, to imagine him tooling along the road with the elegant Kit added much to the aura of each. When Kit Whitman retired in 1963 to return to the ranch to care for her ailing Colden, the Ahwahnee lost an institution, and the house lights dimmed a bit.

THE MUSIC LADY

Nancy Loncaric arrived in Yosemite with husband John in 1937. John was in the hotel division of the YPCC, summer manager at Yosemite Lodge that first year. He stayed on during the war years to keep the lodge, Camp Curry, and Housekeeping Camp operating under the difficult conditions imposed by rationing and the like. Nancy became known as the "music lady," giving piano lessons to interested community youngsters, teaching music appreciation in the local school, starting a rhythm band, and offering the many things that went along with musical enrichment. She made her own niche in a place quite far removed from the musical world and artistic stimulation she loved.

My own recollections of Nancy are of an elegant, exotic-looking woman with strong angular facial features and with great style and flare in her dress. She had her city wardrobe and her Yosemite wardrobe. I loved the designation. Nancy bespoke The City to me in my early Yosemite years—oh my, did she—at a time when I was still missing my own City! Not many years after our entry into the Park, Nancy began spending longer periods of time in Southern California enjoying the much easier access to her beloved *things musical.* What a fascinating woman she was. I have always regretted that our children were not old enough for piano lessons from the music lady and that she didn't linger in Yosemite longer.

John Loncaric retired in 1966, then joined Nancy in the Laguna Hills home overlooking the blue Pacific. With his retirement, our Santa Claus needed a successor. And his were very difficult, black, sooty boots to fill. John died many years ago, but Nancy continued to live in her much loved home until her death in July of 1997. We continued to exchange Christmas cards and notes until the end. Her cards always had a musical theme, and I expect she is somewhere up there now, accompanying those harpists.

QUIET STRENGTH

We thoroughly enjoyed Esther Morgenson and her husband, Dana. With her quiet, unassuming manner, Esther seemed the epitome of the behind-the-scenes wife. Married to yet another "Yosemite institution," she was actually a capable botanist and artist in her own right. We were to know the Morgensons very well, as Charlie and Dana did a lot of backcountry exploring together, and the four of us shared a great love of the Park, Tuolumne Meadows and its environs, the red-rock country of the American southwest and much, much more.

The Morgensons came to the Park in 1944, he as office manager in the Accounting Department of the YPCC, and later manager of the Reservation Office. Upon semi-retirement Dana fell into the best career of all, that of leading the popular summer camera walks for the Company, both in the Valley and at Tuolumne. In this later-year capacity, he captured the imagination of thousands of hearts and minds.

Esther loved to paint. She would often be off across the meadow painting while Dana was teaching and charming on his flower walks. One of these paintings was done in the old ghost town of Bennetville, a short hike in from the Tioga road as it drops over the eastern lip of the pass. It shows an old rust-colored, barn-like building in the foreground with Mt. Dana rising in the distance. I wasn't on that particular Dana Morgenson walk, but the painting hangs in our living room and oh, the memories it holds.

Al Glass captured the essence of Esther so well in his words at Dana's 1980 memorial service: "We can never forget the rich companionship, deep and strong, that Dana shared with Esther. With her quiet dignity, her own rich talents, her resilient strength, she walked beside him through the dark places and the mountain tops of their life together and found a rich reward." Esther died in Sedona, Arizona in 1993. They are both memorialized in the Dana and Esther

Morgenson Wildflower Trail on the Ahwahnee grounds, a fitting tribute.

THE YPCC LADIES

There were a number of special ladies among the YPCC executive staff wives whom I remember with great admiration and respect. These include Elsie Oehlmann, wife of Company President Hil Oehlmann; Muriel Ouimet, wife of Personnel Officer Harold Ouimet, and Mary Proctor. Each was very much a part of an active Valley scene in those fifties and sixties years.

Dete Oliver, wife of Public Relations Officer George Oliver, was in a class of her own with her vitality and enthusiasm. Who else would attempt a bridge party of seven tables in a not-large Curry duplex? There were bridge tables even in the bedrooms. Dete also had a tradition of inviting her Curry Row neighbors' children in for tea parties. If a thank-you note was not forthcoming, there would certainly be no second invitation! Dete lived to the wonderful age of ninety-seven, dying peacefully in 1998.

Mary Proctor came to Yosemite with her Charley in 1935, he to take over the direction of the newly developing winter sports program. They hailed from New England where Charley had starred in ski competitions at Dartmouth. He was a member of the U.S. team in the 1928 St. Moritz Olympics. Both were very much at home in the ski world. When Charlie and I came to the Park the family numbered five. Their young son Billy died of a brain tumor soon thereafter. We'd not yet had the chance to know him, but we shared the close community's great sense of loss. Over the years, we watched Nancy and Peggy Proctor grow up, go off to boarding school, then to college. We went to their weddings in the Church Bowl that marked the beginning of families of their own.

Mary handled many a Wednesday ski-day class for me when I was running the program. She loved the sport and seeing young children take to it. When Charley's 1971 retirement brought their move to the Santa Cruz area, we saw them infrequently, but Mary remained a continuing friend and pen pal. Upon Charley's death some years later, she moved to Colorado to be near family. She remained an avid ski-buff to the end. Mary Proctor passed away on July 18, 2000 in Boulder, Colorado. A few days earlier she had taken an active part in a four-generational celebration of a family twenty-fifth wedding anniversary. Mary lives in my memory as a very favorite lady.

THE NPS HOSTESSES

The Park superintendent's wife of the fifties and sixties had a vital role in the community—and was an important half of a pair. In his autobiography, George Hartzog cites Horace Albright, the second director of the NPS, as saying he would never appoint a park superintendent until meeting—and approving of—his wife.[6] The superintendent's wife, in those early days, was the Park hostess. She welcomed and entertained visiting congressional committees, foreign dignitaries, state and local officials, and other prominent persons. On the other hand, she could be counselor and comforter to the ranger wives in the Park. Betty Russell and Betty Preston, who came with husband John when Carl Russell retired in 1952, each capably filled this multi-faceted job. These two definitely fell into the gracious-lady category. The Prestons retired at the end of 1965, to be followed by Marie and John Davis, another charming, older couple.

For our first two decades in the Park, the Yosemite superintendency was the step before retirement. This changed with John Davis's retirement at the end of 1967 and the arrival of the Lawrence Hadleys. John Davis would be the last person to go into retirement from the Yosemite superintendency in the twentieth century. Future superintendents were younger and moved on to other high-grade positions in the National Park Service. By the late sixties the pace in the Park was definitely speeding up. Among the changes in the wind for the coming decades were those crucial to the role of superintendent's wife. Superintendents' wives were women—and women's roles were changing.

5. Catching Up and Moving On

Stay is a charming word in a friend's vocabulary.
                                        —*Louisa M. Alcott*

Our first half-decade in the Valley had flown by. We were in place and managing to keep up with three small ones, a growing dental practice and a beckoning Park. We were deepening friendships with some delightful people, digging our toes into the various activities around us, and had survived the 1955 flood. We were finding our niche.

The year 1956 brought some positive additions to the Valley. The new Yosemite Elementary School was dedicated that February, with its five classrooms and a welcome multipurpose room. Our telephone system had cut over to commercial phone service, with the result that we could now dial a number directly. Eventually, we stopped missing Donna Donielson's live voice and personal input. The telephone company also brought welcome new telephone company families into our lives, among them the Lashbrooks, Highfills and Schmidts. The new Yosemite Lodge was opened in the spring with much proper fanfare. The old lodge conveniently burned down.

MISSION 66

It was in 1956 too that the National Park Service, Director Conrad Wirth at the helm, unveiled Mission 66. This program brought so much activity, controversy and philosophical change to *our* park that only much later did I realize it was an *all* national parks project. The

NPS had a huge catch-up job to tackle. Not surprisingly, there had been great financial neglect of the parks during and after WWII. All monies had been necessarily channeled into the war effort. Several of the parks had been used by the military to provide rest facilities for returned personnel, e.g. the allocation of the Ahwahnee as an R&R base for the U.S. Navy, while others were used as training areas for the mountain troops. Neglect of NPS buildings, employee housing, and concessioner facilities had taken a toll.

The thinking behind Mission 66 was far-reaching and imaginative, as well as challenging. A huge investment by the government was going to be needed to "fix the parks." In his autobiography[1] Wirth states, "Mission 66 was conceived in 1956 and was designed to overcome the inroads of neglect and to restore to the American people a national park system adequate for their needs." This was to be accomplished within ten years. Wirth felt that Mission 66 could be looked on as a renaissance, the rebuilding of both the national park system and the National Park Service. The estimated cost of this undertaking was $100 million per year for ten years. Wirth and his men put together a cohesive plan to present to Congress. It stated needs, goals, and a practical time frame, both for the doing and for the paying. The Eisenhower administration and the Congress approved the project and Mission 66 was on its way.

For our Park, Mission 66 had six overall goals.[2] The first was to become an ongoing concern: the preservation and protection of the incomparable Yosemite Valley. One facet of this section of the plan in 1956 was to move facilities not directly dealing with the public out of the Park. This meant acquiring land in El Portal for an operating base.

The second goal was to complete the Park's road and trail system. The three main projects were the replacement of the remaining twenty-one miles of the old Tioga Road (what controversy and trauma this caused), the replacement of the seven miles of road between Crane Flat and Carlin to allow Highway 120 west to become an all-year highway, and the completion and upgrading of the long-neglected trail system.

The third goal for Yosemite of Mission 66 was to update provisions for visitor use facilities and services, and the fourth was the construction of new and needed visitor accommodations by the concessioners. These goals were accomplished with the completion of the new Yosemite Lodge and Village Store by the end of the decade, as well as the new Degnan's facility, and the improvements at both White Wolf Lodge and Housekeeping Camp.

The fifth goal was something that has involved us directly over the years: an aggressive land purchase program within the Park aimed at the inholdings in Wawona and Foresta. We had been property owners of one such inholding since 1953 when a friend moved from Yosemite and our Wawona half-acre fell quietly into our laps.

The sixth goal, one that is a perennial for Yosemite, was how best to handle the increase in Park visitation. At the time, the reasons put forth for the noticeable increase in visitation were the completion of the nation's multi-billion dollar highway system and the phenomenal post-war growth in the California population. Whatever the reason, the numbers were rapidly going up.

Over the ensuing few years, some very positive results were seen in regard to the visitor services. There was a much-needed increase in NPS personnel, ranger districts were consolidated and reorganized, lines were drawn on expansion of Valley public accommodations, and the Valley circulation routes were improved. Huge strides were made in the improvement of NPS housing. Old Village, Army Row, and Indian Village were systematically removed. Fifteen new Mission 66 houses were gradually added in the Valley, with twenty more constructed in El Portal. Valley campgrounds were improved and organized into individual sites.

In 1957, the NPS Training Center emerged as an integral part of the personnel development phase of Mission 66. It was set up in our Park to offer two 12-week course sessions per year under the guidance of Frank Kowski and Bob McIntyre, with June Branner as their capable secretary. Twenty-six men from the ranks of "in-take" rangers, naturalists, historians, and archeologists were selected from NPS areas across the country. They were housed in the Valley's Ranger

Club. Anyone who brought a wife and family had to find his own housing, which was scarce. Lois Kowski and Mamie McIntyre were most gracious in welcoming any accompanying wives into the community. I remember going to many a "come-and-meet" coffee at Lois's home. In 1961, the Training Center was moved to newly constructed, permanent facilities in Grand Canyon National Park.

The Tioga Road controversy was one of the most publicized parts of the Mission 66 plan. This road plan had been in the mill since the thirties, but was necessarily shelved during WWII. "Along the Tioga Road" discusses the ramifications of this. Other than the new houses and guest facilities that appeared around us, it was the hue and cry that arose in press and journal concerning the proposed road that really brought Mission 66 home to us. It was not a universally popular project.

Quiet changes were also taking place. Improvements in water and sewage facilities were made, with garbage now hauled out of the Valley. At Happy Isles, the building formerly occupied by the State Fish Hatchery (goodbye to our Overton pals) was rebuilt into the NPS Nature Center. At Wawona, Doug Hubbard made progress on the new Pioneer History Center. At Tenaya Lake the campground at the west end was improved and became the Park's first walk-in campground. In 1959, the new Village Store opened; bringing with it our first wheeled shopping carts. Great progress was made toward bringing television to the Valley. The outside world was gaining a toehold.

ON THE HOME FRONT

In the meantime, more serious matters aside, I was finding Yosemite to be a great place for this "at-home mom." For the most part, this was the only kind of mom around in the late fifties, and the term hadn't yet been invented. We were all at home with our kids—and we had a good time. There was always something to do, after the housework was done and the dinner planned, and more often than not someone with whom to do it. My little ones soon learned that the two or so hours after breakfast were Mom's time to hum around the house, their time to self-entertain (sans TV), and then we could get on with the fun stuff. Sometimes it was a walk with the stroller and trikes, perhaps to the polliwog pond or post office; other times, it was into the car for a trip to the store or to play with friends. Summertime meant scooping up the kids, beach paraphernalia, and plenty of snacks, then heading for one of our favorite river beaches. It might be Sentinel or our own secret beach. It might be to join the Robinsons on the sand plot at the end of the Curry Row. In those early days, Yosemite youngsters thrived on spending a few hours at the river with Mom and the gang.

When the kids were old enough to be outside on their own, I did a quick rattlesnake check before turning them loose in the yard each morning. Our house was one of the closest to the jumbled, rocky, cliff-side slope, and in dry years it was not uncommon to happen upon a snake in our area. Having been just a wall away from a rattlesnake incident when in the hospital birthing Rob, I was a believer. It was during this time that I also became a blue jay-listener, and gained great respect for this bird. Blue jays hate rattlesnakes. If a jay spots one, it stays riveted to its perch, sets up a piercing squawk, and doesn't take its eyes off the snake. Often other jays will rally around and join the chorus. Over the years I've had more than one rattlesnake brought to my attention by these squawking, staring jays.

Another of our favorite pastimes was taking a picnic supper to the beach. The picnic gear would be loaded into the station wagon by the time Charlie rounded the corner from the office and off we'd go. These evening picnics were almost always at Sentinel because we could drive quite close to the beach for convenient unloading. We usually had a campfire, for cooking or perhaps just for gathering around. Some great songfests evolved when Ken Ashley brought his accordion and Doug Hubbard his uke. After a tour of duty in Hawaii, Fran and Doug could also do a mean hula. Anne's second birthday celebration was with the gang at Sentinel where I'm sure she had an Ethel Ashley birthday cake. Somebody took a picture that evening of Anne sharing my lap with her brother Rob, who was born two weeks later.

Children were not a part of adult gatherings in those days. Although baby-sitters were at a premium, there was a definite distinction between grown-up parties and family parties. We had Nancy Moe sit for us as often as she could. The kids loved her, and she was a great favorite of ours, so it was a decided loss that she was at boarding school in Utah much of the year.[3] Since daytime sitters were impossible to find, much trading back and forth of children went on, especially for the early year ski-days.

Certain kid activities became traditional, and reaching the required age for participation became a rite of passage. Seven was the magic age for joining the Burro Picnic outings. Junior Rangers began at eight years, whereas twelve brought a youngster his own Privilege Card, the YPCC-issued discount card. Important milestones, all.

There were memorable grown-up parties along the way, times to let imagination run wild. Rusty and Jane Rust threw a treasure hunt that is still talked about. Who better to come up with intriguingly out-of-the-way hiding places than one who had grown up in the Valley, Rusty. We all learned, and never forgot, where the braided cherry tree stands and where a certain horse-trough can be found. Bob Riechers even wrote a song in honor of the latter.

When the Ashleys lived next door, we joined forces on a scavenger hunt to end all scavenger hunts, complete with rum punch served in a small garbage can. One team adeptly managed to "borrow" Mr. Oehlmann's Cadillac hubcap for a few undetected hours.

The Bullards gave a great Halloween costume party one year further down the Valley in an old, deserted building. The structure had been the mess hall for the old Civilian Conservation Corps camp of the thirties, since demolished. To this day I carry in my mind's eye the image of Ethel as the perfect Barbara Stanwyck, fur coat and all, and Rusty sporting a new-fangled rubber mask and trenchcoat, playing super sleuth Dick Tracy to the hilt.

OUR WORLD EXPANDS

The inevitable entered our lives in a big way toward the end of the fifties. Close friends began moving up, which in our world meant moving out. Except for the very few in-park promotions, advancement in the National Park Service involved a move to another park. The YPCC had gained the reputation for being an excellent junior executive training ground so again, stepping up the ladder in the corporate world could mean stepping out of Yosemite. In the course of fifteen months, spring of 1957 through fall of 1958, we lost four of our dearest friend-families to the outside world: the Munsons to Aspen, Colorado; the Robinsons to Idaho Falls; the Riechers to Medford, Oregon to his own medical practice; and the Ashleys to Mt. Rainier National Park in Washington. None stayed in California, and I was devastated.

When I was able to put things into better perspective, I appreciated two important lessons learned from this hurtful process. The first: putting miles between friends needn't diminish friendships and instead can expand one's own horizons. The second: each family moving from the Park left a spot for new friends to fill. If there was one thing at which Charlie and I became adept, it was giving farewell and welcome-back-to-the-Park-for-a-visit parties. We gradually assumed the role of "those who stayed." Over the years we grew to be the Yosemite touchstone for many friends. The Park claimed a place in the hearts of those who passed through, and they, in turn, claimed a place in ours.

Whether it was tradition or simple necessity, when families were packing and cleaning for the move, friends always pitched in to help. I've cleaned under many just-moved appliances, wiped smudges from acres of warped windowpanes, and packed endless boxes of kitchenware with many good pals. I even packed an entire box with just shoes for Mickey Curry when they moved. I'd never seen anyone with so many shoes! Once, my do-goodism almost did me in. At the time of their impending move from the Park to Rainier, the Ashleys lived next door to us. One evening, after an exhausting day of packing and cleaning, they had been invited out for dinner. Seeing them leave, I knew the coast was clear to go over to finish the one remaining tedious job: the bathroom. I quickly fed my gang, left them in Charlie's charge, and was out the door. In those days, bathtub and basin surfaces were not made from the spray-and-wipe-and-shine type of material we now know. They needed a lot of elbow grease as each had seen several years' and many families' use. I tackled the bathtub, there on my knees, with some ammonia-containing liquid. Didn't quite do the job. Okay, what else cleans the tough stuff? Ah, add some Clorox to the solution in the tub bottom. To this day I can't believe I did this, being an erstwhile science major. Had homemaking, mothering, and the like put all memory of chemical reactions out of my mind? There I was with chlorine gas wafting around my head. I threw open windows and felt stupid, stupid, stupid—and finished the job as fast as I could.

Leave-taking had its social side. Friends entertained for friends, dinner parties being the modus operandi. The bridge/poker group always had a send-off bash filled with poignant moments as reminiscences were shared. Bob Riechers was a master at rendering original bits of humorous poetry to keep the partings from becoming too maudlin. I much preferred the tone of these farewells to the roasts of later years. It is so much more creative to laugh *with* someone than *at* someone. People often left the Valley exhausted—more from that final round of socializing than from the move itself. But then they were off and away, leaving emptiness behind. It would be several years before we made a happy discovery: sometimes friends returned for another tour of duty in our Park.

Ties with friends and relatives in the Bay Area remained strong over the years. Yosemite was a great draw and a place to share. There was a time during the growing-up years when ours was a strained-at-the-seams house, but we managed and could usually find an extra bed for another guest or two. My mom and dad loved to join us, and always arrived with a leg o' lamb, cherries and apricots picked from their own trees that morning, plus bags of other hard-to-get treats. Charlie's mother and father were more the stay-at-the-lodge type, which was okay, too. Shirley, one of my closest friends from college, and Sherry Conner lived in Fresno in the early fifties, and we shared many of the minor holidays with them in Yosemite. Shirley became a second mother to our children, and their Sherrill joined our boys on a number of backpack adventures. We were delighted, too, when my older brother Joe Polhemus and his family moved to Fresno in the mid-fifties, he to practice internal medicine. I also became quite adept at loading kids and paraphernalia into the car to head off to Mom and Dad's in Danville for a few days. Often these trips included cherished reunions with my college mates, sometimes a theater fix.

In 1959, our wanderings began. The incentive was the annual meeting of the American Dental Association, held in New York City that fall. Chuckie was almost eight, Anne was six, and Rob was four. Rob was invited to stay with the Conners, now at home in Alameda. First big trip, huge city, two offspring, two parents: the odds sounded better with two and two and off we went. We flew eight hours on a prop job. The children received much special attention. The pilot invited Chuckie into the cockpit to see the controls. I can't remember that Anne received the same invitation—she was probably invited into the galley to watch the food prep!

We had a grand time in New York. Charlie put in minimal time at the meetings. We did the usual tourist things and loved it all. After visiting the United Nations one afternoon, we went to the theater to see *The Music Man* with Robert Preston. From the buzz, buzz all around us we became aware of Mrs. Khruchshev sitting in the audience just below our balcony. This was their infamous trip during which Mr. K took his shoe off and pounded it on the table at the UN. Nyet, nyet, nyet!

As for the shops, FAO Schwartz toy store was a must, as was Best and Co. This was not the later Best catalogue store but a wonderful store that put out a catalogue called Baby News, and became the mainstay in equipping our household for babies. Living in Yosemite made me an inveterate catalogue-shopper, a practice that brings the shops to one's mailbox. Before our trip ended, we had visited my favorite catalogue stores, L.L. Bean in Freeport, Maine and Carroll

Reed in North Conway, New Hampshire. We had rented a car to tour New England. We could stop as we pleased. After I'd made a purchase at the Carroll Reed Shop, the saleslady said, "Oh, here is Mrs. Reed now." When I said, "I am Marian Woessner," she answered "Oh, yes! W-o-e-s-s-n-e-r from Yosemite." She handled the catalogue orders herself in those days and certainly recognized *that* name. Mrs. Reed graciously took us home for a drink and to show the kids a special vintage car.

As the trip wound down, we found ourselves near Boston visiting another college connection of mine, Natalie Goethals and her growing family. It was sticky-hot, we were tired, and sightseeing had lost its appeal. When the Goethals offered the use of their house on Martha's Vineyard for a couple of days, we jumped at the chance. While waiting for the ferry at Woods Hole, we bought a couple of lobsters and ferreted out a bottle of California wine from the back shelf of a small grocery store. Then onto the ferry and off to the Vineyard. Soon we were dabbling our weary feet in the cool Atlantic. What a delightful interlude. Life works in such strange and wonderful ways. Fifteen years later Chuckie would marry his Dana, just a very few miles from where we sat, in the picturesque little church in Tisbury, on Martha's Vineyard.

The fifties were winding down. Our Yosemite roots had deepened. Yosemite-spawned friends were scattered all over the west, and more had come into our immediate lives: the Slijks, the Morrises, Wes and Dotty Conner, and the Gene Ewings. New Park Service pals included Dee and Dick McLaren, the Betts, Armstrongs, John and Marilyn Adams, and the Branges. Bob and Betty Sharp were back for another Yosemite assignment, and Dorothy and Roland Johnson had moved in down the street, and the Hacketts across the loop. The Metherells swooped through for a training school session and would return in the early sixties. At the school, Erik Bruun was principal, with Glenn Mapes, Thelma McGregor, Jean Leedy and Pauline Trabucco covering the grades. Two of ours were now attending, and Rob would soon join them. As for me, I was preparing to welcome Betsy into the fold. Let the sixties roll!

6. Along the Tioga Road

Wilderness is a whole environment of living things.
—*Howard Stagner*

The section of Highway 120 stretching from Crane Flat to Lee Vining—the Park's own Tioga Road—holds a myriad of family memories. The yearly opening of the road, usually Memorial Day Friday, came to mean the onset of our summer season. The high country was thawing, the trails were opening, the streams were rushing—heaven was closer. Since there are no numbered markers along the road pointing out *our* historical spots or special points of interest, I hereby put forth the "Woessner Guide to the Tioga Road."

FROM CRANE FLAT TO WHITE WOLF

On a hillside above the Crane Flat turn-off can be seen a brown-shingled Park ranger home. In the early fifties this was the scene of many good times shared with the Ashleys. Ash, like most buck rangers, was posted to outlying areas of the Park during his early career. Often a ranger would summer at one outpost, winter at another, and move to the Valley only when school needs arose. Our early knowledge of the Park was broadened considerably by having friends in these outlying areas. We took the bridge and poker groups to the outposts on numerous occasions.

At the Crane Flat junction, the road leading to the Tuolumne Grove of Big Trees (now a walking trail only) veers off to the left, while the other branch continues on toward Tuolumne Meadows. Not far along this main road sits the old Blister Rust Camp, still in use in the early fifties. By the seventies it became the seasonal home of the newly established Yosemite Institute, and the setting for a couple of Yosemite Winter Club cross-country ski and fondue gatherings, held under the fullest of moons. Winter moonlight on the Crane Flat snow-covered meadow offered all the light one needed for an exhilarating ski adventure.

A few more uphill miles along Tioga Road and we come to Gin Flat, with its old sheepherder's cabin. This was a favorite picnic spot in the fifties when we had little ones, didn't want to drive too far, but still wanted to give my mom and dad a taste of the higher elevation beauty, feel, and smell. Oh, the fragrance of those sun-drenched pines. As one approaches Gin Flat, the turnoff to the old Big Oak Flat Road lies to the right, leading to the Tamarack Campground. Dropping steeply down five winding miles through prime forest brings one to the small, rustic campground we used so often when the kids were little. A gentle stream runs through the site, ideal for toddler splashing and the beginning of a fishing career. Tucked away on a side road just through the campground, but well out of sight, lies the remains of an old CCC camp, one cement slab. This was the Sturm's special spot, and it was here we were asked to join them for a picnic supper on occasion. Even here Pat made everything seem effortless and fun. Avery was the amiable bartender, always good for a story or two, and later a campfire. The children loved it as much as Charlie and I.

When the youngsters were older, we explored further down Big Oak Flat Road. One still had car access as far as Gentry, the point where the old road began its steep descent into Yosemite Valley. From Gentry it was a good hike down to the Valley, with here and there a scramble over and around rockslide debris. One day we decided to explore upstream from the point where the road crossed Cascade Creek. After we climbed and rock-scrambled a few hundred yards, we rounded a large granite boulder and found ourselves staring at the most beautifully pristine swimming hole I had ever seen. It was a deep, clear pool surrounded by the warm granite slabs that beckoned sunbathers. A small waterfall dropped from the pool above making a perfect slide for young—and not so young—bottoms. Because the water came from snowmelt and the pool was deep, it had a nip to it: one didn't stay in long. This became one of our favorite destinations in the years before the disintegrating road was closed by barricade at the Tamarack Campground. We did not run into other people there, the one exception being the sighting once of two young male skinny-dippers who dove for cover as we rounded the rocks. That one was a good friend of our daughter Anne caused only momentary discomfort.

The Tamarack Campground has fortunately remained accessible for public use over the ensuing years, with the exception of a couple of summers in the late eighties when NPS maintenance funds were in short supply. We had a memorable supper-picnic there with grandson Charlie when he was but a toddler—*his* introduction to a family tradition.

When we first became acquainted with the Tioga Road, there were several small campgrounds in addition to Tamarack between Crane Flat and Tenaya Lake. Unfortunately, some have since been closed, among them Smoky Jack, Porcupine Creek, and east and west ends of Tenaya Lake. The public was led to believe that these campgrounds would be replaced elsewhere, but one wonders if that will happen. True, the campground at White Wolf was enlarged and "organized," as was the Tuolumne Campground, but of the pleasant, small, rustic campgrounds only Porcupine Flat, Yosemite Creek— with its slowly deteriorating access road—and Tamarack remain.

Before reaching the White Wolf turn off, Siesta Lake pops up on the right side of Tioga Road. The lake has become marsh-like, choking on the organic matter that accumulates each year, but in earlier years it was a lovely little mountain tarn. One early seventies winter, the thermometer dipped well below freezing in the high country some weeks before the first snow fell. Since Tioga Road is traditionally closed only by the first significant snowfall, which hadn't yet arrived, it was still possible to drive over Tioga Pass. Word spread that there were a few natural ice rinks available, and a bunch of us headed for Siesta Lake, skates in hand. Rusty Rust instigated a lively hockey game. Before the snow finally did close the road, various adventurers had skated on Ellery and Tioga Lakes, and even Saddlebag Lake, with its three-mile dirt access road. Other hardy souls climbed to Lower Cathedral Lake and had a truly rare skating experience. There was also some fine skating on the Merced River and Mirror Lake in the Valley that chilly late fall, but the set of perfect circumstances that allowed high country skating happened on only one other occasion during our years in the Park.

White Wolf, with its rustic lodge, was the scene of many dinner gatherings with our friends, at least once or twice a summer. Sitting with good friends on the porch overlooking a meadow filled with vibrant wildflowers, dining on fine mountain cuisine, and absorbing the mellow vibes were the makings of a delightful evening. This old lodge was built in 1926, as the home of the Meyer family. Alice Meyer turned it into a tourist lodge in the thirties.[1] A few years after her death, it was purchased by the NPS. The stipulation of that 1951 sale was that the lodge continue to offer meals and rustic accommodations to the public. The day-to-day operation was taken over by the YPCC and has been concessioner-run ever since.

White Wolf Lodge and campground lie on a spur road branching from the Highway 120/Tioga Road corridor. This byway is a part of the old Tioga Road, which then led on past Harden Lake, eventually dropping down into Aspen Valley and on to Carlin. We explored this old road a time or two before it was closed at the White Wolf Campground. In the sixties it became a "fire road only" and its gate was locked.

White Wolf is the jumping off place for—or the termination of—several choice high country hikes. For day hikes, especially with smaller children, we often covered the trail into Harden Lake or up the hill to Lukens Lake. In our earliest years we could set up camp at Harden, but it has since been made into day-use only, as has the Lukens area. Both are deemed too fragile and too accessible to survive the onslaught of present-day campers. There is a richly rewarding day hike to the "wild flower terrace" lying just over the edge of

Harden Lake's meadowland as the trail begins its descent into Pate Valley. It is a breathtaking, veritable feast of color at prime time during the summer. For longer hikes from the White Wolf trailhead, Pate Valley, and Ten Lakes offer themselves. We once hiked down from Tuolumne Meadows, through Pate Valley, to exit the backcountry at White Wolf. It is a steep climb out of Pate, and I was pleased with myself for making the long upward pull in not too shabby a time. Pate Valley, on the Tuolumne River, is noted for its rattlesnakes and its Indian petroglyphs. We were pleased to only view the latter. This was one of the places my mom and dad had always spoken of with fondness and I cherished walking in their footsteps those many years later.

During that trip, we had passed Jim Snyder's trail crew camp a mile or two above Pate Valley. Unfortunately, it was midday and an almost deserted camp. Trail crews and their able foremen[2] have a special place in Yosemite backcountry lore. Every hiker has seen the results of the hard labor and intricate skill that go into trail building and maintenance in backcountry Yosemite. Jim Snyder was a master craftsman.

THE OLD TIOGA ROAD

Just beyond the White Wolf junction is the turn-off to the Yosemite Creek Campground. This narrow, twisting road was our access to the high country for the first decade of our Yosemite life. It was the beginning of the "last twenty-one miles," the only part of the old Tioga Road still in use in the early fifties. From the outset of our Park years, we loved Tenaya Lake and its environs. The best kind of Sunday, away from the telephone and a call back to the office, was to climb into the car, picnic lunch, beach towels, and kids in tow, and head for Tenaya Lake. Even knowing we had that infamous stretch of narrow, twisting, rough, often one-lane road ahead didn't deter us. Charlie developed his own style of aggressiveness in handling the road. Tailgating until the offender finally, in desperation, pulled into a small turnout was the name of his game. I spent a lot of time cringing in the passenger's seat. I knew I was going to be the one to get the dirty looks—or worse—as we edged by. Drivers facing that stretch of road for the first time were absolutely terrified. The looks on many of the faces, coming or going, were studies in disbelief, fear, anger, or desperation. By the mid-fifties, trailers and other over-sized vehicles were becoming more common. The Park Service eventually put restrictions on their passage, allowing them to go through only during the evening hours. Later, when we took up sailing and often towed our small boat to Tenaya, we had occasion to truly appreciate the new Tioga Road. We simply could not have trailed the boat over the old road with its endless manipulations and frustrations.

The old road veered up to the right through the pine forest soon after the White Wolf junction. It wound its way around and down to the low point at the crossing of Yosemite Creek, past the welcoming small campground, then climbed steeply up through lovely aspen growth and over the ridge above Porcupine Flat. It continued past the turnoff to the small Porcupine Creek campground, with its trailhead to North Dome, climbed past Snow Flat to the small tarn at the May Lake trailhead, and there dropped more steeply down to skirt the edge of Tenaya Lake. Three miles beyond the lake, the new section of the road was again joined near Fairview Dome above Tuolumne Meadows.

We had many adventures along that stretch of the old Tioga Road, including our memorable "you can't get anywhere from here" trip. We were in our much-loved 1952 black Ford convertible, with just three little kids then, and were on our way to Tenaya Lake. Down we drove to the Yosemite Creek crossing. We hadn't progressed more than a few hundred yards up the other side before vapor lock struck. Sinking feeling in the stomach. There were few adequate turnouts on that stretch so Charlie deftly backed the car down the hill to the creek. And there we sat. We decided to scrap the trip, sensing that it could be something more serious than simple vapor lock. When the convertible finally started, we turned around and started back up the other side toward home. We got about five hundred yards up that not-as-steep road when the car stopped again. We couldn't go east, we couldn't go west. We sat for a couple of hours hoping the engine would cool enough to make it up the hill. The kids played in the creek, we ate our lunch, I fretted, and we waited. The car refused to start! Finally we decided Charlie would hitchhike home, get the station wagon, and come back for us. Fortunately, it wasn't hard to get a ride in those days. Anyone stranded on that road had the pity of anyone traveling it. That three attractive young ladies were the rescuers didn't faze me, although we've chuckled over it since. Two or three hours later back Charlie came and home we went. The overnight rest seemed to do the trick and the frivolous convertible's engine performed with great assurance the next day when we went back to rescue the car.

THE TIOGA ROAD CONTROVERSY

We had been in the Park only a few years when we became aware of the ongoing controversy between the Sierra Club (to which Charlie had belonged since early college days) and the National Park Service (our neighbors) over the proposed new Tioga Road that would replace the last twenty-one-mile stretch of old, substandard road. Construction had begun in the thirties, but the war had halted work on any additional new road sections. Planning resumed in the late forties and early fifties. The NPS put forth the route that later became the accepted one, while various members of the Sierra Club Board of Directors and of the club itself favored a high-line route,[3] which would have placed the road in the vicinity of Ten Lakes, along the north and east slopes of Mt. Hoffmann and behind Polly Dome. Active in the Sierra Club drive were David Brower and Ansel Adams,[4] while the Park Service standpoint, locally, was championed by Park Superintendent John Preston. After much study, the Yosemite Advisory Board composed of William E. Colby, J.P. Buwalda, and Duncan McDuffie supported the NPS stand.[5]

No sooner had the route controversy been settled than a hue and cry went up about the road standards, from the engineering standpoint. How wide should the lanes be? How large did the turnout viewpoints need to be? Should the elevation of the road skirting Tenaya Lake be raised? We would pore over the Sierra Club Bulletin each month to learn the latest from that standpoint. We would talk to our Park Service friends to hear the latest at home scoop. It was a shock to learn one day that the whole thing had put John Preston in the hospital. Heart attack? Exhaustion? We didn't ever really know, but he was in the good hands of Avery Sturm and was soon out and back into the fray.

After lengthy studies and discussion over the proposed road standards, the decision was made to keep it a park road, not create a high-speed highway. It was to be two ten-foot-wide lanes with two-foot shoulders on each side. The road was to be elevated a few feet at Tenaya Lake. I remember a time or two when the lapping lake water threatened a bit of the old road during a heavy snowmelt spring. It seemed wise to raise it above that threat. The turnouts were planned. The battle quietly went underground.

Construction began again in 1957. The road was completed in 1961, at a cost of $5,250,000. A dedication was held on June 24, 1961 at Olmsted point. Those troubled years saw a growing rift between the Sierra Club and the NPS. To many conservationists, the scarring of the glacially polished granite dome at what became Olmsted Point was an unforgivable desecration. Statistically, the Tioga Road is the highest trans-Sierra crossing, reaching, at Tioga Pass, an elevation of nearly 10,000 feet. To many, it is the most scenic route in all of California and one of the outstanding roads in the National Park System.[6] It did not come easily. Friendships were lost over this project, groups were split, and ideals were tarnished. No, it did not come easily.

We, Charlie and I, did not yet have enough history in the Park to have the deep feelings about the Tioga Road issue that so many around us seemed to harbor. We were onlookers—and, after all, the new road would make it far easier for us to get to the high country on our days off. But through this highly publicized battle I became fully aware of this truth: Yosemite is *the* sacred cow to multitudes of people. Everyone has an opinion about how to care for the Park. This insatiable interest in the well-being of our Park has only increased in the intervening years. In the nineties, we found ourselves in the midst of the Arch Rock Road controversy. We do have history with that unique piece of road, and we deplore some of the changes that have been made. I am reminded of some of the arguments of the fifties: excessive width of roadway, overblown turnout needs, no high-speed highways. Overdoing what is really needed.

ALONG THE NEW TIOGA ROAD

Now when we head for the high country, we do not turn onto the small winding road that led through the Yosemite Creek campground, to go on up the hill and beyond. We continue over the new Tioga Road, the "sparkle road" as our granddaughter, Heidi, so aptly named it when a small girl. The roadway was made from crushed granite containing quartz. Decades later it sparkles still. As the road cuts through the granite hillside, a profusion of wildflowers brightens the sides of the roadway—scarlet gilia and magenta pride of the mountains in abundance. A fine overview of the Yosemite Creek drainage unfolds at the same time one's eyes are lifted to the heights of Mt. Clark in the distance. The panorama of mountains all around is almost overpowering as one gradually descends toward the Yosemite Creek crossing.

Just before the Yosemite Creek crossing, the trail to Ten Lakes begins its climb. I have done that trail just once but loved the trip. Charlie and I did it alone together, in the early eighties, after our young were out of the nest. We camped our first night at Ten Lakes, an area notorious for marauding bears, but were bothered by none. The next day we dropped down behind Mt Hoffmann, and came up around the mountain to find a perfect campsite in Hoffmann's shadow. It was a drought year, and one has only to pass those dry streambeds and empty potholes to gain renewed appreciation for the snows of winter. The third morning we continued to skirt the backside of the mountain until we joined the Glen Aulin/May Lake trail. We came out at the May Lake trailhead and found the bike Charlie had stashed for the pedal back to the car at Yosemite Creek. After leaving the popular Ten Lakes area we had encountered very few people on that trip. There *are* unpopulated trails to be found if one seeks them out.

Continuing along the Tioga Road we come to the North Dome trailhead. Here, the old dirt road leading to the small Porcupine Creek Campground was left to return to nature after the campground was closed in the late fifties, but the trail to North Dome follows its traces in the beginning stretch. This trail is an excellent choice for launching a beginner into the charms of the backcountry, as it has no great ups and downs. There is a secret arch to search for along the way and a splendid view opening up from the Dome itself. Looking across the Tenaya Canyon at the face-on view of Half Dome is spectacular. Half Dome cannot be seen at this imposing angle without a hike. One either hikes out to North Dome or hikes the Tenaya zigzag trail between Snow Creek and Mirror Lake.

Charlie took Anne on the North Dome hike one day when she was a youngster, just the two of them. In her writings she recalls not really wanting to go, but grudgingly she joined her dad. Mid-way, while sharing their lunch on a rock, she remembers "simultaneously realizing two things; first, that I could *do* that long hike and, second, that I *enjoyed* it! I liked being exactly where I was!" A mountaineer was born that day. Charlie took granddaughter Heidi on that same hike when she was also about eight. He took a picture of her sitting on "shoe rock" just as he had taken Anne and Chuckie's years before. Shoe rock was a family-given name. It was a perfect replica of "Old Mother Hubbard's" high-top shoe—cast in granite.

Leaving the new road for awhile, the bit of old road leading to the trailhead for May Lake is a charming wander through forests and meadows, past the old Snow Flat ranger cabin, then up the hill to the tarn at the jumping off place to May Lake. There is a High Sierra camp at the lake but it has been the least visited by our family. The short, steep one-mile trail up to the camp didn't offer the away-from-civilization feeling we usually sought. One Father's Day, however, after parking small Betsy with the Browns at Badger, the rest of the gang headed up to May Lake and kept on going, to climb Mt. Hoffmann. I'd always been told that one could see the firefall from Hoffmann and, yes, there was Glacier Point in the distance. It was a great climb—and I had "bagged" my first peak. Chuck relates a story of three young lads (himself, Ken Metherell, and Rob Johnson) packing their homemade kayaks up this steep trail to make camp for a couple of nights and do some fishing. They endured a memorable hailstorm—to catch and eat some tasty trout.

Back on the new road, the view from Olmsted Point is grandly spectacular. Without digging into old wounds too much, it must be acknowledged that this road has opened up a magnificent panorama to millions who could not have seen it any other way. Looking across at the grandeur of Clouds Rest, down into the Tenaya Canyon, then out over the splendor of Tenaya Lake, with peaks to the right, granite domes to the left, and then letting the eyes soar on to the majesty of Mt. Conness is still, to me, one of the greatest views of the world. It truly speaks to the essence of the Yosemite high country.

Because Tenaya Lake and Tuolumne Meadows played such major roles in our Yosemite lives, each merits a chapter of its own. But between them on Tioga Road lies the trailhead of a fisherman's trail climbing up to the Cathedral Lakes. We've ascended that steep trail many times, as it is a short cut to choice views, lakes, and good day hikes. We've climbed up to Lake of the Domes, usually hopping with frogs, to the pass above Upper Cathedral, and scrambled over the ridge to descend to Budd Creek. Some in the family have climbed Tenaya Peak, others, Cathedral: still others simply sat by the lake and absorbed the beauty. The wildflowers can be abundant and spectacular along the trail. After a great day of poking around the lakes, it was often a wrench to drop over the edge for that climb back down to earth and to the hum of civilization that was the Tioga Road.

BEYOND TUOLUMNE MEADOWS

Often, as we headed east toward Tioga Pass, hunger pangs would hit about the time we headed up out of the Meadows. We would stop to take in the view of the Dana Fork of the Tuolumne River off to our right, with its grassy wildflower patches on the banks, and choose this perfect spot for our picnic. Soon we'd again be on our way, the long drive to Colorado or maybe just a hike to Parker Pass ahead of us.

The trailhead for the passes, Mono and Parker, is just a bit further along the Tioga Road and we've often headed out from here on a day hike. I never approach that first glacial moraine on the trail without thinking of Dana Morgenson and of my continued quest to find a Steer's Head, that elusive, tiny, very pale pink flower that grows in sandy soil just as the snow is receding. It is the one flower in Dana's *Yosemite Wildflower Trails* I have never found. He told me it grows here on this moraine and I am still seeking it—and recalling his great love for these mountains.

My dad, too, loved the Sierra and their abundant and varied wildflowers. He carried his heavy Jepson flower guide wherever he went on the trails, and was quite an authority in his own right. The trail to Parker Pass runs through a small valley beside Spillway Creek. Years ago we scattered Dad's ashes in this valley's meadow. What better place for him to rest than in this place so beautifully carpeted with wildflowers.

Up that same trail and over Mono Pass, Betty Johnston and I backpacked one day in the late seventies. Camping isn't allowed in the Spillway drainage because the creek is the Tuolumne Meadows water supply; so one must drop over the pass a short distance to find the first permissible camping site. We had a delightful evening, felt ourselves quite capable, and tucked ourselves under a sheltering rock for the night. Unfortunately, Betty developed a fierce headache in the night. We bailed out early in the morning. While walking down the trail, we spotted a figure approaching in the distance. As we neared, the clothing seemed of a greenish hue, and yes, it was an NPS uniform and yes, it was daughter Anne. She was a backcountry ranger that summer, stationed in Tuolumne, and out on patrol. Were we glad to see her! She assured Betty that indeed it was altitude sickness, that a lower elevation would most certainly help, and I think she may even have supplied some welcome aspirin. We made our descent slowly, passing the weathered old miner's cabins along the way.

TIOGA PASS AND BEYOND

One can't approach the kiosk at Tioga Pass without being reminded of Ferdinand J. Castillo, "Mr. Greeter." It is hard for me think about Ferdinand without a certain sense of sadness. Our first contact with him was when he was a seasonal ranger in the Valley in the fifties. In his spare time, he would help the kids with swimming lessons at the lodge pool. Dr. Bob (Riechers) tells a story of going along on an emergency carry-out call in the Bridalveil area with Ken Ashley and a new seasonal ranger, who happened to be barefoot but covered the rocky, uneven ground as quickly as any of them: That was Bob's introduction to Ferdinand.

Most people remember Ferdinand as the smiling, welcoming person on the gate at Tioga Pass, often with a joke, always with helpful information. If one was traveling west, he sang out, "Watch for deer in the road." If heading east it was, "Watch for rocks in the road," as one drove away. On many an occasion, if one were expecting friends from over the pass, Ferdinand would call down to the Valley, "The Ashleys are on their way." He rarely forgot a face, and was never too busy to welcome a tourist to *his* Park. He cared for the surrounding area as if it were his garden, and soundly scolded those who were seen to be treading on his alpine tundra.

Perhaps it was a sign of the times, a cliché I have come to hate, but in this world of speed, hurry, and haste, it was deemed by the powers-that-be that Ferdinand was slowing down access to the Park with his meeting and greeting, and he was removed from his beloved job in the Tioga Pass entrance station. He lived only a couple of years longer. Fortunately, Ferdinand had been the earlier recipient of the Yosemite Alumni Award, an award given annually for outstanding Park community involvement. He *had* been made aware that he was much appreciated in his own right. It was beyond standing room only at Ferdinand's funeral in Sonora. When the road opened that summer, a memorial gathering was held at Tioga Pass. He was a man who left his mark on the hearts of many.

From the Tioga entrance station parking area, the trails to Gaylor Lakes to the north and Mt. Dana to the south take off.

Gaylor is a steep, short trail leading to some lovely small lakes, noted for superb fishing, and to some old mining buildings up on the ridge—a great area to explore. During the late fifties, NPS Chief Naturalist Doug Hubbard was instrumental in the historic restoration of these buildings. They still stand today, a memorial to the area's mining past.

I've climbed Mt. Dana only once, but have been on its flanks many times. After my own children had grown up and were off to summer jobs, I did the climb one day with Anne Hendrickson, her son Vik, and Danny Wilson. I could never call this hike hospitable. The rocks seem unforgiving as you climb over them near the top, but we made it, the views were outstanding—and I'd bagged one more peak!

Although outside the Park, the walk to the old mining camp of Bennetville from the Tioga Road is a yearly favorite of ours. The snow leaves this eastside slope by June so the trail is open before other high country spots are accessible. It's a fine place to go when you have the high country urge and the snow lingers around Tuolumne. This walk was a great favorite of the Morgensons—and another place Dana told me to look for the tiny Steer's Head. Our friend, ranger Dick Ewart, often led walks into Bennetville. It has always been a popular hike for the novice because so much can be seen in an easily accessible stretch: unfolding wildflower displays, mountain tarns, a rushing high country stream, and the old buildings of the Great Tioga Mining Company. About halfway along the trail Dick would momentarily disappear behind some rocks or trees to emerge in the guise of an old miner, to continue the walk in character.

Beyond the "mining trail to Bennetville" marker, the Tioga Road begins its drop down the eastern slope of the Sierras into the Mono Basin. The descent is gradual at first, passing Tioga and Ellery Lakes and the turn-off to Saddlebag Lake. Saddlebag is the jumping-off point for a lovely hike down Lundy Canyon. The multi-hued columbine of July and August or the vibrant aspen leaves of autumn make this hike a highly rewarding, albeit steep, endeavor in mid- to late summer. We descended that canyon with Rusty, the Johnstons,

Connie Metherell, Jan Robinson, and others, many times. Jane Rust was always our faithful car-shuttler, meeting us at the bottom, and dinner at the Mono Inn was our reward.

Once past the turn-off to Saddlebag Lake, the road curves sharply, passes "Oh My Point," and becomes a steep descent into the Mono basin. This is the section of the Tioga Road that, in descending, has brought many a flatland Midwesterner to his knees, and, conversely, vapor-locked many a car on the ascent toward Tioga Pass. Heading east, it is a spectacular climax to an equally spectacular trip across the Sierra Nevada. Heading west, it is the challenge that must be met before one reaps the rewards of the Park's beauty. It is a stretch of the Tioga Road not easily forgotten.

7. Christmas in Yosemite

The moon on the breast of the new-fallen snow
gave the lustre of midday to objects below.
—Clement C. Moore

The words "Christmas in Yosemite" bring back so many cherished memories. Some Christmas traditions we came to know as only-in-Yosemite experiences, unique to the Valley. Other holiday moments became treasured because of the friends and loved ones who were a part of them. The sparkling setting of Yosemite in wintertime, often under a blanket of snow, increased the pleasure of both.

A CHILD'S CHRISTMAS

For children the holiday season was magical. The major event was a visit from the real Santa Claus, who stopped by the Curry pavilion each Christmas Eve just before setting out on his North American rounds. Excitement had reigned for days, when finally children were allowed to don the new Christmas outfits and families headed across the Valley to Camp Curry. Often moonlight *was* reflected "on the breast of the new-fallen snow."

Letters to Santa had been written some weeks earlier. Parents helped the preschoolers, but the others wrote their own letters at school and were very specific about their wants. The teachers used infinite tact to steer requests away from bicycles or electric trains as these were out of bounds financially. Christmas of a youngster's third grade year was the cut-off point for this largess. After that it was a bag of candy for each. At last Santa arrived, with laughter and jingling bells. All the well-coordinated pieces fell into place to spark a wonderful evening. Sacks and sacks of gaily-wrapped packages appeared, carried by Santa's pixie-capped helpers. There were oohs and aahs as coveted dolls, ice skates, pogo sticks, Tonka trucks, doll buggies, special-that-year games, fuzzy animals—even skis—were given out, each gift bearing a personal tag. Our youngsters grew up knowing they had been in the presence of the real Santa. None of those sit-on-Santa's-lap-and-smile department store pictures adorn their scrapbooks.

Of course, all of this wonderment didn't really appear by magic. It was a true and genuine gift to the younger children of the community from the Yosemite Park & Curry Company. The YPCC planned and paid for the entire endeavor. Three or four of the executive wives, lists in hand, went to an understanding toy store in Fresno on a Sunday early in December—stores normally being closed on Sundays in those days—and made the selections. If a requested item was not found in that particular store, someone was assigned to look elsewhere. The children were not to be disappointed. Skis and skates were found in a store specializing in winter sports equipment. The women then set to work typing the gift tags and rechecking the lists.[1]

Shortly before the big day, a larger group of women gathered in the Ahwahnee Indian Room to wrap the gifts, secure the tags, and check off each child's name and gift on the master list. This festive occasion became a favorite part of my Christmas season. Daytime sitters were scarce in those days, and this was the one time when Charlie would close the office and come home to take care of the children.

I began my wrapping stint during the era when the Ahwahnee was closed from the end of October until the week before Christmas. The wrapping-party was held a couple of days before the hotel reopened—and about one day after the heat was again turned on. It could be bone chilling, so we all bundled. What fun it was to see the toys, and of course I had to check to find what was in store for my own four. After all the gifts had been wrapped and all the names had been checked off, tea and cookies were served, and we knew that Christmas was once again close at hand.

When the Ahwahnee Hotel began staying open to guests all year, the wrapping gathering moved to a private meeting room at the Yosemite Lodge. Then in the very early seventies, when the numbers of children became too great, and the YPCC was about to change hands, these wonderful Christmas Eve parties came to an end. Though there continued to be places where parents could quietly bring gifts for their children, and a Santa-clad person gave them out, gone was the magic of visits from the real Santa Claus.

AN ADULT CHRISTMAS

The Sturm Christmas Open House was another anticipated Christmas tradition. It was a festive adult community occasion. Everyone—two or three hundred people—was there. It was an afternoon gathering at Pat and Avery Sturm's home and people were expected to come, stay a respectable amount of time, then leave to make room for the next guests. There were always the few, however, who interpreted the invitation to mean come and stay. One year, Pat decided she would thin the crowd by asking half to come between two and four, and the other half to come between four and six. She forgot that everyone knew the last couple of hours were the most fun. The two-to-four people came at quarter to four, and the four-to-six people came at quarter after four—and everyone stayed. It was wall-to-wall bodies, and the idea was hastily scrapped.

Tom and Jerrys made from scratch, beaten eggs and all, were the libation of the day, although there was always a punch for the abstainers. Tasty open-faced sandwiches seemed to appear by the hundreds from the upper regions of the house. Once I was asked to go up to bring down more trays of food. There I found several beds literally covered with trays of sandwiches. There were no caterers in those days: these were Pat's doing. Later, came the "little supper" for anywhere up to twenty helpers. Out came elegant casseroles, sliced ham, salads, all followed by Christmas cookies and cakes. Such an easy, gracious hostess was Pat, a conjurer of abundant sustenance.

Pat delighted also in decorating for the holidays. The usual wall hangings came down at Christmas to be replaced by glistening large gold stars and draped garlands. The Christmas tree wasn't put up until after the Open House but always sparkled for the staff party, usually a night or two later. All the medical/dental staff and their spouses were invited for Tom and Jerrys, a buffet supper, a gift exchange and carol singing—with Pat at the keyboard. For some members of the staff, far from home, this *was* Christmas. These were warm, loving occasions as Pat and Ave donned their Santa hats to direct the gift exchange. In 1955 this cozy gathering was blatantly interrupted by the phone call that reported rising floodwater in the Valley. It was a call for help, and all strong backs left immediately for Superintendent Preston's home to raise the furniture above the reaches of the invading river.

Many of the loveliest traditions centered around the Yosemite Chapel. In our early years, the Christmas Music by Candlelight offering was a favorite, usually presented the week before Christmas. In December of 1951, after Charlie and I attended for the first time, we drove peacefully home through the falling snow. Within an hour I was off to the hospital in anticipation of my baby's birth. Could this explain his calm, stoic nature in growing up?

As our children grew, we became involved with their Sunday school and the ensuing Christmas presentations. Never good at creating costumes, I was delighted when the children were cast as a shepherd, wearing a cinched-in bathrobe of their father's, or as the seated Madonna with a pale sheet to cover head and body.

The chapel Christmas Eve candlelight service began at eleven o'clock. A huge wreath with a cheery red bow hung on the front wall, and smaller wreaths adorned each window. These had been lovingly made, locally, in the weeks before Christmas. Candles flickered in the wall sconces and on the altar. We shared this joyous occasion with our Park visitors, and I recall vividly the fragrance of pine wreaths and boughs mingled with the elegant scents from the fur-coated Ahwahnee Hotel guests. The service culminated in the lighting of a small taper by each parishioner. Carrying the candle and singing a last hymn of joy, we left the chapel—and Christmas was upon us. Excitement and peace were in the air as we greeted our Catholic friends who were just arriving for Midnight Mass. We missed this part of the Christmas Eve exchange when, in later years, the Catholic services moved to the Visitor Center.

Other holiday traditions came and went over the years. In our earliest years in the Valley, the Chief Ranger and his wife gave a party a few days after Christmas. It was then that I learned my first "there is a pecking order" lesson. We arrived home early in the afternoon from what was to be our only Christmas away from the Valley. I had forgotten the party hours and called a neighbor to ask. She testily informed me, "I wouldn't know, we aren't a high enough grade to be invited." This was a concept I had not sensed in the Valley until now, and I added the lesson to my growing knowledge of the ways of our new world.

YOSEMITE'S BRACEBRIDGE DINNER

The famed Bracebridge Dinner is fashioned on Washington Irving's 1812 description of a festival held at Squire Bracebridge's pre-Elizabethan manor house in England. It had been adapted, under the direction of Donald Tresidder, for presentation at the Ahwahnee Hotel in 1927, the year the hotel was built.[2] Tresidder soon called on the musical expertise of Ansel Adams and the artistic help of Ted and Jeannette Spencer. Eugene Fulton was assigned to be music director a few years later. The soon-to-be-celebrated Bracebridge Singers were drawn from the Bohemian Club in San Francisco.[3]

The Bracebridge Dinner became a hallowed tradition for many a Park guest and a once-in-a-lifetime occasion for thousands more. Quite a cadre of locals centered their Christmas planning around participation in the pageant. A youngster who made his debut as a small village minstrel might advance over the years to the costumed monkey, the regal bearer of the Baron of Beef, or even the delightful Lord of Misrule. Traditions grew out of traditions. While no one in our family became involved in the production end, all have been guests for dinner at Bracebridge Hall a time or two, thanks to their hosting grandparents. The senior Woessners loved this celebration of Christmas.

Many tales circulated about the various idiosyncrasies of a few of the long-standing guests at the Bracebridge. A favorite was that of the older couple who took a large, elegantly dressed doll to dinner each year to sit with them at their table for three. An imagination can run rampant concerning that threesome!

In 1978, when there were still just the Christmas Eve dinner and the two Christmas day seatings, Charlie and I were invited to portray the Visiting Squire and Lady for the later Christmas day dinner. This was a heady, treasured experience. We donned the costumes for which we had earlier been fitted, and gracefully entered Bracebridge Hall to partake of the feast as honored guests. The other participants at our magnificent raised banquet table were the professional cast members who had, therefore, feasted with gusto at the earlier seating. It was a lovely meal, the hour was late, and Charlie and I were hungry. While others at our table barely nibbled, we fully enjoyed the feast. The hotel guests at the front tables must have noticed that the visitors at the groaning board were far out-eating the household. But the household was still thirsty, so no one stinted on the wine service. By the time the festivities were over and we stood with Squire Bracebridge and his Lady at the dining room doorway, we, too, felt we were bidding farewell to our guests.

A most gracious touch was extended to the Visiting Squire and Lady by the YPCC in the form of an invitation issued to their family members to be dining room guests for the dinner and pageantry. Family members in residence with us were daughter Betsy (laid low with the flu), and daughter and son-in-law Anne and Chas Macquarie. This being one of their Tuolumne Meadows resident ranger winters, they had skied down from the Meadows for a family Christmas. After rustling up some appropriate duds, they joined the celebrants in the dining room and did complete justice to that feast of many courses. Who better to enjoy such a repast than a couple who had skied those many miles to get there?

Humans can never fully depart from reality, and thus it was with the Bracebridge Dinner, too. Eugene Fulton, the effervescent, capable director of the pageantry, suffered a fatal heart attack in Yosemite on December 24, 1978. In the age-old tradition of the theater the show went on, under the assumed-directorship of his daughter Andrea. She has filled this role capably ever since. In later years the number of Bracebridge seatings increased to five. The additional two are offered a few days prior to Christmas.

FAMILY TRADITIONS

As the children grew older, some or all of us tried to get to San Francisco in the weeks before Christmas. Always it was a visit to grandparents, perhaps also to see the *Nutcracker* ballet or to hear the *Messiah,* but certainly it was to enjoy the magic of the floral displays at Podestas, the giant Christmas tree in the City of Paris, and the wonderfully animated Christmas windows at Macys.

Flooding closed the Park twice at Christmas during our Valley residency. In the 1955 flood, the Park was closed for five of the Christmas days. We were invited to share the Rust's festive Christmas dinner since our parents couldn't get into the Park as planned. Many locals went to a simplified, less costly, but lovely Bracebridge. Only two of the Bracebridge singers had arrived in the Park before the water rose. They, Fran Hubbard (choir accompanist), and the chapel choir came through with a warmly welcomed musical offering, and a legend was born. Santa, too, made the detour away from Camp Curry to greet the children in the glowing warmth of the Ahwahnee Great Lounge. Floods came again in the mid-sixties, but this time we were able to leave the Park by noon on Christmas day to head for my aunt's in Santa Barbara. The flood of 1997 considerately waited until New Year's Day. The Christmas revelers had come and gone.

Sometime in the early seventies, I decided to create my own Christmas tradition. Because things like this are more fun when planned with a friend, Ti Shackelton and I joined forces to host a Christmas coffee for our Park friends. We chose a weekday morning before school let out for the holidays, to help with the sitter situation, then sent out the invitations. Traditionally we invited about 150 friends, did not bother with an RSVP, and waited to see who would turn up. I cherished my freezer at times like this because I could bake ahead and store. Christmas decorations went up, the engagement cups came out of mothballs, the silver service was given a sparkle—and the party was on. Our average turnout over the years was about sixty percent. It just wasn't everyone's bag and also by then more women had entered the work force. We didn't encourage the bringing of small children but the nine-to-twelve stretch of hours gave ample time for shift exchange sitting. Coffee and tea were served, with a dollop of rum or brandy if welcomed. I loved to decorate the house and the gathering was a festive one. This tradition continued until we moved to Wawona in 1987. A couple of friends continued the idea for a while, and then others took over in the form of a cookie-exchange party.

One year Chuck showed up from college with several friends in tow two days before the Monday coffee. They planned a cross-country ski outing into the backcountry above Little Yosemite and needed a place to organize their gear, which included eating and sleeping. Sunday found packs, food, and ski gear all over the living room, and bodies seemingly all over the house. They planned a Monday morning take-off up the trail. It was ultimatum time and I announced mine. I would serve breakfast at six, and they were to be out the door not a minute past seven. Then came two frantically busy hours between the last boot that clomped out the door and the first high heel that stepped daintily in. The last vestige of ski paraphernalia was quickly tossed up the stairs to fall where it landed—and out came the fancies. We made it! And I was still "good ol' Mom." I call that storing up brownie points.

Another time when I wondered if perhaps I had overextended a bit was the year we hosted the joint medical/dental group staff Christmas party the evening before the morning coffee gathering. At least I only had to clean the house once. After the Sturms retired, the hosting of the staff party was passed around each year. It was an honor to portray Mr. and Mrs. Santa, remembering all the times we had shared the largess of Pat and Avery.

CHRISTMAS HOMECOMINGS

A very different aspect to the joy of the Christmas season was added in 1966. It began as the homecoming from boarding school; later, college; eventually, careers and marriages. Chuck started the exodus, as a freshman at the Colorado Rocky Mountain School in Carbondale, Colorado. We hand-delivered him to school in the fall but winter travel by car was chancy and time-consuming. Hence, we depended upon the good old California Zephyr to get him home for Christmas in those earlier years. We met him at the depot in chilly, foggy downtown Stockton that first December. What a strange sensation it was to not even recognize my own firstborn as this person alighted from the train. There he was, looking a foot taller, with hair down to the shoulders, bundled in a huge down parka. The encompassing hug, however, had not changed and our boy was home. With him, that Christmas, the outside world of youth in the late sixties entered our lives.

In later boarding school years, the train became passé and standby plane flights were the custom. There were no Denver to Fresno flights as yet so we had to drive to San Francisco and hope that our children had made the plane. Somehow they always materialized through the expected passageway, until the one holiday when we became more dejected by the moment as the flow of passengers ebbed, trickled, ended—and no Rob! Just as we were wondering what to do next, a tap on the shoulder announced his safe arrival. He had made it onto another airline. Now Christmas could begin.

Once the kids entered their respective colleges, all in California, we saw them often enough that the Christmas homecoming didn't hold quite the same sense of excitement it had during boarding school days. Our first year with holes around the Christmas table came in 1972, when Anne was studying in Grenoble, France, and Chuck had taken a year's leave from UC Davis to work as a ski instructor at Aspen Highlands. In my Christmas list book, I call this the "scattered Christmas." Charlie's mother had recently died so his dad joined us for a quiet Christmas in Yosemite.

Our first Christmas to be blessed by the addition of a grandchild came in 1976, when Dana and Chuck brought four-month-old Heidi west from Vermont. It was a wonderful homecoming. Heidi was introduced to both her Woessner and Polhemus great-grandfathers and we had a true Woessner family reunion. It was to be a milestone, because we've not been able to get everyone together at Christmas since. It has proved too far to travel for too many people through too much winter weather.

LATER CHRISTMASES

For many years, until his retirement in the mid-nineties, Derrick Vocelka was Santa Claus to the local children in the Valley. He went around to various homes throughout the Valley on Christmas Eve. He would find the sack of packages hidden outside the house, then come ho-ho-ho-ing through the door to dispense the gifts. Unfortunately, when this tradition began, our children were far too old for the fun. But one Christmas—out of the blue—I received a call that Santa would be stopping at our house that evening and I'd better make the appropriate arrangements. Several of our grown-up gang were home for the holidays and the Cramers were stopping in for Christmas cheer at some point. I scurried around, wrapped and tagged gifts, and put them in a sack to surreptitiously stash where Santa could later find them. All went well, the Cramers arrived, the sack was in place, the time approached. And then the doorbell rang, heralding the arrival of—Laurel Munson, dropping by to see Anne! Quick thinking, plus a conveniently available and appropriate wrapped package saved the day. Tag written quickly for Laurel's gift, out the back door, around the house, gift added to the pile in the nick of time. Not five minutes later Santa appeared at our door, sack on back. As gift tags were read, and presents dispensed, "To dear Laurel from Santa" rang through the room. I'll never forget the stunned look on Laurel's face. In an instant her childhood faith had been rekindled. "There really is a Santa!"

The year we moved to Wawona had the potential of being a grim

Christmas. None of our family were with us. I still felt displaced in our new home, had met few Wawona people, and felt quite lost. The season was saved when my brother Joe and his Nancy invited us to come to Fresno for Christmas dinner and the night with them. We jumped at the chance and joined a lovely Polhemus Christmas. In my heart, however, I sorely missed our kids, our Yosemite home, and our Valley. I've grown up since then, but still hold close the magic that was Christmas in Yosemite Valley. It was a place of loving traditions and magnificent winter beauty, with a big splash of basic goodness and Godliness thrown in. It was home.

8. The Changing Sixties

The growth of true friendship may be a lifelong affair.
—Sarah Orne Jewett

The sixties rolled in with conflicting joys and concerns: great joy on the home front with the advent of Betsy, concerns nationally and internationally with roiling civil rights tensions in the nation and the increasing unsettledness abroad. Our family looked forward to a few more years of togetherness before jumping into the boarding school years, and we made the most of them.

AN ASSORTMENT OF ACTIVITIES

Betsy came into the fold in September 1960. No baby could have been more joyously welcomed than she. Weighing in at ten pounds and already chubby-cheeked, she looked two weeks old at birth. There always seemed to be someone around to cherish her when she was awake, and she thrived. In the preceding month another girl-child had been born at LMH, Julie Harders. These two would go through twelve years of school together, be a part of each other's weddings, and remain lasting friends across the miles and the years. The ties of Yosemite had begun for another generation.

My first Yosemite book discussion group also came into being in the opening sixties. This was a facet of life I sorely missed, eagerly welcomed, and enjoyed in its various forms throughout our Valley years. This early format was a Great Books discussion group conducted by YPCC's Stuart Cross around a large table in the YPCC orientation room. Stuart's professorial background made him a natural for leading provocative discussions. Stuart and Great Books kept our rapt attention for about four years. In succeeding years, as people and ideas changed, a variety of methods were tried. By 1969 the "group" was a course sponsored by the Merced College Extension Division with the amiable Edward Bean coming up from Merced to lead some lively discussions. When it became unrealistic for the college to financially justify his long drive to Yosemite, we continued on, limping at times, but always eager to share book ideas and opinions. Fran Scoble contributed much as an appointed leader in the later seventies. On her departure, the pattern of rotating-leader developed. In the mid-eighties, Mary Ellen Gorman was the glue that held us together. The Book Group, as we called ourselves, was my sacrosanct evening-out. It delights me to report that, at this writing, there is still an active, ongoing book discussion group in the Park.

The enrollment in Yosemite Elementary School had climbed to 136 students. An inspired project to provide the school with its own library was begun in 1961 under the joint auspices of the Parent Group and the Lions Club. Charlie was chairman of the library planning committee. The venture was kicked-off with a highly successful fund drive. No one was spared from eager solicitation—not gas station attendants, not grandparents, not a single approachable adult. The donation of appropriate books was also welcomed (*appropriate* being the definitive word). The new library was housed in the school's multipurpose room. Moveable protective covers were custom-made for the shelves, since the room also served as a basketball court in inclement weather. Later, when school enrollment dropped, the library was moved into an unused classroom, where it remained and flourished over the years. Some years the school had a dedicated volunteer librarian, among them Helen Johanson, Paula Davis, Patti Reilly, Diana Johnston, and Mary Vocelka. Other years, the library was manned by a group of mothers working assigned days. The library lived up to all expectations as a valuable community gift to the school, both in its collection and with its all-volunteer management.

Other happenings in the Valley during the early sixties included the instigation of the Ansel Adams Photography workshops, the arrival of the Bill Henning family, he to be our minister, and the exodus of the NPS Training Center to the Grand Canyon. In the spring of 1962, the Park played host to the Shah of Iran and his Queen, Farah, and to President Kennedy later that summer. The President's visit involved much fanfare, excitement, and a special rocking chair. In the fall, PBS's KQED was gratefully welcomed into our viewing lives. In 1963, upon the retirement of Walter Fitzpatrick, Rusty Rust took over as postmaster. Thus began the open door/open heart policy that held forth at the post office for almost thirty years. Arlis Carter became the assistant. The Snowflake Room at the Badger Pass ski area was opened on the upper level to jazz up the ski lodge fare with genuine Ahwahnee cuisine. It proved difficult to continue brown bagging it for some of our four as they watched their buddies, whose dads were "all meals, all units" Curry executives, disappear up into the Snowflake Room for a gourmet lunch.[1]

The Bob Smiths became our neighbors to the west, and Frank and Kathy Betts were to the south. New friends included the Gary Browns, the Wayne Howes with their four boys, Dr. Walt and Judy Morgan, the Hendricksons (back in Yosemite after military service in Germany), the Merrys, Englishes, Shackeltons, and Joneses. As the decade moved on, we came to know the Worthingtons, Warnocks, Flemings, and the Don Crosses. On the flip side, we were again bidding farewells: the Slijks off to Chula Vista, the Morrises off to Hal's own Plaza Books in Santa Cruz (he became my personal book shopper), the Conners to San Luis Obispo to pursue an academic career at California Polytechnic University. Park service farewells saw some friends off to other national parks: the Branges to Everglades, the Armstrongs to Zion, the Betts to Grand Canyon, and the McLarens and Rick Andersons to Sequoia.

By 1962, Chuckie, Anne, and Rob were able to travel further than to our favorite river beach for a picnic. That summer my dad and brother Rob joined us on our first trip to the newly constructed Sunrise High Sierra Camp. Toddler Betsy stayed in the Valley with my mom and an expectant Aunt Liz. It was a lovely three-generational outing, with Dad spreading his love and knowledge of wild flowers to his three grandchildren. When we absolutely had to head home the following day, we parted company in Long Meadow. From there, the various paths leading homeward reflected the varying abilities of the hikers. Chuckie and his Uncle Rob headed for the Valley over the view-filled Clouds Rest trail. Anne and her dad were off to climb Tenaya Peak before descending the Cathedral Lake fisherman's trail to join the remaining threesome at the car below. On our chosen path, my dad, small Rob, and I had a nice, unpressured meander through flower-filled meadows and past glistening lakes under the bluest of skies.

A few weeks later Anne and I joined my parents for a performance of *Kismet* in San Francisco, a treat for these mountain ladies. It was the last such occasion I would share with my mother, as one morning, less than a month later; she just didn't wake up. Mom was such an avid Giants/Willy Mays fan that we decided perhaps her heart really had been broken by Willy's failure to win the 1962 World Series.

MISSION 66 AND OTHER OUTSIDE INFLUENCES

The Mission 66 project, conceived in 1956 by the National Park Service to bring a renaissance to the parks, was moving to completion in Yosemite. Construction on the new stretch of Tioga Road began in the summer of 1960—with all the emotions still rampant. It was expected that one season would see it finished, but the road was not actually dedicated until the end of June 1961. Principal speaker at the dedication was Assistant Secretary of the Interior John A. Carver. The setting was Olmsted Point. Other participants were NPS Director Wirth, Will Colby (former secretary of the Sierra Club) and our Superintendent, John Preston. In his speech, Carver seemed to make light of the years of trauma connected with the building of the controversial road when he said, "If the Park Service is to have roads they might just as well be good ones."

Other Mission 66 projects progressed: the winterizing of the

Wawona Hotel, the remodeling of Camp Curry, the addition of new lodge accommodations, and twenty new NPS houses in El Portal. A new school was also in the plans for El Portal. It is interesting to read a quote from then Assistant Superintendent Keith Neilson in a 1960 *Yosemite Sentinel:* "El Portal may someday be the largest town in Mariposa County." It hasn't happened yet, nor does it seem likely to happen. The years have shown that most people, when moving from the Park, pass El Portal by, opting to buy equity-producing homes in the Mariposa or Oakhurst areas.

CAMP 6

Charlie had many patients who returned to the Park and to tent living in Camp 6 summer after summer. This was the loyal cadre of men serving as seasonal park rangers and naturalists. They were, for the most part, educators, and brought their families with them. They were dedicated to their two careers, teaching school and rangering, and these careers jibed well timewise. The summer crowds in those days didn't arrive in hordes until the schools were out and, conversely, dropped off with the Labor Day school-openings. It was a win/win situation for both the National Park Service and for the teacher-families.

Camp 6 was located between the Village Store complex and the Merced River. It had the privacy of forest cover and a lovely, often private, stretch of swimming beach nearby. In later years this was our favorite spot for a quick after-work dip. In addition to the NPS employees, many YPCC summer employees, church student helpers, and other seasonal employees and volunteers were housed in Camp 6. When Charlie needed summer dental student housing, this was where it was found.

Most of the NPS tents were double-length, two-sectional affairs: one section for sleeping, the other for living. If family size warranted, a private tent or trailer could be incorporated along the side. The area was served by communal bathhouse/restroom facilities. The nearest person to the booth answered the public telephone and delivered the message. Proximity to the Village Store was a convenience, and the discount program was intact and applicable to seasonals. Because of the bear problem, food storage could be tricky, and refrigeration space was necessarily limited, so food buying was pretty much on a day-to-day basis.

Convenience, camaraderie, and outdoor living in a beautiful setting were the key to the popularity and success of Camp 6. The group of regular seasonal families occupied the same sites year after year. They became part of the summer Yosemite community life. Many names come to mind including the Easterbrooks, Russells, Merlin Millers, Grays, Pimentals, Potts, and McMillans. Good summer substitutes for the various bridge clubs came from this group.

The Jim Ices were among the Camp 6-ers. Their daughter Linda, when husband Len McKenzie was appointed Yosemite's Chief of Interpretation for the NPS, returned in the eighties as part of the permanent community. Linda became active both as a Girl Scout leader and as the Yosemite Elementary School secretary. After Len's job moved to the Bay Area, Linda returned often to hike in the high country. The Ice's grandson, Jim McKenzie, is carrying on the tradition and is currently on the NPS rolls in Yosemite.

The seasonal interpreters lived in their own small Camp 19 enclave, on the south side of the river, in our earliest years. With its demise, these families were absorbed into Camp 6. The Brubaker family was part of this group before moving on up to White Wolf, where they were active for many summers. Lloyd Brubaker headed up the summer Junior Ranger program at Happy Isles in the years of our children's involvement.

The phasing out of the dedicated bunch of seasonal teacher/rangers began in the seventies. The demise of the convenience of Camp 6 living as a result of wind damage, and the increase in needed specific training for all protective division rangers (i.e., law enforcement school) were two of the reasons for this change; another was the gradual extension of the Park's busy season. It no longer jibed with the school vacation span. By the end of the decade, this congenial symbiosis was a thing of the past.

THE CHANGING OF THE GUARD

In October of 1963, the NPS Superintendents' Conference was again held in Yosemite. As concessioners, we were invited. It was during this "conference of challengers," as it became known, that NPS Director Conrad Wirth announced his upcoming retirement. The following evening we attended the conference-closing banquet at the Ahwahnee. A prevailing sense of sadness enveloped the crowd, a group composed of NPS employees and concessioners who had worked with Wirth for many years. Wirth was a dedicated National Park Service careerist who radiated a sense of civility and kindness. Word was already out that Associate Director George W. Hartzog had been appointed to assume the directorship the following January. There was the strong impression of a knife-in-the-back having been inflicted.

It is fascinating to read versions of this episode in Wirth's autobiography *Parks, Politics and the People*[2] and Hartzog's *Battling for the National Parks*.[3] It seems that if there was a knife-in-the-back, it came from Assistant Secretary of Interior John Carver, not Hartzog. Carver was not fond of Conrad Wirth and felt the NPS to be "insular, rigidly bureaucratic and politically unresponsive." Even before Carver came to the Superintendents' Conference to give his infamous address, it had been set up, with Secretary of the Interior Stuart Udall's blessing, that Wirth's retirement announcement would be expected and accepted, Hartzog would be named to succeed him.

Carver's pet seemed to be the newly created Bureau of Outdoor Recreation, and he felt the NPS (i.e., Wirth) was ignoring this bureau and its directed assumption of some former NPS duties. In Carver's address to the NPS leaders at the Yosemite Conference, he stated, "When all else fails, the Park Service seems always able to fall back upon mysticism, its own private mystique. Listen to this sentence: 'The primary qualification requirement of the Division Chief position and most subordinate positions is that the employees be imbued with strong convictions as to the "rightness" of NPS philosophy, policy and purpose and who have demonstrated enthusiasm and ability to promote effectively the achievement of NPS goals.'" Carver went on to say, "This has the mystic, quasi-religious sound of a manual for the Hitler Youth movement. Such nonsense is simply intolerable...."

Wirth writes in his book that the auditorium was full of angry people after Carver's speech. Carver returned to Washington immediately, held a press conference that resulted in a story published the next morning stating that Wirth had been fired. At the same time, in Yosemite, Wirth was giving his long prepared letter of retirement to the just-arrived Secretary Udall. So it was that we in the Valley had very much been privy to all the emotional ins and outs of that particular NPS "changing of the guard."

MID TO LATE SIXTIES HAPPENINGS

The Centennial of Abraham Lincoln's designation of Yosemite Valley and the Mariposa Grove of Big Trees as "The Yosemite Grant" (to be administered by the State of California) was celebrated on June 30, 1964. This act was the basis for the later state and national park systems. In 1872, Yellowstone National Park was created and thereby officially becoming the first national park. There are those Yosemite loyalists, however, who feel our Park was first, certainly in designated intent, if not in nomenclature.

On December 22, 1964 with almost fourteen feet of snow and a forty-three degree temperature at Badger Pass, a heavy, warm rain began. The Valley was alerted and the flood plan, which John Preston had spearheaded after the 1955 inundation, was put into motion. Flood-prone buildings were evacuated—including the Preston's house—gauges were monitored, precautions were taken—and the waters rose. The Bracebridge Dinner was again disrupted, the locals were invited, and Santa again found his way to the Ahwahnee rather than to Camp Curry on Christmas Eve. The waters ebbed, clean-up commenced, and life went on. Fortunately, the chapel had been raised earlier that year so the damage inside was not as great as in 1955.

The Wawona Pioneer History Center was dedicated in September of 1964. Two years later construction began on the new Valley

Visitor Center, and the concessioner stable operation launched into its second hundred years. Horses, and the need for them, had been in the Valley a long time, under several different operators. In the new-friend department, Don and Peggy Baldwin were settling into the Valley, he as our protestant minister. Father Bob Thornton began his stint as resident Catholic priest. All three of these people contributed much to various facets of community life. Peggy became a strong plus for all theatrical endeavors.

Lots of moves were afoot. We lost the Currys to Southern California and Disneyland, the Metherells to Yellowstone, the Hubbards to Washington, D.C., and the Martischangs to Rocky Mountain National Park. With great joy, we welcomed the Robinsons back from a stint in the outside corporate world. Art became Vice President in charge of Administration for YPCC. The Bryan Harry family moved into the vacant Hubbard house down the street, he to fill Doug Hubbard's Chief Naturalist's position. The Wurglers were back in residence, Jim having completed his stint in Vietnam. There were new friendships to be made with the Briggs, the Utterbacks, the Barbees, the Ivan Millers, and the Hickmans in the Valley, also with the Hartmans in Wawona. The Dick Marks family would arrive before long to live around the corner and become part of our Christmas Eve tradition.

I wonder whether not wanting to go through a third flood had an influence on John and Betty Preston's decision to retire at the end of 1965. After his thirteen years of dedicated, caring concern for Yosemite Park and the community, John and Betty were affectionately feted as they moved into retirement. John and Marie Davis came to fill the superintendency.

THE TIES BEGIN TO LOOSEN

For our family, 1966 brought the first eighth grade graduation, Chuckie's, and the fall saw our first trip to deliver one of our own to the Colorado Rocky Mountain School in Carbondale, Colorado. The campus was a rustic collection of buildings set in the lovely Roaring Fork Valley under the shadow of Mt. Sopris, a feel not unlike home.

The Yosemite Arts Guild was organized in 1967 under the auspices of the YPCC and the guidance of Art Robinson. This was a generous gift to the community, and we all enthusiastically responded to its offerings. Over the next few years the guild sponsored a great variety of cultural happenings to which the community was invited. Several musical groups performed in the Ahwahnee's Great Lounge; among them the Fresno Philharmonic, a jazz group, various vocal and string ensembles, and, one year, the Southern Oregon College Choraliers. Drama groups were invited to put on plays. One year a popular film festival was organized. Charlie and I served on the Art Guild Advisory Board at one point. Unfortunately, these activities ended with the advent of the new Park concessioner in the seventies.

Anne Hendrickson and Char Wilson organized the first cooperative play-school for the Yosemite community in the latter sixties. It became a successful venture involving many mothers of preschoolers. In the beginning, it was housed in a Visitor Center facility and was active two mornings a week. All mothers were expected to contribute time and expertise. Since then, some form of preschool program has existed in the Valley and the seeds were sown for the day care center that would fully materialize in 1983.

Fall 1967 found us again preparing for the boarding school trek across to Colorado, this time to deliver both Chuck (when one starts high school, one's mother is expected to drop the "ie") and Anne. We had looked long and hard for a coeducational boarding school as it would be more convenient to have the two of them in the same place, and thinking they would like to be in the same school. I'm not sure the latter idea had much effect on the eldest of the four at the time, however, as Anne later professed to being roundly ignored by her brother much of the time. After hours spent affixing nametapes to Anne's clothing and linens and refurbishing Chuck's gear, we packed the trailer with all of the above, light camping gear, and mere essentials for the rest of us—and we were off. Often, along the way, I thought of my paternal grandparents, each of whom came west as a child in a covered wagon with the family's worldly goods aboard. Here we were, making the trip in reverse two generations later. At times, out in that arid, barren Humboldt Sink I felt very much the pioneer.

ISIE

Somewhere in the confusion of our takeoff in 1967, I had been told the name of the new teacher who would join the staff at the local school to teach the fifth and sixth grades. At some point as we were tooling across the vastness that is central Nevada and Utah, the name popped into my head and I was struck with the realization that it was a very familiar one. Could it possibly be the Isabel Tinning whose Aunt Margie had been a dear friend of my mother's from college days at UC Berkeley? Could it be the same Isie Tinning who had knocked the socks off her many friends and admirers at Cal, just a couple of months before I entered Cal, by quietly entering the Dominican Order of the Roman Catholic Church and disappearing from the outside world? I couldn't wait to get home to find out.

Yes, it *was* the same Isabel Tinning. And on the day we met, I gained a delightful new friend, one to whom I had old ties even though we had never seen each other before. Isie had left the Dominican order the previous spring and there was not a better place than Yosemite for her entry into a secular school system and a welcoming community. She brought a quiet, yet witty, sense of serious teaching to her students. Rob just missed having her as a teacher, but they became good friends over the years she shared our lives. Betsy eventually was a part of Isie's classroom, for two appreciated years.

Isie added a gentle, intelligent sparkle to our dining table and our lives. She and I shared a similar Bay Area/Cal Berkeley family background and many a chuckle over Herb Caen's daily column in the *San Francisco Chronicle*. We joined her at the Tinning family home at Fallen Leaf Lake near Tahoe on several occasions, for good fun, chancy fishing, and chilly swimming. Isie partook of all Yosemite had to offer, reveling in the freedom and grandeur of the trails while sharing her Park with numerous nieces and nephews. She stayed in Yosemite for six years, and then felt the need to venture forth into new areas, both career-wise and geographically.

Isie's next adventure took her to Keystone, Colorado, where she worked with Bob Maynard at the Keystone ski area for a couple of years. Finally the tug of roots pulled her back to the Bay Area, where she had been raised and still had close family ties. The perfect, small house in Belvedere was found, across the street from the yacht harbor on San Francisco Bay. What a cozy home it was, with always a favorite cat. She went to work for Wells Fargo in the very stressful job of crisis counseling. This was re-entry into the real world in spades.

Isie came up from Marin to join us for both Anne's and Betsy's weddings in 1978 and 1983. She too had developed the special ties to Yosemite that snag so many people. How lucky for us that a teaching position had come open in 1967 and that Isie appeared in our lives. Another treasure was lost when she died of cancer in November of 1984.

HARTZOG'S VOICE

More changes came to the Valley in early 1968 when Director of the NPS Hartzog began to make his voice heard in the Park. Stuart Cross succeeded Hil Oehlmann as president and general manager of YPCC. Oehlmann became board chairman, and Mary Tresidder became honorary board chairman, having retired from active participation in the company. The NPS Master Plan was in the works. A UPI story made public a letter from Hartzog to Stuart Cross proposing: elimination of such crowd-drawing attractions as the famed firefall and the vaudeville entertainment at Curry-sponsored campfires, to be replaced by more ranger/naturalist talks.[4]

The next elimination on Hartzog's list was the Wawona golf course, which as of this writing hasn't happened. Rafts and air mattresses were prohibited on the Merced River. Air mattressing down the Merced was great summertime sport. Dotty Power and I shared some fine floats, including the time her bathing suit was snagged by a just-cast fishhook as we floated under Sentinel Bridge. The prohibition did put a damper on floating for some of my Park Service wife cronies. Cooler heads prevailed and the ban lasted only one season. Hartzog's plan was also to designate specific swimming beaches along the river but this did not come to pass until the closures in the seemingly inhospitable nineties.

Then followed two excellent, and now proven, Hartzog proposals: the setting up of a shuttle-bus system in the east end of the Valley and the instigation of the one-way Valley road system. These both came to fruition in the next few years, as did the closing of the east end of the Valley to private cars. For the Valley campgrounds Hartzog proposed restriction of the number of campsites and the instigation of a reservation/use fee system. Both of these inspired programs were later accomplished.

Several public-input meetings sponsored by the Master Plan Study Team followed Hartzog's proposals. Copious survey pages were filled out by hundreds of interested individuals. The primary concerns expressed there would resurface in the nineties, with the Valley Implementation Plan. Who should have access to the Valley, by what means, and what types of amenities should be made available?

The first visible change in the Valley scene was the elimination of the firefall. James McCaulay, innkeeper on Glacier Point, initiated the firefall in 1872 for the enjoyment of those below.[5] Great chunks of red fir bark were gathered and ignited on the edge of Glacier Point. As darkness fell these glowing embers were pushed over the cliff, falling freely through the considerable stretch to the next ledge. In 1902, after a hiatus of some years, David Curry reinstated the custom. Great production was made in the calling of the firefall from Camp Curry, the answer floating down from above and the lilting strains of the *Indian Love Call* filling the air[6]. In these late sixties Hartzog felt the firefall created Valley gridlock and was inappropriate to the naturalness of a park. The folders of NPS correspondence forthcoming indicated that the public of all ages did not let go of the firefall easily or graciously. Many Yosemite residents gathered near the Church Bowl, a spot that afforded a wonderfully open view of the Point, on the night of January 25, 1968. The last firefall was a beautiful sight, as the cascade of embers fell on and on and on. We sang *Indian Love Call* and raised a tearful toast, as it all became a memory.

THE SIXTIES ROLL OUT

By the end of the decade, we had two off in boarding school and the other two very much involved in the local school and activities, and I was ready to venture into something more. It dropped into my lap when the Olivers announced retirement and Gene Ottonello, at the Credit Union, was looking for someone to take Dete Oliver's part-time job as his assistant. I jumped into it, putting in a few hours twice a week. An accountant I wasn't, so I had to pick up the basics quickly. I found that I thoroughly enjoyed dealing with people. Some of them were strange and wonderful, for I remember Charlie being accused of raising his dental fees for a particular person because I (his wife) was privy to how much money said person had stashed in the Credit Union.

The Olivers' retirement was the beginning of an exodus of the delightful group of old timers who had welcomed us into the Park almost twenty years before. All too soon the Otters, Ouimets, Breckenkamps, and Cramers followed the Olivers' lead. After a relatively short stay in the Park, Superintendent John and Marie Davis were also ready to retire. Larry and Mary Hadley soon moved into the superintendency to become the first family in the superintendent's house in our Park years.[7]

Meanwhile, the country was in turmoil. Repercussions of the war in Vietnam were widely felt and the Park was experiencing its share of the waves. The turbulent years were upon us, with the biggest changes yet to come. So many facets of the life of our community were to be affected in the following decade.

9. Betsy's Birthday

Tuesday's child is full of grace.

—*Anonymous*

Our youngest's birthday came to be the harbinger of fall in our earlier years in Yosemite. Betsy was born the day after Labor Day, the
sixth of September 1960. I went to the hospital early in the afternoon
and she was born about four o'clock. The next morning Rob—Dad
by the hand—walked off to his first day of kindergarten with Pauline
Trabucco. It was truly the end of summer and the beginning of the
school year. But it also marked the end of Charlie's busiest season,
and could often herald a much-needed vacation. The Yosemite Elementary School staff was very understanding about such things.
Many Park breadwinners just couldn't leave the job during the busy
summer season.

Labor Day came earlier the next year and Betsy's first birthday
found us well into our vacation travels. We were at the Ashleys' in
Mt. Rainier. We had driven up through northern California, Oregon, and on into Washington to reach the Ashleys' new park. It was
our first time to see them since their leaving Yosemite so it was a
joyous reunion. Betsy was introduced around, then the older kids
were off and away with Janet and David. Here we were, Betsy's birthday at hand, and where else could one find a more proficient birthday cake baker than Ethel Ashley? That birthday cake, however, was
not to be. Ethel had gone over the handlebars of her bike in a downhill plunge a few days earlier and was suffering from sore ribs and a

broken hand. We were made painfully aware of this when Charlie tried to give her a hug in greeting.

The next morning, however, we scattered over the hillsides gathering wild huckleberries for a birthday pie. Since Ethel's good stirring hand was out of commission, by default *I* was expected to make the piecrust. I can only say that for me it was comparable to being asked to do the honors in Betty Crocker's kitchen. Somehow I managed, the one birthday candle was affixed and lighted—and the pie promptly disappeared. The mouthwatering flavor of wild huckleberries can cover a multitude of sins. Birthday number one in Mt. Rainier National Park was the first of many on-the-trail birthdays for Betsy.

ANOTHER BIRTHDAY, OTHER ADVENTURES

In 1963, Betsy again had the chance for an Ethel birthday cake. By now, the Ashleys had moved to Yellowstone National Park. We wanted to check out their new surroundings, and to see another world famous park. This opportunity to view other parks through the eyes of our NPS friends was a gift that only increased over the years. The experiences proved invaluable.

When we left home that Labor Day weekend, we headed over the Sierra and on around the Mono Craters to the dip road—a family name for the undulating stretch of Highway 120 between the Craters and Benton Station. A very special and long-planned event was to take place that evening. It was the weekend of the High Sierra Centennial Climb and thirty Sierra peaks were scaled that day. The climb honored the one hundredth anniversary of the Whitney survey team's exploration of the Yosemite peaks. At 9:00 P.M. a light was to appear on the most southerly peak, Mt. Whitney. As soon as that light was visible from Mt. Russell, a flare was to be lit there, and so it was to continue in a northerly direction until all thirty peaks were aglow, the last in line being Cloud's Rest, Half Dome, then a special firefall from Glacier Point. We stopped the car at a high point along the road hoping to catch a glimpse. Soon we were rewarded by seeing the lights come alive atop Mts. Ritter, Banner, and Lyell—a thrilling sight. We oh-ed and ah-ed awhile, then went on our way to find the night's camping spot.

In those days, we always camped our way across the country. Motel money for six was not available in our budget unless the elements ordained otherwise. We carried with us the basic gear for a simple camp supper, overnight camping, and an equally simple breakfast. It worked well, giving the kids plenty of time to run and stretch. This method of travel also meant we had neither reservations to make nor deadlines to keep.

We arrived in Yellowstone after a couple of days, eager for our first glimpse of that huge park. In the Ashleys we had excellent tour guides, and Betsy had a superb Ethel birthday cake. All of us were much impressed with the wildlife: bison, elk, and moose, to say nothing of the grizzlies spotted occasionally off in the trees. We soon learned to be alert on the trail: this park was less hiker-friendly than Yosemite. The geysers and hot pools, the colorful mineral deposits and travertine waterfalls, the variety of terrain all fascinated us. Our few days there whetted our appetite for more, and we returned to Yellowstone several times in later years.

From Yellowstone, we headed south to Grand Teton National Park, where we set up our camp at Coulter Bay. Finding a campsite after Labor Day was never a problem in those days. Again, we found a former Yosemite friend, in the person of Dick Stenmark. He and Charlie were soon making plans for a climb of the Grand Teton. None of the youngsters were yet of an age or inclination to go along (how that would change over the years). While the men climbed, the rest of us filled the day exploring the wonders around us. Ours was a nice campground in a spectacular lakeside setting. Its restroom holds two enduring memories for me: it was the only National Park Service restroom I have ever seen with hot running water, and on its wall hung the mirror in which I spotted my first gray hair! Must have had something to do with the climb of the Grand Teton in progress.

As the late afternoon came on so did the rain. I awaited Charlie's return from the mountain eagerly. We made the best of that night but left the next morning with our U-Haul trailer full of soggy camping gear. We headed south into Colorado to spend the night in a welcoming motel in Craig.

Leaving in the morning, we headed east over Rabbit Ears Pass. At mid-pass we had a short time-out while Charlie changed the fuel pump. I was amazed that he just happened to have a spare. In response to my asking "how come," he admitted that these station wagons were notorious for going through fuel pumps. In fact, he went on, he had brought the car's registration papers in case we had to abandon it somewhere along the line. I wasn't quite sure how to absorb that bit of news.

At Kremmling we turned south, driving through the lovely Blue River valley to the site of the Dillon Dam project. This area would eventually become Lake Dillon. Little did we imagine then that Rob would settle here in the late seventies and that nearby Keystone would become one of our favorite and oft-visited ski areas. Then came the long pull over Independence Pass (elevation 12,000 feet). Would the station wagon make it pulling a trailer? Yes! Much cheering. Down into Aspen we dropped. It was still pretty much an unsophisticated old mining town in 1963, with a certain rustic charm. On we went to look over the Colorado Rocky Mountain School in Carbondale, a possible high school choice for Chuckie. We must have looked a well-worn bunch by then, but they accepted Chuck three years later anyway.

We continued across western Colorado, Utah, and into Nevada. At some point along the way Charlie began to feel rotten. As we passed through Ely, and began the seemingly endless pull across to Tonopah, things were becoming a bit edgy in the car. We ate an early picnic supper along the way and now darkness approached. In that free-range country, a driver needed to be on constant alert for cows meandering on the roadway. We had passed through Currant Junction and were on a long stretch of barren, unvarying road—at times as many as twenty to thirty miles with nary a bend. A time of reckoning was at hand—a miserable dad, the threat of smacking into a cow, darkness falling, and a gas gauge telling us we were not going to make it to Tonopah without a refill—when we topped a rise and saw the lights of a small someplace in the far distance.

This was our introduction to Warm Springs, Nevada: a gas pump, a faded BAR sign in front of a tavern/office structure behind the pumps, a couple of old motel rooms across the highway, and a few smaller shacks clustered around the main building. Charlie said he couldn't go any further, so into the bar he went to see what he could find us for the night. Yes, they could put us up in the building across the road, but we had to pay right then. It had been one of those "have everything ready, the car packed and we can leave when I finish with my last patient" type of trips, and it was I who had purchased and signed the traveler's checks. Therefore it was I who had to go into the smoky, partially filled barroom to make payment. Charlie was so miserable he was barely functioning. Not being very brave about this sort of encounter, I scooped up my best defense, three-year-old Betsy, and with her in my arms headed off into the building. Up to the bar we went—to sign the checks as quickly as possible. The bartender, however, was not to be hurried, and stated loudly that he wanted "to buy this cute little boy's mama a drink." In the next breath he instructed a crusty old codger sitting at the bar to go across the street and change the sheets. Yup, that was no overnight motel across the way! Declining the drink as graciously as I could while edging toward the door, Betsy and I retreated to the waiting family.

We took the barest of essentials into our night's home-away-from-home and surveyed the situation. Sure enough, there was ol' Slim changing the three double beds as best he could after the evening's libations. There were two connecting rooms with a bathroom of sorts and no locks on the doors. My last request of Charlie, before he painfully collapsed into bed, was that he please hang his newly purchased Stetson on the post at the foot of the bed to inform anyone bursting in that there was a "real man" in there. Chuck and Rob shared a bed, as did Anne and Betsy. Looking at the grungy sheets, then at my baby, I decided she would go into her sleeping bag to sleep on top of the bed. In spite of my concerns, I must have died, for the next thing I knew it was morning. After a brief panic, I discovered Betsy and bag had rolled off the bed and there Betsy peacefully slept, face-down on the gritty carpet. But the night had passed, we all survived, and Charlie was feeling better. When the tank was filled, I paid a chastened and sober manager for the gas. Off we went to Tonopah, a heavenly breakfast and more than a few chuckles.

IN OUR OWN BACKCOUNTRY

Birthday number four was another memorable one. Charlie and I left Tuolumne Meadows, heading for Smedberg Lake in the northern part of the Park, with five youngsters and four burros. One of the burros carried a lighter pack, and on top of that pack sat Betsy. It can't have been very comfortable. Many times her caring brother Chuck talked her up hill and down dale.

The first night on the trail found us in Cold Canyon, a mile or so up from the Glen Aulin junction. I was impressed by how much Charlie knew about the care and packing of animals, knowledge gained during his summers at Echo Lake. Soon, he had the boys—Sherrill Conner was with us—and Anne into their assigned jobs and a routine was established for the trip. That night we celebrated Betsy's fourth birthday with singing around the campfire. Our second day found us up and over the ridge, making the steep descent into, then rise out of, Virginia Canyon. We camped in Matterhorn Canyon that night. By the afternoon of the third day we were setting up our campsite on the shore of glistening Smedberg Lake. What a magnificent setting. Nearby smaller lakes Doe and Sister afforded great swimming and warm rocks for sunning. We basked, and with diligence managed to keep kids from frying.

In retrospect, I have always been impressed at Charlie's cool composure on that trip, three days out in the wilderness with a quite inexperienced helpmate, five youngsters of ages ranging from four to twelve, and the care of four pack animals. But it worked and we had a glorious time. The kids and Charlie fished, we hiked, swam, ate simple campfire meals, and introduced the kids to the first of their long-remembered "happy-jollys," those special evening times around a campfire. To this day we have a couple of campfires at family reunions if possible.

Toward the end of our stay, Charlie decided he would like to make the 1,000-foot descent to Benson Lake, a distance of about five more miles along the trail. The older boys and Anne went along. Rob opted to stay with Betsy and me. My parents had made trips to Benson Lake in their earlier years and had given glowing reports of its beauty. I hoped to get there someday, but this was not to be the time.

When the others departed, Rob, Betsy and I finished our camp chores and decided to meander down the lake toward a campsite whose flickering fire we had seen the evening before. With a four-year-old, it *is* pretty much of a meander. Betsy and I were delighted that nine-year-old Rob had chosen to stay with us. The three of us had good fun exploring the flora and tiny fauna along the shore. How lovely to have a kick-back day in this pristine spot. When we reached the camp the fishermen were off at another lake, but the Indian packer-cook was in residence. We had a good chat with him and found that the party was out of one of the pack stations on the Sierra's eastside. What I did not need him to tell me, as he knowingly assessed the clouds in the distance, was, "Those clouds have snow in them." He had already told me his group was moving out that afternoon. The kids and I soon headed back toward our own end-of-the-lake campsite. We still had a few hours before Charlie's return, and this Nervous Nelly began to ponder the fate of one man, one greenhorn turning into a basket case, five kids (even more responsibility in that one was not our own), and four burros, three days out from civilization—in a snowstorm!

Charlie and the kids returned to tell of a great hike and a splendid few hours cavorting in and around the lake, and the pull for my eventually getting to Benson Lake only got stronger. The snow did not materialize and we started for home the next morning, making the outward journey in an impressive two days.

By the time Betsy turned five, she had started kindergarten, and was allowed a traditional birthday party with small friends around the table with all the trimmings. What a strange, new experience. However, after a week of school for all four, we took off on our usual fall trip, this time to Zion National Park and the southwest.

THE SURPRISE PARTY

Birthday number six was a true family project. We were taking Chuck off for his first year of boarding school at the Colorado Rocky Mountain School in Carbondale, Colorado. It was a traumatic time for this mom, saying goodbye to her fourteen-year-old first-born as he headed out into the world, so I decided we could use a bit of a diversion. We would throw a family surprise birthday party for Betsy wherever we happened to be camping on September 6. The five of us didn't mention a word to her about her upcoming birthday. We would be well on our way by the time school began, and Betsy and her friends were not yet into knowing whose birthday was when. The mail was easily intercepted and incoming grandparent packages were squirreled away. Everyone had a package for Betsy, wrapped and hidden away with the luggage. It was a full trailer, with all of Chuck's off-to-school requirements (blankets, towels and the like), our camping gear, everyone's personal stuff, and, in a secluded corner, a portable birthday party.

We were in Arches National Monument (later made a National Park) for the birthday. On our way into the park, we stopped at a Moab market to surreptitiously pick up a decorated birthday cake and some fresh produce. In those days it was still possible to find the perfect camping spot in those wonderful, relatively undiscovered parks. We succeeded, and set up our camp by some great red rocks and low cliffs. It was mid-afternoon and bodies were tired of sitting so long in the car. The suggestion that the kids head over the rocks to do some exploring, with Betsy in tow, was jumped at. Charlie and I had a grand time setting up the surprise: balloons, fancy paper tablecloth and napkins, party hats and favors, a mound of presents, and a six-candled birthday cake in the middle of it all. Back they came at the designated time and what surprise and joy were written on that young face as she took it all in. This was one party where the givers had every bit as much fun as the honoree, and it proved an excellent way to keep our minds from the eventual purpose of our journey, that of delivering Chuck to boarding school the following day.

The next morning we awoke, knowing that this was the day. We had better than half a day's drive still ahead of us so we got on with it. We arrived at the school at the designated time and did the appropriate things and met the people we needed to meet, then unloaded our Chuck, his gear and his person. One lesson we learned right then, and continued to practice for years, was that when parents drop a youngster off at boarding school it is of no benefit to anyone to hang around. The rest of us spent a subdued night in the motel in Glenwood Springs, then were up and heading for Rocky Mountain National Park early the next morning.

We continued on to see friends from earlier Yosemite days—in Rocky Mountain National Park, in Denver, and again in Yellowstone. But my strongest memory, gained that first day after our leaving Chuck, was how soon "the mantle is passed." We paused somewhere on a high pass in Rocky Mountain National Park to take a short hike, have our lunch, and look for Bighorn sheep. A "short hike" with Charlie goes on until all are weary, and then he goes on alone just a bit longer. This time Anne kept up with her dad every inch of the way, even after the rest of us had proclaimed enough. She was taking over for "the big boy."

CANYONLANDS, A NATIONAL TREASURE

The next on-the-road birthday was number twelve—1972. We were again on the way to take a child off to boarding school, our Rob for his senior year. Chuck was two years into college, and worked summers at the Tuolumne Meadows Chevron Station, so he wasn't with us. Anne had been working at the Tuolumne Meadows Lodge but came with us as she was recuperating from an ankle sprain. She had finished a year at UC Santa Cruz and would soon be off to France for a year of study at the University in Grenoble. So off the five of us went over the now familiar route to CRMS.

Since we had a new 4-wheel drive Jeep station wagon, we

planned to stop and explore a bit of Canyonlands National Park enroute. We had come to love that park over the years, and we still get back as often as we can. We added adventure to Betsy's birthday as we learned there are ways and ways of driving a Jeep over the likes of Elephant Hill. On our first attempt, we badly scraped the bottom of the vehicle, resulting in an oil pan leak. Rob accompanied his dad back to Moab for the necessary repairs. Our next adventure was a quick exit from Salt Creek Canyon just before a flash flood came roaring through. I've never seen so much water rushing over the side cliffs and, soon, down the center of the canyon. We made it out, and then watched the torrent pour over the brink of the next cliff and into the Colorado River, far below. It made us all true believers of the very real danger of flash flooding in dry creekbeds. Although the birthday didn't hold center stage that year, we did have a party— cake, packages and all.

NUMBER TWENTY, IN THE FAR NORTH

Betsy's last away-from-home birthday before she moved to her own home was her twentieth. This one found her at Wonder Lake in Denali National Park while on a trip to Alaska with her dad. Rob had been working on a fire crew in Kenai that summer. I had gone to England with a couple of friends. Chuck and Anne were both married and off in their own worlds. Dad and Betsy finished their summer jobs and took off on an Alaskan adventure of their own. They soon met up with Rob, his summer job also finished. Betsy had a warm reunion with her friend from pre-kindergarten days, Kris Brown. Pat and Gary Brown were stationed in Denali National Park. Kris had just married and was living nearby.

When Betsy turned twenty-one, she and I were the only ones at home. Her siblings no longer lived in Yosemite and Charlie was off on a backpacking trip with Wes Conner. In the Park there is only one place to celebrate such an auspicious occasion: the Ahwahnee Hotel, of course, so off we went. We had her first legal drink together in honor of the occasion, a special dinner, and singing waiters (she *hated* that).

In 1983, Betsy celebrated her birthday by being married four days later in a lovely ceremony in the garden of the Superintendent's Old House. We gave her, with much love, to Kerry Grande of Waterville, Washington, whom she had met at Humboldt State University. Thus ended for us the wonderful adventures wrapped around Betsy's birthdays. They had been great fun, and the family had covered a lot of territory together in the celebration of them.

10. Those Granite Walls

All things are sweetened by risk.

—Author unknown

Worlds within worlds.... There was another group of Yosemite aficionados in addition to those of us who lived and worked in the
Valley, and those who came for brief visits to enjoy the Park's grandeur. This was the growing community of serious rockclimbers,
young men from the Bay Area, the Central Valley, and Southern
California who were intrigued by the feats of the climbers of the thirties and forties—Salathe, the Bedayns, Brower, and company. They
came to Camp 4 to be challenged by the granite walls that surrounded Yosemite Valley. This group eventually became a part of our
lives—both directly and indirectly.

OUR AWARENESS KINDLES

In the fifties and early sixties we were fascinated by the action taking place on the cliffs around us. If anyone got wind of a climb in
progress the word spread rapidly and the best vantage point was
sought. Steve Roper's *Camp 4—Recollections of a Yosemite
Rockclimber* provides a fascinating extension of my own knowledge
of what took place on the Valley walls and spires during those
significant years. The book also gives an insightful glimpse into the
life of that other world: Camp 4. Our own world was touched by
theirs in that we became avid spectators of the big climbs, recognized
the climber faces around the Park, and became very aware of grow-

ing media intrusion into our peaceful Valley. With the press interest in these first ascents the Valley, on occasion, became a circus.

Climbing was not unknown to the Valley prior to the first assault of El Capitan, begun in the summer of 1957. The El Capitan climb, done in stages, and successfully completed in November 1958, was, however, the first to so completely capture local and press attention. The route of ascent was later named "The Nose." Warren Harding, working with a variety of partners, spearheaded the climb. With him, on the November day when he topped out, were Wayne Merry and George Whitmore. We were among the rapt audience below, spending as much time as possible in El Cap meadow, flat on our backs, binoculars in place. We were enthralled. El Capitan had been conquered.

In September 1960, The Nose was again the scene of activity when Royal Robbins, Chuck Pratt, Tom Frost, and Joe Fitschen attempted the first continuous ascent of El Cap. This was not a fixed rope, or "siege," climb, as the 1957-1958 climb had been.[2] The four men lived on the cliff for the seven days it took them to complete the challenge. This time I wasn't able to be down in the El Cap meadow. I was holed up in Lewis Memorial Hospital, where Betsy was born just as the climb began. For days anyone not nailed down to hospital emergency duties—or having a baby—was down in the meadow looking up. It was a lonely old hospital stay, but a real coup for Yosemite climbers. Hence, Anne's birth was celebrated with Edmund Hillary's conquest of Everest, and Betsy's with Robbins and company's first continuous ascent of El Capitan. She and I went home the day they reached the top.

In the early sixties I was far too busy with four youngsters to be more than marginally aware of the major advances in climbing technique and equipment that were making possible these first ascents. I was aware, however, of more climbers becoming familiar faces around the Valley. One evening in the mid-sixties we were invited to Anne and Rog Hendrickson's for dinner, along with a few other locals. Anne mentioned they had invited some of the climbers from Camp 4, so dress down—jeans would be appropriate. We had just turned up in our cleanest jeans when in the front door walked Liz Robbins looking absolutely smashing in a chic white outfit—right out of Camp 4! So much for the "who wears what and when" idea. In addition to the Robbins, we met Chuck Pratt and Yvon Chouinard. Chouinard was beginning to make a name for himself with the climbing hardware he was designing and using. Chuck Pratt had become one of the regulars in the climbing circle and a Valley persona as well. The occasion was a fascinating glimpse into that other world.

Climber Warren Harding became a familiar Valley figure in those years, as did Steve Roper (we all knew of the *Valley Climbers Guide* he had written) and Galen Rowell. A few climbers stayed around in the wintertime to teach skiing, including Kim Schmitz. Glen Denny was really one of our own in that he was a YPCC employee, then a climber. Herb Swedlund undoubtedly dated some of the nurses, as I remember him well. Wayne and Cindy Merry became great, continuing friends of ours. Daredevil Rick Sylvester definitely left his mark in local lore with his antics. Probably his most notorious was performed in February 1972, his parachute ski-jump off El Capitan. He intended to use this sequence in a movie he was making, but things didn't quite go the way he had planned. His parachute deposited him in a tree rather than in a meadow, his camera failed him, and the Park Service nailed his camera crew. The catch-the-NPS-unaware-and-run caper had not worked out.

REVERBERATIONS

There was one aspect of this group/these times that was disturbing to the Park establishment. This was the conflict that developed between the group trying to live where it needed to live to avail itself of the granite walls—with little collective income—and the group trying to provide visitor services for the paying public. On many occasions we observed the systematic food scrounging that developed in the lodge cafeteria. The lodge lounge was often used as the Camp 4 lounge, with all the grubbiness such use brought with it. The YPCC had a rough time keeping a lid on the situation. Yes, "The

Park belongs to the People," but the paying guests didn't always see this in quite the same light as the Camp 4 dwellers. The proximity of the lodge comforts to Camp 4 aided and abetted the freeloaders. We were privy to many tales from our establishment friends and know that these were not the easiest of times for the concessioner.

Another highly publicized climb took place in the Valley in 1970. Warren Harding and Dean Caldwell joined forces to make what turned out to be a twenty-seven day first ascent of an El Cap route named the "Wall of Early Morning Light."[3] We were all involved in this one—the press wouldn't let us not be. Harding liked publicity and he got it! Our good friend Pete Thompson was the National Park Search and Rescue ranger, so we had his input, as well. A stalwart collection of climbers was at the ready in case rescue was needed. When someone interpreted a movement of Harding's to be a distress signal, the call went out for the rescue helicopter. Harding furiously waved off the rescue, later vowing a signal had never been made, and the hue and cry went up over who would pay the helicopter expense. We were all very much aware of that furor. There were banner headlines in newspapers around the State as the climbers approached El Cap's summit. When they topped-out, a barrage of TV cameras was there to capture the moment. Amid the hoopla surrounding all this was a sense of disgust toward the publicity-seeking duo. We later heard that the friendship between the two men soon dissolved.

In light of the confusion, the aborted-rescue fiasco, and all of the notoriety that came in the wake of the climb, the National Park Service saw the need for a well organized Search and Rescue division. The SAR was founded in 1971. With the popularity of climbing ever increasing, more hikers in the backcountry, more water-related sports, a trained SAR team became essential. A good summation is given in Tim Setnicka's *Wilderness Search and Rescue*.[4] "The crux of SAR theory is that rescue is a transportation problem—of rescuers to the victim and the victim to safety." Later added to the trained teams in the Park, with their volunteer backups, were search dogs, which proved very useful. The helicopter became indispensable.

Since 1983, the NPS has leased one, with pilot, to be stationed at the Crane Flat lookout during the summer season.

Rescues can be enormously expensive. Who should pay? This question surfaced more and more frequently. In the early seventies former climber Raffi Bedayn came to the Valley on numerous occasions to work with the NPS and the climbing community on the possible development of some form of an insurance plan. Such an arrangement had been adopted successfully in European climbing communities. Unfortunately, the idea never took hold in Yosemite.

A pleasant offshoot of Raffi Bedayn's trips to the Park was getting to know both Raffi and Barbara Bedayn. Barbara was instrumental in getting our community involved in the AFS weekends. Through her contacts we began to host a group of American Field Service students for a weekend in Yosemite. These young people were foreign exchange students who were living with families in the Bay Area for the year. Valley and El Portal homes were opened to these students, and it proved a truly broadening experience all around. The program continued for several years. Additionally, when coming to Yosemite, Raffi would stop at the farmer's market in Berkeley, load the back of his pick-up with seasonal fruits and vegetables, then head for the mountains to hold his own farmer's market for the produce-starved locals of Yosemite. A thoughtful, interesting couple, they.

"IF YOU CAN'T BEAT 'EM, JOIN 'EM"

The Yosemite Climbing School was founded in 1969–70 under the auspices of the YPCC and the direction of Wayne Merry, Loyd Price assisting. The colorful "Go Climb a Rock" T-shirts blossomed prolifically around the Valley, bringing criticism from some in the climbing community, who felt their sport was being commercialized by two of their own.[5] Be that as it may, the climbing school caught on, and hundreds of novices, including our two boys in their younger years, have availed themselves of its expertise. In the late nineties the school began winding down. There are so many climbing walls and so many self-styled guides these days—and so much bootleg guiding—that there is less demand for the commercial lessons.

Camp 4 was renovated in the early seventies. The renovation included the closing of the upper reaches of the camp, the instigation of a fee plan, and a name change. It now appeared on Park maps and directional signs as Sunnyside Campground. It remained the last unrestricted camp in the Valley, and still a walk-in. Since it was first-come, first served and could hold six persons per site, it was the place people were sent to look for a spot when all the reserved campgrounds in the Valley were full. During the turmoil of the seventies, there was often a hodgepodge of types and ages using the campground. Eventually, the search and rescue volunteers were assigned their own special area and, later, a Park ranger was put in residence.

SEARCH AND RESCUE

During the spring months of the early eighties, I worked seasonally for the NPS Backcountry Unit with Ron Mackie and Laurel Munson Boyers, filling in until the summer seasonals came on duty. We worked out of a room abutting the chief ranger's office on the second floor of the Valley District Building and shared our not-large office with the SAR division, Mike Durr and John Dill. It was cozy! Although two phones could be ringing off the wall and people coming and going, much was accomplished, and I gained insight into the actions and interactions of SAR. Both of these men were extremely dedicated to their jobs, but for John Dill, it was his life. He was meticulous in detail and driving in perseverance. Already knowing the following saga, I came to appreciate his expertise even more.

On January 3, 1982, while daughter Anne and her husband Chas were resident winter rangers in Tuolumne Meadows, a plane enroute from Mammoth to the Bay Area disappeared over the Sierra. Aboard were an eleven-year-old boy, his mother, and his stepfather. That evening, Anne and Chas were alerted by an eastside Inyo National Forest ranger to the possibility that the plane may have gone down in the vicinity of Tioga Pass, the area of its last radio transmission. During that night the already deep snowpack received an additional nineteen inches.

The next morning, after contact with SAR ranger Mike Durr in the Valley, Anne and Chas set out on skis for Tioga Pass. Finding themselves sinking to their waists in the fresh snow, they changed to snowshoes, strapped the skis to their packs, and slogged on. It took them two hours to cover only the mile and a half to the summer ranger cabin at the end of the Meadows. They pushed on for another mile or so but falling darkness forced a return to the summer ranger cabin for the night.

By morning's measurement, Anne and Chas calculated that another four feet of snow had dropped in the preceding twenty-four hours. Leaving the cabin at nine, they spent an exhausting seven and a half hours covering the seven miles to the Tioga Pass ranger cabin, taking turns breaking trail. After another overnight in this cabin, they spent the whole of the next day searching the Dana Meadows/Gaylor Ridge/Tioga Pass/Tioga Lake area—to no avail.

The next day, day number five, the ground search was called off, and Anne and Chas returned to Tuolumne. The midnight oil was still burning brightly in the Valley SAR office, however. In a final attempt to find the downed plane, an Angel 3 helicopter was summoned from Lemoore AFB near Fresno. The helicopter, with Ranger Jim Sano—who knew the terrain well—aboard, picked up Anne and her gear in Tuolumne Meadows. From the air they searched the areas Anne and Chas had covered in the ground search, then flew a search pattern along the ridge between Gaylor Peak and Mt. Conness. After several passes, Sano spotted a plane nosed into a 45-degree snowslope three quarters of a mile east of the summit of White Mountain. Spirits rose, and the avalanche danger was assessed.

An approach to the plane on skis was deemed plausible. The party returned to the Meadows, dropped off Jim Sano, and picked up an equipped Chas. Back to the crash scene they flew. Anne and Chas, with their gear, were set down on a flat spot on a snow ridge north of the site. To lessen the chance of avalanche, they decided on a direct downhill walking approach for the last hundred feet. On finding a fracture in the snow with a slight slippage, a potential avalanche condition, it was decided that Anne would wait above this line while Chas carefully descended to the plane.

Once there, Chas rapidly began to shovel snow off of the plane's canopy. Could it be possible that the taps of his shovel on the plane's surface were being answered by a cry from within? Yes, yes, it *was* a human sound. Chas shouted the encouraging words up to Anne that there was a survivor. Anne radioed the news to the Angel 3, and then descended to join Chas in the digging.

Donnie Priest was found alive, after five nights in the freezing plane wreckage with two dead bodies and no food. Donnie later told of having slept much of the time. As Chas lifted Donnie gently from the plane, he discovered that Donnie's feet were bare and his pants were frozen around his legs. They wrapped him in Anne's parka, then put him into her sleeping bag. A crewman was lowered from the helicopter, and the three of them painstakingly loaded Donnie into the hoist-apparatus. He was carefully raised and safely secured inside the Angel 3. So began his evacuation to Yosemite Valley, then on to Fresno.

Anne and Chas remained on the mountainside, and continued to probe the wreckage. Both the mother and stepfather were found in their seats and frozen solid, apparently killed on impact. The rescue helicopter, by now low on gas and daylight hours, was forced to abandon the original plan to return for Anne and Chas. Therefore, after documenting vital information, the two spent the remaining daylight hours of their exhausting, never-to-be-forgotten day skiing the considerable miles back to their Tuolumne Meadows home.

In his official statement, Donnie said that when he saw that shovel coming through the window he knew it was the happiest day of his life. Through a strong will, this brave lad had survived, although the severe frostbite necessitated the amputation of both feet just above the ankles. He adapted well to his prostheses, and came back to the Park a few months later to express his thanks. Anne, already in Nepal in the midst of her Ama Dablam climb, had to miss the festivities, but Chas well represented the duo at the Ahwahnee luncheon celebration.

John Dill's persistence in spending hours plotting the plane's radio transmission blips on a Park map was widely credited with narrowing the route-direction-line of the plane and with the eventual location of the wreckage from the air. This is a dedicated and determined man.

FAMILY PARTICIPATION

Although climbing, per se, was phased out of our boys' lives when their working-summers in Tuolumne Meadows ended, they have each kept a great interest in hiking, backpacking, and "bagging the fourteeners" (climbing peaks over 14,000 feet)). Betsy, like her mom, was never even tempted by the thought of climbing. The "granite walls of Yosemite " did, however, have a lasting effect on one in our family. That it was Anne, I have since attributed to the fact that while awaiting her birth I was completely caught up in Maurice Herzog's *Annapurna,* the account of his successful climb of that peak in the far-off Himalaya. Also, just a few days before Anne's birth, Edmund Hillary had succeeded in his bid to be the first to conquer the summit of Everest. Climbing-vibes were in the ozone.[6]

As Anne grew, she showed signs of her dad's love of adventure. She felt the challenge of the high mountains and had the guts and common sense necessary to meet the challenge. She climbed while at boarding school in Colorado and while summering in Tuolumne Meadows, a mecca for climbers from all over the world. It was there, in 1976, a young British climber walked into Anne's life and never went home. Two years later, Anne and Chas Macquarie were married in a lovely Valley meadow. Yosemite Falls thundered in the background, granite walls sparkled with the glisten of spring runoff, and Half Dome was a majestic presence with its white crown of snow. After a brief delay for Anne to complete a NPS law enforcement training obligation, they were off to Alaska for a honeymoon that included the climbing of Mt. McKinley (Denali) by two different routes. Anne's ascent of the Cassien Ridge route was the first ever by a woman.

Summers for the two were spent in the Tetons with Anne a climbing ranger for the NPS and Chas a mountain guide for Exum Guide Service. Winters were spent snowed-in at Tuolumne Meadows in the capacity of resident winter rangers. Over several years they formulated plans for a challenging feat: an ascent of Everest. Somewhere along the line a group of planners merged and the wheels began to turn. Climbing skills were honed on a trip to Pakistan in 1981. Anne was the only female on that adventure. Then in the spring of 1982, Anne was invited to be a member of the American Women's Himalayan Expedition to climb Ama Dablam, a 22,800-foot peak in the Khumbu region of Nepal.

Coincidentally, Charlie and I were putting together our own April 1982 trip to Nepal with a Mountain Travel group. We signed up to trek the Kali Gandaki Gorge, worked hard to get into shape, enplaned to Kathmandu, bussed to Pokhara and were on the trail for about two weeks. It was a glorious experience—and I reveled in it. The views of Annapurna, Machhapuchhare, and Dhaulagiri from our various campsites were breathtakingly beyond description. This was the trip of a lifetime, one that left me with new insight into why people "go to the mountains." Although being so completely wrapped up in the challenges and experiences of our own trip kept us from dwelling on the dangers of Anne's, she was never far from mind.

After our trek of about eight miles a day for those two weeks, enjoying the mountain-sightings, the smiling Nepalese, the colorful donkey trains (we were well beyond any roads), the rhododendron trees, the rushing streams—even the thrill of the swaying bridges— we were back in Pokhara, and soon, Kathmandu. Two days after returning to the Mala Hotel, we received the joyful news that Anne had successfully led the second group of four in their summit attempt on April 22, 1982. The first group, also four, had summitted two day earlier. All eight women had made it, were safely down and would hike to Namche Bazaar to await their flight out. Unfortunately, we would have to leave Kathmandu before Anne arrived, but we did take a scenic flight to view Everest and Ama Dablam the next morning. We felt very close to Anne as we looked down on that rugged grandeur.

With us on our homebound flight out of Kathmandu were members of another American team who had successfully climbed Mt. Cholatse in the neighborhood of Ama Dablam. In the party were Galen Rowell and Verne Clevenger, both of whom we had previously known in Yosemite. They reported seeing Anne and party after the climb, and that all were well. Music to a mother's ears! Home we flew with very full hearts.

THE BIG ONE

Meanwhile, Chas, Jim Sano, and others were readying for their fall 1983 Everest expedition. They finally received the hard-to-get climbing permit from the Nepalese government. Hundreds of T-shirts needed to be sold, sponsors found, decisions made, and a climbing team selected. Their game plan was to have an equal number of men and women in the climbing party, and to attempt to put the first woman on the summit. The logo was "American Men and Women on Everest." By this time Anne was a year into a Master's program at UC Berkeley, but was able to make the necessary arrangements for a leave of absence.

After months of training and preparation, the team departed for Nepal at the end of July 1983. It was terribly hard to say good-bye to Anne and Chas this time. So much good and not so good had occurred in our lives that year. A section of my heart went on hold the day Anne and I parted. Charlie left mid-September to join a group trekking to the Everest basecamp, the moral support party. In this party were our old friends the Burtons, Dick Ewart and new friends Mary and Ned Barker. I stayed home and lived in limbo. While holding such positive thoughts for the team, I still had to come to grips with the knowledge that Anne and Chas would put their lives on the line, literally, many times. I well remember, with love, the thoughtful friends who called just to say, "I'm thinking of you, it can't be easy;" still chuckle over those who said, "How could you let her *do* this;" and wonder about those who said nothing.

The upshot was that the team didn't quite put a person of either gender on the summit, due to the weather closing in and the near-depletion of their oxygen supply. In the larger sense, they were highly successful in getting everyone down and safely home. All of these thoughts have been much in the minds of this family since the Everest tragedy of 1996. "Success" has been given a new perspective. In December of 1983, with Anne's homecoming, I experienced the rebirth of a special daughter. Anne gave up serious climbing in ensuing years, confiding, "When you have children, Mom, everything changes." Chas still climbs as time permits, and they are raising two very fine backpackers. Climbers? We'll see.

Are these Himalayan adventures important to my story of life in Yosemite? Not really. But Yosemite, per se, is very important to the story of these Himalayan expeditions. Yosemite fostered the challenge, nurtured the ability and strengthened the drive—in all of us.

11. Tenaya Lake: Close to Heaven

"O, World, as God has made it! All is beauty."
—*Robert Browning*

In the summer of 1949 a grand adventure came my way. I had completed my medical technology apprenticeship and had a couple of months to fill before starting a job at the University of California Medical Center in San Francisco. I jumped at the invitation to join forces with three similarly between-jobs friends to explore the west, a daring undertaking for four young ladies in those days of the forties. We had a great time covering the states from Mexico to Canada, from California on the west to Colorado on the east, eight in all. Where we had no welcoming connections, we camped. Toward the end of our six-week caper, we found ourselves in Glacier National Park on the shore of Lake McDonald. It was the loveliest place I had ever seen and I carried the memory away with me.

It was winter when I arrived in Yosemite, Charlie and I having been married on a January afternoon. The Tioga Road would be blocked by snow for several more months. Finally, on Memorial Day weekend, the barricades were moved aside. Eager to explore new worlds, we headed toward Tuolumne Meadows. Past the White Wolf junction, past Yosemite Creek, past Snow Flat we went. Just beyond the May Lake trailhead, the old Tioga Road descended steeply and Tenaya Lake came into view—with the first sight, I knew I was home. Here was a setting lovelier than Lake McDonald—and it was in my backyard. There was no doubt in my mind that this lake would become the hub of future family adventures and the gathering place for camaraderie with old and new friends.

When we first went to the lake to picnic with our babies and toddlers, we still traveled over the last twenty-one miles of the original Tioga Road. It could be quite an undertaking. Often, as the snows melted into the lake, Tenaya lapped over the roadway.

In the early fifties we could drive into a primitive, beach campground at the east end of the lake. With small children and the necessary gear, parking near the beach was a boon to fathers. We camped here often before the access road was closed to private vehicles. There was an old ranger station, then still in use, at that end of the lake. We felt worlds away from the summer bustle of the Valley.

As our friendships and children grew, we often joined forces with other picnicking families. Someone threw in a baseball and bat, others floating devices, everyone food to share, and off we would head to Tenaya. The time our car failed to get us out of the Yosemite Creek depths, we were to provide the cold drinks, and I had to hope the gang wouldn't get too parched when we didn't show up. We learned quickly which beach could be the windiest and which had the fewest mosquitoes.

In the later fifties, we camped in the campground at the west end of the lake. We could park quite close to the lake's outlet, then wade across the shallow stream toting smaller kids and camping gear. Our camp was set up in an ideal open sandy patch about twenty-five feet from the lakeside. This end of the lake, with its sandy bottom and gradual drop-off, proved a perfect spot for small swimmers and paddlers. When the new section of the Tioga Road was opened in 1961, the area was designated a walk-in campground. Two areas were provided for parking just off the highway, and gear toting took on a more serious dimension.

THE ADVENT OF SAILING

John and Mickey Curry brought their first sailboat, a Lehman 10, into the Park and into our lives the summer of 1962. The advent of the new stretch of Tioga Road made trailering a sailboat to Tenaya finally feasible. Our now-favorite gathering spot was the north side beach, where boats could be launched. One summer of experiencing the fun of crewing for John, and we, too, had the bug. We were a week on the beach in southern California that fall—and came home with a sky-blue, ten-foot Sprite atop the station wagon. There was much discussion about a suitable name. I offered *Setting For Six,* since the funds earmarked in my mind for a new dining set had been detoured to the boat purchase. A tactful compromise was reached with the *Betsy-Anne.* Since ships are traditionally feminine, this didn't put the boys' noses out of joint. We bought the necessary trailer, and our family sailing days began with the *Betsy-Anne's* maiden voyage on Tenaya Lake that fall. We took the traditional Christmas card photo of the four children sitting in our new boat, and agreed it was more appealing than one of the group sitting around a new dining room table. Then we bided our time until the next summer's Tioga Road opening.

June 1963 found us waiting eagerly for the lake ice to melt and the water to become hospitable. As a little warm-up and a new adventure, the Currys, Bevingtons, and Woessners pulled two boats over Tioga Pass to Mono Lake. At that time there was a convenient launching ramp (left high and dry in later years). This was the fateful day when we learned that the winds of Mono Lake can be strong and tricky, and the brine solution of the lake a miserable, rash-producing bath. One minute John Curry was sailing along smoothly, the next minute his boat was over. John and Bob Bevington were both dumped into the choppy lake, and the struggle to right the boat began. The whipping, swirling wind made it impossible. Charlie and Chuckie took the mast off our boat and paddled out to attempt to pull John's boat to shore. No luck. Finally, a passing kind soul with a powerboat in tow took pity on our motley crew, launched his boat, and successfully towed the capsized boat to shore. What a cold bunch of dripping, miserable sailors! We repaired to the nearby Mono Inn for warmth, food, and a stiff warmer-upper—and to discover that collectively we had a mere token amount of cash. Fortunately, John had one of those quite new plastic inventions called a credit card. Our honor was saved, we dined well—and never again put our boats into Mono Lake.

By the next summer, our outfit had an official name: The Tenaya Lake Sailing Club. Thanks to Mickey and John, we now had club banners, even an organized regatta. We were now a fleet of four: John, in a new Satellite; Wes Conner, who had bought John's Lehman and renamed it the *Sharondipity*; Earl Pomeroy, in his yellow *Banana Boat* and our *Betsy-Anne*, with Chuckie crewing for his dad. Commodore Curry had figured out an intricate handicap system (none of the boats being of the same class) and set a challenging racecourse in and around the tree-trunks protruding from the lake's surface. This was in the early days of orbiting satellites, and when a bystander on shore bellowed, "The satellite is going over," we all eagerly looked skyward—as John's Satellite unceremoniously dumped its crew into the lake. Earl sailed on to take winner's honors.

The next summer saw the addition of two more entries in the regatta and in the sailing community: Roger Hendrickson in his red *Pohono* and Spencer Grams with his Flying Dutchman Junior. Grams was the winner of that race. When he moved from the Park that fall, we just couldn't let his boat go down the road with him. We bought it and renamed it *Thunderhead*. We, in turn, sold the *Betsy-Anne* to Dale Devine, who trailered her off to Rocky Mountain National Park and out of our lives.

We had many years of family sailing. Young Chuck became a fine sailor and carried that love into his later life on the shores of Lake Champlain in Vermont. Although the boat remained a part of future Tenaya gatherings, the real impetus for the regattas left when John and Mickey Curry headed south in 1966.

I was sorry that our dear friend Dana Morgenson, purist that he was, didn't approve of sailboats on Tenaya. Certainly motors had no place on Park lakes, but I felt the white, flowing sails skittering quietly down the lake added another dimension to Tenaya's beauty.

TENAYA CAMPOUTS

Spurred on by tales of joint-family camping escapades at Tenaya by an earlier generation, Eileen Berrey, Anne Hendrickson, Mickey Curry (who returned often for camp outings), and their all-boy bunch of offspring took on a similar endeavor for several summers. Theirs was a three-family/one camp arrangement, with Ellie Nishkian turning up when she could join them. Since we Woessners were already a bunch, we set up our own campsite just down the beach when we joined the group. The dads might come on the weekend, a day-off, or even just for dinner occasionally. We had great fun, good times, and hilarious adventures. That David Curry is still alive after wrapping a garter snake around my ankle attests either to my paralyzing sense of shock or to his fast footwork in getting away. We often had our sailboat along, and it proved a good food storage haven. Food was stowed aboard, then the boat was anchored many yards out from shore, well out of bear range. The alternative was to carry the food all the way to the car. Bears were not as worldly-wise about ice chests and car break-ins in those days.

One of our more memorable nights was spent surviving a strong Mono wind that suddenly came whipping down the lake. While strains of, "it's a Mono, it's a Mono" echoed through the camp, we valiantly tried to hold down our tent and prayed that the boat's anchor would hold. The boys had quickly moved the sailboat further out into the lake so it wouldn't be slammed against the rocks or shore. The hatches were battened, the campfire extinguished, and into the tent we jumped to join Betsy in her assigned duty of keeping it from blowing away. Not a lot of sleep was had that night, but we did a lot of singing in the tent as the wind continued to howl. Unbelievably, all was calm the next morning—and the boat had weathered the storm. Anne paddled out in the kayak to retrieve it while I finally got a bit of exhausted sleep. That night was the stuff of family legends, and we were all tickled that we had coped so well without ol' Dad and could return the boat to him intact!

We were also right there on the shores of Tenaya that auspicious day in the summer of 1969 when Neil Armstrong walked on the moon and took his "giant step for mankind." We felt quite close to that particular moon—it looked huge. A thrilling event.

After we had jumped into the seventies, with the older three working at various jobs and pretty much out of the nest, I decided I wanted to do something to gather our favorite friends in our favorite place. Thus began our annual Woessner Tenaya Picnic. Since the guest list might be thirty or more, organization was crucial. Charlie and I arrived early with the sailboat in tow, filled with ice chests and other picnic paraphernalia. We established a beachhead in our favorite, semiprivate spot on the north side beach. The menu was pretty basic: prepared-ahead fare and libations to suit the occasion. My real coup was to figure out how to have warm, crunchy rolls way out there in the wilderness. This I mastered by putting them into a large, metal, covered casserole on arrival, setting the pot in the sun, and voila, hot rolls by picnic time—my own solar oven. The guest list changed as people came and went, but the hardcore group included the Rusts, our sailing pals from Belvedere, Stuart and Judy McKelvey, the Sturms (up from the Ranch), the Berreys and Johnstons, Jan Robinson (now in Mariposa), the Powers, Saulsburys, and Shackeltons. Other friends camping at the lake were invited to join us, and we were always tickled when Marte Miller could break away from the Tuolumne Lodge. Organized entertainment was superfluous, but Charlie or Stuart usually gave sailboat rides before the afternoon was over, and swimming was always part of the action. But the main entertainment was shared camaraderie, good conversation, and general contentment.

In 1975, The Women's Group, Gail Thompson in charge, branched out to sponsor a breakfast/regatta at the lake. Three years later, the Yosemite Winter Club made the move into summer activities with its first annual Tenaya Picnic at the east end beach. This handed me the opportunity to bow out of hosting our annual picnic, while still having the joy of being at Tenaya with a group of good friends. The Winter Club gatherings involved a much larger and age-diversified group with activities ranging from sailing, volleyball, and swimming, to log-raft building and sand castle construction. The club, Gerry Smith in charge, put on an excellent barbeque that first year, and the picnics continued well into the nineties.

A SPECIAL GATHERING PLACE

Tenaya was always the place to rendezvous with friends coming back to visit the Park. When our great bunch of Ashley, Robinson, Riechers, and Woessner kids were working at Tuolumne in various summer jobs, parents sometimes came from afar to visit and there was always a Tenaya picnic. Bob and Marifran Gallison came over from Tuolumne stays to join Winter Club gatherings on several occasions. The lakeside was often the setting for a let's-get-together kind of quiet visit, such as the good meanders around the lake I've had with Char Wilson as we caught up on each other's lives. Our old launching beach became a favorite place to stop for a quick sandwich and respite en route to other places—and a place to share with the grandchildren later on.

Two days after our Betsy and Kerry's wedding in September 1983, our family gathered at Tenaya: Chuck and Dana with daughters Heidi and Betsy Anne from Vermont; Rob and Amy from Colorado; Betsy and Kerry, soon heading back to college at Humboldt State University; and Charlie and I, joined by Kerry's brother David from Washington; and friends Don and Peggy Baldwin. We donned our American Men and Women on Everest T-shirts, proposed a good luck toast and sent a long, rousing cheer out into the atmosphere to our climbers, Anne and Chas, then well along on their trek to Everest basecamp. Standing on that particular beach, I think we all felt a little closer to them.

My sixtieth birthday rolled around in 1987, just before we were to pull up our Valley stakes and move to Wawona. Betsy and Anne decided Mom should have an occasion to mark the rite of passage. They put it together—guest list and food, including a sailboat on the birthday cake. It wasn't even a toss-up as to where it should take place: There we all gathered, on the beach at Tenaya. The real surprise had come the night before with thumping footfalls on the porch that turned out to be Rob and Amy, just arrived from Colorado. Another rollicking Tenaya picnic fell into place with many good friends in attendance. The newest addition to the clan, Anne and Chas's son Charles Alexander Macquarie, age 5 months, slept quietly in a nearby tent for much of the afternoon. In this peaceful manner, his entrance into the world of Tenaya was made.

In the years following our 1987 move to Wawona, we did little sailing. The added forty-five minutes through the Park on ever-busier roads became enough of a deterrent that we usually settled for just meeting the Macquarie family, over from the east side of the Sierra, for a picnic and swim. Often, Chas was among the climbers on the nearby rock walls. Tenaya's granite was another mecca for climbers.

In the early nineties, the last campground at Tenaya was closed. This family deplored the action. True, the sanitation system was out-dated, and yes, NPS maintenance dollars may have been in short supply right then, but to completely do away with what had been a wonderful—and appropriate—experience for Park visitors seemed shortsighted. As we fondly remembered our days of camping in that gorgeous spot, we felt a sense of loss for those who would never have the experience. Another campground was lost along the Tioga Road.

On my dresser stands a heart-tugging picture of small grand-daughter Anna Macquarie walking hand-in-hand with her gramps along the beach at Tenaya. It is much like a similar picture taken thirty-six years earlier of Anne walking with her dad—the same special lake in the background, the same tickly sand between the toes, the same delightful radiance shining from the faces, and probably a similar tasty picnic lunch tucked inside. Tenaya is the one place in my life experience that remains timeless, there for the ages. As it wraps its aura of contentment around me it becomes my cherished haven.

12. Tuolumne Meadows and the High Country

O, I could sing such grandeurs and glories about you.
                                        —Walt Whitman

Tuolumne Meadows holds much history for our family. Its environs were the setting for my first backpacking experience and of many ensuing trips. For Charlie, it was the scene of snow and glacier surveys, the camaraderie that came with them, and much, much more. For our older three, it was a home-away-from-home in the summers between their eighteenth birthday and the departure into the real world. Tuolumne has been the setting for quiet enjoyment with good friends, rollicking camping expeditions with the family, and expectant take-offs on favorite trailheads. It was a major element in our Park life.

Tuolumne is the gateway to the spectacular northern and eastern Park backcountry wilderness. It is the hub of trailheads. A favorite trail drops down to Glen Aulin to branch at the High Sierra Camp, one arm heading down past Waterwheel Falls to the Tuolumne Gorge and Pate Valley, the other leading up through Cold Canyon to the Matterhorn, Smedberg, and Benson Lake splendors. Another Tuolumne trail takes off to Cathedral Lakes, Sunrise Ridge, Clouds Rest and Echo Valley—eventually leading down into Yosemite Valley. Still another trail heads south along the Lyell Fork of the Tuolumne River to Mt. Lyell, and on along the Pacific Crest/

John Muir trail. A branch of this trail climbs the Rafferty Creek drainage to the Vogelsang Peak area with its glistening high elevation lakes. The trails beyond Vogelsang High Sierra Camp lead either up over Vogelsang Pass to Lewis Creek or down along Fletcher Creek, both leading into the Washburn/Merced Lakes country, and finally to the Valley. The Young Lakes trail, skirting Ragged Peak as it stands sentinel over the lower, middle, and upper lakes, is another offshoot of the Glen Aulin trail. There are a number of worthwhile, short day hikes out of the Meadows: to Dog Lake, Budd Lake, Lembert Dome, Elizabeth Lake, or the fisherman's trail along the west side of the Tuolumne River from Pothole Dome. We've done them all and reaped the rewards: the smell of pine on a warm day, the sight of a marmot quickly scampering from sight, the delight in finding a tiny alpine or Sierra gentian blooming along the trail, the gasp for that second wind that must come during an uphill climb, the beauty of a clear, crisp stream flowing over and around smooth, sparkling granite. Culminating all is the breathtaking magnificence of a pristine mountain lake when that last rise is topped.

SODA SPRINGS

In our early years of camping with the youngsters in Tuolumne Meadows, on those eagerly anticipated out-of-the-office weekends, we put up our tent in the small Sierra Club campground at Soda Springs. The prime spots were those along the river. Since it was a first come, first served system, these sites filled quickly, but a second small camping area had evolved on the knoll above the access road just before the springs. Both of these camps afforded delight for small children, with great wandering-around potential. The spring, with its covered shelter, Parsons Lodge and the McCauley cabin were old, *old* and meant history to the kids. Our friends the Burtons were the caretakers for a summer or two in the later fifties, and we loved visiting them in the McCauley cabin, their summer home.

The first homesteader in this area was John Lembert, who built a cabin on the site of the present Parsons Lodge in 1885.[1] A few years later, he put the protective structure over the bubbling Soda Springs.

The waters of Soda Springs enhanced many a good shot of whiskey in earlier days. Although now roofless and open to the elements, this cabin still stands.

Following Lembert's death, his brother sold the homestead to James McCauley, proprietor of the Glacier Point Hotel and originator of the firefall. A new cabin was built in 1904, and the McCauley brothers began using the Meadow as summer pasture for their cattle, brought up from the ranch at Big Meadow in Foresta. Upon his death, McCauley's heirs put the property on the market in 1912. Fearing the land might fall into the wrong hands, William Colby, then secretary of the Sierra Club, took an option on the holdings. Within a year, the purchase price was raised within the club through member subscriptions. Three summers later, a stone lodge was built on the site of Lembert's original cabin. It was named Parsons Memorial Lodge in honor of Edward Taylor Parsons, a dedicated Sierra Club member and early environmentalist who had died the preceding year. Parsons Lodge is a handsome, rugged stone building that eventually became a meeting place for Sierra Club members and a display background for club and Tuolumne memorabilia. The aforementioned small camping areas developed around the lodge for the use and enjoyment of club members, and the original McCauley cabin became a home for the area's caretakers. During our years, Fred Eissler and Lee Verret are names that come to mind when remembering dedicated families who filled this role for the club.

One summer, Charlie and Rob hauled our tent trailer to the Soda Springs knoll campground where Rob, joined by Tom and Allen Berrey, camped, fished and hiked for a glorious week. Chuck and Anne both worked in the Meadows by then so there were advisers at hand if needed. This experience whetted Rob's affection for the high country, and in another couple of years he too worked there.

By the later sixties, it was becoming increasingly difficult to maintain the intent of the Soda Springs campground. To quote from Elizabeth S. O'Neill's informative article on the Edward Taylor Parsons Memorial Lodge: "It was no longer easy to uphold the traditions of sanitation, decorum and mutual respect among campers that had been taken for granted by earlier generations." This speaks to the heart of what was being seen in other parts of the Park—and the nation.

The Sierra Club was also having second thoughts about the appropriateness of an environmentally concerned organization maintaining an in-holding within Park boundaries. This was influenced by the NPS's new aggressive policy in regard to in-hold purchase. The upshot was the club's sale of the 160 acres of land and the three buildings thereon to the National Park Service, in 1973, for $208,000. The gate was closed at the YPCC stable road junction, the knoll campground went back to nature, and the river section became a walk-in campground. A seasonal park ranger was housed in the McCauley cabin. 1976 saw even the river sites closed to campers, and by 1979 all three of the structures had been accepted onto the National Registry of Historical Places. Three decades later, the area still draws history lovers of all ages.

THE HIGH CAMPS

The history of the High Sierra Camps goes back some eight decades, to 1916.[2] In that year, the Desmond Park Service Company set up tent lodges at Tuolumne Meadows, Merced Lake, and Tenaya Lake. In 1919 the company was bought out, to be renamed the Yosemite National Park Company. This outfit in turn merged with the Curry Camping Company in 1924 to become the Yosemite Park & Curry Company. Along with this merging of capital and executive ability came the long hoped-for expansion of high country hiker facilities. Tent camps at Boothe Lake and Little Yosemite were added. By 1938, further changes had moved the Boothe Lake camp up the hill to the present Vogelsang setting, obliterated both the Little Yosemite and Tenaya camps, and added two new camps. The new camps were May Lake, beneath the grandeur of Mt. Hoffmann, and Glen Aulin, beside the thundering Tuolumne River with its cascading falls. These five camps—Tuolumne, Merced Lake, Vogelsang, May Lake and Glen Aulin—became known as the High Sierra Camps. Mary Tresidder's own Sunrise Camp completed the loop in 1961.

The High Sierra Camps are all situated near either a stream or a lake, and each has a distinct character. They are opened when snowmelt and accessibility dictate, usually mid-June, and closed soon after Labor Day. The basic camp layout consists of tent cabins on concrete platforms, usually with four cots, a central table, wood stove, and candles for light, and a main canvas lodge housing the dining area and kitchen. Sanitary facilities have varied over the years but are always provided, albeit with some restrictions in the case of Vogelsang.

The lodge at Tuolumne is by far the largest and most luxurious of the camps, by nature of its being car-accessible. It is usually the jumping-off place for hikes to the other high camps. The addition of the Sunrise Camp made possible a very popular six-day-hike loop trip. The comforting thought of having a bed and hot meal waiting at the end of one's seven- to ten-mile trek each day keeps the camps filled to capacity every summer. In the eighties, the clamor for reservations necessitated the institution of a lottery system. We have friends who have learned how to handle the system adeptly: With infinite patience and persistence on the telephone, they manage to return to the High Sierra Camps year after year.

Although Charlie and I camped at Boothe Lake with friends in 1950, the fall before I joined him in the Park, and walked through the camp at Vogelsang, I did not stay in a high camp until 1958. That year my dad, who loved to hike in the Sierra, invited seven-year old Chuckie-grandson and me to join him in a visit to all the high camps. My mother could no longer handle that high an altitude so remained in the Valley. Chuckie and I accepted with alacrity.

Sunrise had not yet been added, so ours was not to be a loop trip. We started at the May Lake trailhead on the old Tioga Road. It was a good place to get our legs under us with just the one steep mile up to the May Lake High Sierra Camp. From there we dropped down to Glen Aulin next morning and spent the remainder of that day exploring the environs. The next day it was up along the bouncing, churning Tuolumne River, with its spectacular cascades, to overnight at the Tuolumne Meadows Lodge—and have a shower!

We were early on our way the next morning, and climbed the Rafferty Creek trail enroute to Vogelsang High Sierra Camp. There we found friends in the form of Pete and Malinda Minor, camp manager and camp cook par excellence. Pete was the son of old family friends. The crews at the camps in those days were college kids out for the summer. They were imaginative, personable, hardworking, and capable.

The following morning found us on down the Fletcher Creek trail to Merced Lake. The beckoning scenery along the way made this long hike seem a breeze. Merced Lake is the largest of the off-road camps and, for some reason, my least favorite. Perhaps the trip-is-almost-over twinges color my outlook. Nevertheless, here we again found a friend, Jerry Mernin, then a summer seasonal ranger.[3] We also met the engaging DeMartini brothers, who came each summer from homes in the Bay Area for a long stay at the camp. Lots of good stories and history were shared around the campfire that night.

The next day meant down the trail to home. This was our longest trek, and the trail got dustier and more crowded as we descended through Echo Valley, Lost Canyon, Little Yosemite, and on down past Nevada and Vernal Falls, to end at Happy Isles in Yosemite Valley.

It was a joy to be with my dad, still going strong in those days, and to be with my first-born, now proving to be a fine hiker. Chuckie learned much from his grandfather on that adventure—and so did I. This was the first time Dad and I had hiked any distance together. We had genuine camaraderie, some good chuckles, and some hot and heavy games of "Go Fish!" I would wish for everyone the opportunity to have a three-generational trip at some point in a lifetime. It is a memory forgotten by none of us.

Having Tuolumne Meadows and Vogelsang to share with friends was one of the great pleasures of our Yosemite life. I have had the joy of being on many a high camp trek with a variety of friends and family. Vogelsang is easily my most visited camp. Nestled as it is in an exquisite alpine meadow by the small mountain stream flowing out of Fletcher Lake, it is one of the smallest of the high camps and one of the most beloved. We have rendezvoused there with the Riechers, down from Oregon. We have hiked the trail and tented with the Gallisons and Plumbs, home from Colorado and northern California (both Bobs were raised in Yosemite). I have hiked to the camp with former college pals to introduce them to its beauty, then added the thrill of a scramble up to lovely Hanging Basket Lake. I have shared Vogelsang's ambiance with Valley friends, including two hikes sponsored by the Yosemite Women's Group, organized by Donna Mackie and Anne Hendrickson. I remember the fun of being with Jody Wurgler, Ti Shackelton, and Barbara Wendt on those trips. It was magic to stroll through a paradise of red and yellow monkey flowers ablaze in the rocky nooks and crannies near Ireland Lake, a memory carried home from one of the trips by Fran Scoble, Maggie Gehen and me.

One September day in 1976, Charlie and I passed through Vogelsang with packs on our backs, and continued up and over Vogelsang Pass. We nodded to Gallison Lake, then contoured around to Bernice Lake, where we spent the night. In the morning we hiked on down the Lewis Creek trail, and eventually reached Merced Lake after a couple of wandering, exploring days along the high trail to Isberg Pass. At each Ranger Station we passed, Little Yosemite being the last, we asked for possible messages: Our first grandchild was due and we'd left a sketchy itinerary. Chuck and Dana's Heidi arrived to claim first grandchild honors a few days after we arrived home from our glorious change of pace.

YOUNG LAKES

I have packed into Young Lakes on two occasions. Only the setting was the same: clear mountain lakes tucked beneath Ragged Peak and Mt. Conness. The earliest trip was a family venture in August of 1963 when we joined three generations of the Macaulay family for a long weekend. The second trek was twelve years later, a trip organized by Women's Group activity chairman Donna Mackie. The outings couldn't have been more diverse.

The first trip found the six of us headed out of Tuolumne Meadows along the Young Lakes trail with two burros, one for our camping gear and one with three-year-old Betsy atop. Hours later we rounded the bend at Lower Young Lake and found a joyous reception and a fine-looking camp, the Macaulays having been there a week. It was an old-home weekend for me. My mother had been in college with Polly Macaulay, wife of Ed, and I had been in college with Anne Parrish Macaulay, wife of son Ted. Completing the welcoming party were Anne and Ted's three youngsters, Peggy, Susan, and Teddy, plus Ted's sister and husband. A third generation connection was born on the spot. Although the busy season precluded our staying away from the Valley and Charlie's dental practice more than two nights, we made the most of each hour. There were no great hikes or climbs on that particular trip, but there were some active young fishermen and fine evening campfires, complete with stories, reminiscing, and s'mores. Betsy was already a trooper—no one gave her a chance to be otherwise. It was a difficult place to leave when Monday morning rolled around.

The Women's Group trip in the mid-seventies was a kick. Donna had recruited about a dozen of us, then husband Ron also decided to come along. I'm still not quite sure why. Did Donna think we needed his fine backcountry expertise? Or did he think we needed his backcountry expertise, the idea being to go along to help us versus having to rescue us later? What I am sure of, however, is just who learned the most on that adventure: Ron Mackie. We still refer to the caper as "the greening of Ron" in that he found women could be quite capable in the wilderness.

Capable—as well as persevering and uncomplaining—for with packs straight or askew, feet blistered or not, everyone made it to camp in a respectable time and in a fine humor. Tents were set up in no time, cooking areas selected, and happy hour was underway. As evening approached, the campfire question came up. Stands were firmly taken pro and con as to whether we were above the 9600' campfire cut-off elevation or not. The argument got hot and heavy for a while, the purists pitted against the romanticists. Ron wisely stayed out of that one!

Sharing the laughs and beauty on that trip were Barbara Wendt, Ti Shackelton, Clarisa Garza, Anne Hendrickson, and Eileen Berrey. Completing the group were Jeff (a.k.a. Mary) Karraker, Gail Thompson, Gretchen, B Weiss, the Mackies and myself. The food bags were properly hung that night—not an easy feat, as the bears had definitely smartened up in the decade of the seventies. To string a rope high between two trees, or find the right high branch to toss a rope over, then to use a long stick to counterbalance two food sacks at a level above a bear's reach was never easy. Even with this precaution, and while the rest of us gratefully slept, Anne and Ron took turns driving our furry marauder away. How does one discourage a hungry bear? Not easily. Any available method that works—be it making noise, tossing rocks, or appearing aggressive—is termed successful.

It was on to climb Mt. Conness the next morning. We hadn't counted on a recent snowfall that still covered the slope between Upper Young Lake and the summit. Some of us had neglected to bring dark glasses (surely losing points in Ron's book). I was one of these, as I don't like to hike in glasses. The field of white snow was blinding, however, and I tried to improvise with a strip of paper and two tiny pinholes. It worked for awhile, but light-headedness from the altitude set in, and I returned slowly to camp. There I found Barbara in the first aches of a flu-onset. Since we had both planned to part from the group that afternoon anyway, we packed up, left notes of farewell, and began our slow trek back to civilization.

It wasn't until a couple of days later that we heard the rest of the saga. The two stalwarts who did make the summit were Anne and Jeff—a little spirit of competition there. The others turned back sooner or later. Donna suffered an extremely painful case of snow-blindness and spent an excruciating night in camp with little or no sleep. In the morning she bound her eyes against the searing sunlight as Ron literally led her down the trail. She was in pain for days. It was a lesson etched in stone for all of us.

JUST PLAIN FUN

August 1967 found the children and me camping in the Tuolumne Campground for a couple of weeks. August truly is the month to be in Tuolumne—and camping. It is the time when the shooting stars of the heavens put on their most glorious show, and the wildflowers in the meadows try to outshine them. It is also, traditionally, the time when the mosquito population begins to abate. This was our last summer to have Chuck with us. He would be sixteen the next year and involved in a YPCC summer job. Charlie helped us set up camp and came up as often as he could get away from the office. We had with us almost every means of mobility one could imagine: feet, sailboat, boys' bicycles, car, and Bessie.

Bessie had come into Anne's life that summer via the kindness of Bob McGregor. Bob, whom Anne and Kathy Metherell adored, was the head wrangler at the NPS stables. Knowing about girls and horses, he had found, through his contacts in Hornitos, a horse with the right amount of spunk and, more importantly, in need of some tender, loving care for the summer. The match was made, and Bob brought the mare to the Valley. Anne and her dad made the necessary arrangements to board the horse for a nominal fee at the Curry stables, and a special summer began for this fourteen-year-old. With the help of the Company, Bessie, as Anne named the mare, went along with us to Tuolumne. She was hauled up in one of their horse trailers to be kept at the Tuolumne stable, at that time over near the Tuolumne Meadows Lodge, Mogue Morris in charge. What a memorable time Anne had exploring the trails of Tuolumne astride her Bessie.

I don't remember where we parked the boat—certainly not in the campground—but it was used on the occasions when Dad came up. We swam, we explored the Meadows, we cooked in camp, we had our happy-jolly campfires—and we got dirty! Being the mother of the group, I was delighted to find four appropriately sized black sweatshirts in the Tuolumne store at just about the time even tolerably decent shirts gave out. These became the uniform for the rest of the stay.

Charlie came up to help dismantle the camp when our two weeks ended. Getting home was a logistical puzzle. Betsy was easy. She was just about seven and Mom's buddy, so she and I trailered the boat in back of the loaded station wagon. Chuck and Rob had ridden their bikes all over Tuolumne Meadows and now decided to ride them as far as Tenaya. There they loaded the bikes into the boat and hopped in with Bets and me. Anne and her dad were far more creative—and challenged. They had to get Bessie home.

They solved the dilemma by alternately riding and hiking the twenty-two miles of the Muir Trail to the Valley, over Cathedral Pass and along the Sunrise Trail to Nevada Falls, down the horse trail to Happy Isles, and home to the Curry stables. About every three or four miles, the positions switched and the rider hiked. Even Bessie seemed none the worse for wear. In this day of campground reservations and restrictions, far more expensive stable boarding costs, and simply the hassle of trying to do innovative things in the Park, could this caper be repeated?

WILDERNESS PERMITS

The late sixties and early seventies brought an ever-increasing number of backpackers to the Park. The easily accessible areas of the backcountry wilderness became inundated with people, resulting in far less than quality camping experiences. The need for some form of control became a National Park Service priority.

By the time I went to work in the Yosemite Backcountry Division in the early eighties, the wilderness permit quota system was well in place. This had come about neither quickly nor without dedicated research. By 1971, the NPS and the U.S. Forest Service had set up a joint fire/travel permit program to cover their combined wilderness areas. Two years later, Dr. Jan van Wagtendonk, research biologist, introduced and outlined specific travel zones for the Yosemite backcountry. The study of these zones and their carrying capacities evolved into specific set limits on numbers of people in an area at any given time. 1974 was deemed the "public education summer." Permits were checked, the program explained, but citations were not yet issued. In 1975, the permit requirement began being strictly enforced in the Park. Two years later, using gathered information, the trailhead quotas were set up. These were specific entry numbers for each trail leading into the studied zones. Permits for half of each trailhead quota were issued by advance reservation. The remaining half were issued on a first-come, first-serve basis within twenty-four hours of trail take-off. Lines formed early at the Tuolumne permit kiosk during the height of the season, and long waits could ensue. It always paid to think ahead and to have an alternate trailhead in mind.

The majority of backpackers hiked just one or two days into the backcountry from their chosen trailhead. These camping areas became easy pickings for the clever, hungry bears. Many a novice backpacker rued not taking more seriously the instructions on the proper method for successfully hanging food sacks. As the bears became more and more savvy, the best intentions of even seasoned hikers could end in frustration and hunger—for the people, not the bears. The introduction in the late eighties of the bear canister as a part of necessary backpacking equipment has saved the trip for many a traveler. These are cylindrical food storage containers made of a tough PVC material that fit inside a backpack. A coin is used to open the lid. (So far, the bears do not carry pocket change.) The late-nineties addition of sturdy bear boxes at many trailheads and parking areas in the high country also proved a great boon to hikers and cut down on car break-ins.[4]

A SWANSONG

What I now know to have been my last high country backpacking adventure did not take off from Tuolumne Meadows per se. It could have, but the time factor dictated that we start from Twin Lakes, a day's hike shorter than the route out of the Meadows. I was to finally realize my long-held dream of seeing Benson Lake. My mother and father held great affection for this backcountry lake in its pristine setting. In my youth, the name became synonymous with High Sierra beauty. Now, in August of 1985, I was ready to get there.

Charlie, Wes Conner, and I drove over Tioga Pass to enter the backcountry near Bridgeport. Our trail climbed past Barney Lake, up to Peeler Lake, and on over to Kerrick Meadow, where we camped the first night. In the morning we continued down Kerrick Canyon and up over Seavey Pass to make our last drop down to Benson Lake. And there it lay, truly the alpine jewel I'd pictured, with its sparkling surface and the distinctive long, sandy beach on one side. This was the same beach and lake that Anne, Chuck, and Sherrill Conner had reveled on twenty-one years earlier when Charlie brought them down from our camp at Smedberg Lake. This time, the three of us had a fine two-day camp-out, some swimming and exploring—but for me the getting there had proven to be as much fun as the being there. I'd made it in fine style, held my own with those two old pros, and could now retire fulfilled—for retirement, it proved to be. Backpacking and disintegrating knees are just not symbiotic.

Tuolumne Meadows was the 1996 setting for my last meandering hike, last game of Poohsticks-under-the-bridge, last time of togetherness at our favorite TML with Marifran Gallison, friend from my earliest Yosemite days. Marifran and Bob moved from the Valley soon after they were married in the fall of 1951, but returned whenever possible for their Yosemite "fix." Throughout all the years, Marifran never ceased to remind me of how very lucky I was to be able to live in the Park. She died most unexpectedly in March of the next year. Nowhere do I feel her presence more deeply than in Tuolumne Meadows. And yes, dear friend, I do know that I have been *more* than lucky.

We have had the joy of introducing various grandchildren to Tuolumne Meadow's beauty, challenges, and camaraderie. Nothing could be cozier than being tucked into a TML tent with three small grandchildren, each eagerly absorbing tales of a parent's growing-up adventures. Now they hike the hikes and climb the domes in the footsteps of their parents. Our beloved high country will be left in capable, appreciative hands.

13. Summers in the Meadows

Wilderness is the beauty of nature, solitude, and the music of stillness.

—*author unknown*

I envy the opportunity our older three had to work and live for several summers in Tuolumne Meadows, but take solace in the knowledge that the experience was wasted on none of them. They cherished those summers and made the most of them. They reveled in the beauty of nature, in the solitude that wilderness can bring, and they heard the music of the mountains.

The magic age for getting a summer job involving Company housing was eighteen. Marge Cromer, of the YPCC Personnel Office, went out of her way to help local youngsters obtain jobs at Tuolumne or in the High Sierra Camps. When Chuck reached eighteen, having worked two live-at-home summers in the Valley station, he was a natural to step into an opening at the Chevron station in Tuolumne.

The next summer, 1971, found Anne also moving to the Meadows. Her home for three summers would be the Tuolumne Meadows Lodge (TML). She started as a maid, under the guidance of Martha (Marte) Miller, and in a couple of summers worked her way up through pantry-worker and sidehall-server to become a full-fledged dining room waitress. One summer Marte turned up with costumes from the Austrian folktale *Der Freichutz* (from her winter's stint with the Fresno Opera) and the waitresses took on added character. With her plaited hair, Anne looked like a *Fraulein* fresh from a Swiss chalet.

Rob, when eighteen, also headed for Tuolumne, having landed a camp-helper job at TML. His duties ran the gambit from wood splitting, stacking, and delivery, to floor and bathroom cleaning, to maintaining and lighting the Coleman lanterns each evening. These were still pre-electricity days at TML and lanterns provided illumination for the dining tent, lobby, rest rooms, and walkways. Food was kept cool with the use of a generator, turned off at night. Ice was at a premium so thirsty guests drank their whiskey neat. The lodge employees were housed, as they are now, in tents below the main lobby/dining/kitchen complex.

There was great camaraderie among the gang working at TML in the sixties and early seventies. It became the summer home for many Valley offspring and for others who came back often enough to seem local. The names Worthington, Ponti, Field, Kinneson, Richards, Sano, Meneguzzi, Swanson, Mooers, and Faubion blended well with the second-generation Valley names Ottonello, Robinson, Ashley, Munson, and Woessner as they rang through the tents and trees in those years. To quote our Rob: "The best parts of being at TML were the active group of people working there, the centralized location affording access to some of the best backcountry in the world, and the fact that the Lyell trailhead was literally just outside the backdoor." The competitive spirit took hold in seeing who could accomplish the most challenging feat or cover the greatest distance during a split shift. Anne loved her split shifts when she achieved the dining room job, but recalls with a bit of chagrin the few times she was late for dinner duties because her chosen climbing route had taken longer than anticipated. Anne and Rob each worked summers under the management of both Marte Miller and Dillon Gillies.[1]

Over in the store/Grill/gas station area, another group of comrades formed. The SOBs (Standard Oil Boys) lived in the tent area behind the store, as did the Grill and grocery store employees. Of this time and place Chuck writes, "I still feel the two full summers spent in Tuolumne Meadows were amongst the most amazing of my life—over eighteen (thus an adult), away from home, not in school, with a bunch of like-minded and similarly interested peers, living free-and-unfettered in one of the world's most beautiful spots. 9,000-feet above sea level, everyone active and in great shape, and doing wonderful things together. Working at the gas station, living behind the store, meals in the Grill, knowing the climbers and packers, get-togethers every night, climbs, hikes, fishing, photography, sailing, trips to Leevining bars, sunrise from the top of Lembert Dome. Climbing (and falling off of) Fairview Dome. Waterwheel Falls— the list goes on."

Chuck's immediate boss and friend was Ken "Bear" Anderson. Mike Harrison, long-time family friend, and Dan McHarg were other SOBs. In the Grill were manager Ann Baker, Diane Henneberger, and two who have continued their dedication to the Park: Lisa Dapprich and Linda Ede. The Ashley's daughter Jan, back in Yosemite after an absence of more than a decade, worked in the store, as did Mariposan Joe Ritter. Dennis and Carol Brady were the store managers.

Chuck spent much of his off time, as did the other two, honing his climbing skills. The seeds of climbing had been sown in the Valley, and then nurtured at school in Colorado. Now the challenges lay all around them, and they had the time to explore and test their skills. Tenaya Lake was the hangout for a quiet day off or between shifts. One summer the sailboat stayed at Tuolumne and was often out on the lake, one of our younger generation at the helm.

By the time our Betsy was eighteen the hiring practice had changed. The unions had arrived in the Park, and YPCC employees could bid on the various jobs. The positions at TML were much in demand by those who had worked the winter season in the Valley or at Badger Pass. Few local faces appeared at TML after the mid-seventies, though the returnees began to feel local after a few seasons. Betsy would never experience a working summer at TML.

MARTE ⌈A.K.A. MARTHA MILLER⌉

Usually, when having a stay, or even just dinner, at TML, we hope Marte Miller will have a free moment to join us by the rushing Dana fork or, better yet, for dinner. No one is more a part of the ongoing Tuolumne Meadows Lodge scene than she, a delightful lady of many facets who has been in our life almost as long as has Yosemite. Our children were fortunate to have Marte as a factor in their Tuolumne Meadows careers, whether as a supervisor or as a friend. One can't think of Tuolumne Meadows and TML without thinking of Marte.

When we arrived in the Valley in the very early fifties, Martha's parents were counselors in Camp Curry's Boy's Town, the summer home for the YPCC male seasonal employees. The Millers were among Charlie's first patients, and he enjoyed them immensely. In the winter, the family lived in the Carpinteria Valley just south of Santa Barbara, where Martha and her sisters were born. This was my first tie with Martha, as my mother was a native Santa Barbaran. I had visited relatives there every summer, both as a child and, later, with our own children. I grew up cherishing many of the same beach and mountain sites as Martha.

Martha's parents introduced their family to Yosemite, Valley and high country, in the forties and a lasting love affair began.[2] Hers were the wonderful kind of parents who encouraged adventure and opened doors of inquisitiveness, and this was not lost on Martha. She spent many hours hiking with the Valley ranger naturalists, to the top of the various falls or to wherever that day's scheduled trip might lead. She spent a week with ranger friends in Tuolumne one summer, hiking each day with Dr. Carl Sharsmith as he led novices into the discovery of the Meadow's many treasures. Seeing it through his eyes, she was touched for life by the wonders of the Range of Light.

Martha tells a wonderful story of wanting to become a ranger naturalist during her teen years. Her dad encouraged her to talk to someone over in the NPS museum, even accompanied her, to find out what courses she should take in school to further this goal. Whoever was behind the desk that day heard her out, and then with great authority told her to think no further of that career because the field was restricted to men!

What do you do to be able to stay in your beloved mountains if not allowed access to the NPS portals? You jump into the tourist service business with the Yosemite Park and Curry Co. That is just what Martha did. One of her high school summers was spent as a helper at the Vogelsang High Sierra Camp. Maid work and waitressing at TML and food service at the Yosemite Lodge, Camp Curry, and the Mountain House at Glacier followed that beginning.

By the early sixties, Martha was into her ski-teaching winter career at Badger under Nic Fiore's tutelage. She became one of his first female certified ski-instructors. Soon joining her in this endeavor were Hap Johnson, Patty Walker Anderson, and Char Spranger Lockwood. The bastions of this male-dominated profession had begun to crumble. In 1964, Martha participated in the Winter Olympic Games in Innsbruck as a representative of the U.S. Ski Association.

Gradually, the two loves of Martha's life merged—mountains and music. She was able to dovetail a career in the performing arts with her ongoing one in the hotel management business. Through an introduction to James Schwabacher, a frequent visitor to Yosemite, Badger, and the Ahwahnee, her first contact with the San Francisco Opera management came about. The upshot was a dedication to an apprenticeship and learning program in opera production and direction. She worked in the performing arts field for many a winter/spring season, returning to the Park in time to organize the opening of TML and assume command for the summer. Working with Art Robinson, Marte, as she came to be known, often brought symphony and opera to the Park, to both Tuolumne Meadows and the Valley, under the auspices of the Yosemite Art Guild of the late sixties and early seventies.

Marte's musical knowledge and hotel savvy have made her an integral part of the Ahwahnee's Bracebridge productions at Christmastime. Her involvement with the Bracebridge began under the direction of Ansel Adams and Jeanette Dyer Spencer. She went on to work with Eugene Fulton and, following his death, continues to work closely with Andrea Fulton. Along with Washington Irving and hundreds of Ahwahnee guests, Christmas at Bracebridge Hall has become a tradition for Marte as well.

Following management assignments at the Wawona Hotel, Big Trees Lodge, and the Ahwahnee, Marte became manager of TML. She has held forth in that capacity for many summers, with an occasional hiatus, including three years in the mid-seventies when she managed White Wolf. Having worked for her at TML, Anne and Rob both hold great respect for Marte's abilities. Miller Cascade, a lovely series of small falls behind the lodge, was named in Marte's honor by an earlier group of employees.

Travel and horseracing now claim Marte's away-from-the-Park time. Again showing her dad's influence (she claims he had her reading racing forms before she could decipher her first grade reader), she is now part owner of several racehorses and keeps up with their activities all over the country.

There are few, if any, interesting regions of the world unvisited by this adventuresome lady—and she finds friends and acquaintances in many of them. The TML camaraderie is something unique.

Former employees remain lasting friends, while frequent guests become old friends. We have loved being a part of this family—vicariously, through our kids, and actively, through our stays at Tuolumne Meadows Lodge and our friendship with Marte.

ENTERING GOVERNMENT SERVICE

The age requirement to enter any branch of seasonal government service, e.g. National Park Service or U.S. Forest Service, was twenty-one years. In 1973, while still attending UC Davis, Chuck left the Meadows for an NPS summer seasonal job as resident ranger (another tent) in Little Yosemite Valley, above Nevada Falls. His resident days in Tuolumne Meadows came to an end, to fade into fond memories.

When Rob turned twenty-one, he headed off to Lake Tahoe to a U.S. Forest Service fire crew job. The following summer found him back in the Park, stationed at Lake Eleanor, just north of Hetch-

Hetchy, as a member of an NPS fire crew. He, too, had closed the curtain on Tuolumne Meadows as his home away from home. Many days off, however, were spent on quick trips to the Meadows for a breath of Tuolumne air.

Anne's career with the Company faded at the end of her 1973 summer as turning twenty-one opened her door to NPS employment the following summer. Unlike her brothers, Anne's new challenge kept her in the Tuolumne Meadows environs for yet another decade. Her entry job was once again at the bottom of the totem pole, that of fee collector in the Tuolumne Campground kiosk and at the Tioga Pass entrance station. Long-time Valley friend Sonja Hoie joined Anne in this endeavor. By 1976, she and TML friend Laurel Munson entered the backcountry division—and back into a kiosk she went. This one, however, was the wilderness permit issuing station near Tuolumne's government stable and ranger station. It was to this kiosk, later that summer, that a young British climber was attracted. In just this manner, Chas Macquarie entered Anne's life, affections, and future.

After a summer of permit work, Anne at last landed the perfect job for her abilities, interests, and energies—backcountry ranger. Patrolling the backcountry could involve day hikes, overnight ventures, or even longer backpacking excursions. Her only bone of contention was that Walt Castle, government stock-boss, did not yet allow any of his horses to be assigned to females. Anne was not only one of the first female backcountry rangers, she was one of the only unmounted backcountry rangers. She often joked about her developing belief that very few mounted patrol rangers got off their horses to break up the illegal fire-rings discovered along the way.

For three summers Anne remained a backcountry patrol ranger in Tuolumne Meadows. After she and Chas were married in 1978, they began a five-year stint as winter patrol/resident rangers at the Meadows. It couldn't get much better than this—knowing and living in Tuolumne Meadows in all of its seasons.

Tuolumne Meadows remains one of the greatest come-back-to places in the world for people of all ages. One meal around a large table in the Tuolumne Meadows Lodge dining room with even strangers can result in a wonderful and spontaneous outpouring of affection for—and personal history with—the Meadows. Everyone has a tale to share. Our children have some of the best.

ABOVE: Our Valley home for thirty-seven years
BELOW: The family complete, Christmas 1960

ABOVE:
Pat and Avery Sturm

RIGHT:
Jan and Art Robinson

ABOVE: Tenaya Lake welcomes the *Betsy-Anne*
BELOW: On a Tuolumne outing

Gearing up for a ski race…

…and going for it (Betsy)

ABOVE: Betsy with Secretary of Interior Rogers Morton in 1971,
post-riot Park tour
BELOW: Anne and Bessie on the Tuolumne Meadows-to-Valley Trail

RIGHT: Rob climbing
at Tuolumne Meadows

BELOW: Tuolumne
home for winter
rangers Anne and Chas

LEFT: The Christmas coffee with Ti Shackelton

BELOW: Betsy backpacking the trail to Vogelsang

ABOVE: Marian and Charlie at Tioga Pass, enroute to Tuolumne
BELOW: Marte Miller, skiing her favorite backcountry

ABOVE: With Marifran Gallison at our favorite high camp
BELOW: Tenaya Lake: Charlie, Nic Fiore, Bob Gallison

ABOVE: Rusty and Charlie on a high country day

RIGHT: Skating on the Merced River: Jane and Rusty Rust

BELOW: Our pondering fisherman, Chuck

Anne and Chas's wedding, 1978

RIGHT: Eileen Berrey and Isie Tinning

BELOW: First grandchild, Heidi, on North Dome hike with her grandfather

ABOVE: NPS seasonals, one early summer: Betsy, Marian, and Anne
BELOW: Horse patrol summers for Betsy

ABOVE: Betsy and
Kerry's wedding, 1983
(Anne and Chas
already on the way to
Everest)

RIGHT: Clockwise
from author: Charlie,
Bob and Carolynn
Riechers, Jan
Robinson, Ash and
Ethel Ashley

ABOVE: Young mothers' bridge club, four decades later: Carolynn,
Jan, Jane Rust, Ethel, author, Sue Munson, Hazel Overton
(Kathy Bevington deceased)

BELOW: Vermonters: Chuck and Dana (née Stevens),
with Betsy, Trevor, and Heidi

ABOVE: Nevadans:
Anne and Chas
Macquarie, with
Charlie and Anna

RIGHT:
Coloradoans:
Rob and Amy
(née Riesman),
with Emily
and Catie

ABOVE: Wyomingites: Betsy and Kerry Grande, with Collin and Jacob
BELOW: The ultimate adventure: trekking in Nepal

End of the trail

14. Ski Trails

Skiing is not a way of life, skiing IS life.
—the Woessner Family

We came to Yosemite because the dental practice was close to ski-ing—a truth I have never doubted. Charlie was already an avid skier, having worked winter weekends at Tahoe's Echo Lake while in dental school. I, on the other hand, had to learn. I vividly remember the sinking feeling I got as the final turnoff to Badger Pass hove into view: I had to do it. Eventually I reached that very real plateau when skiing becomes fun. It took a while, with several pregnancy time-outs, but I have always been glad that I persevered—in spite of be-ing anything but a natural athlete. Badger Pass and skiing were major factors in the life of our family. These many years later, what plea-sure to have a day of three-generational family skiing—be it in Ver-mont, Colorado, Jackson Hole, Tahoe or Badger Pass.

A BIT OF HISTORY

Donald and Mary Tresidder returned from a mid-twenties holiday in Europe with an enthusiastic interest in skiing. The possibility of introducing the sport to Yosemite was considered, then duly stud-ied. The upshot was the establishment of a ski school in the Park in 1928. It was the first ski school in the west, with Ernest Des Baillets hired to be its director. The slope near the Company stables in the Valley was the site of the first downhill endeavor. Soon, a ski-tour-ing hut was built at Snow Creek below Mt. Hoffmann for those who

ventured further afield. The roster of early-day ski instructors passing through Yosemite reads like the *Who's Who* of early western skiing: Jules Fritsch, Sigi Engl, Hannes Schroll, Fred Iselin, Gordon
Hooley and, of course, Luggi Foeger, who was holding forth as Ski
School Director when we arrived in Yosemite. Each of these men
eventually went on to make his mark as additional ski areas were
established in the west.

By 1933, the Wawona tunnel was successfully completed, and
both the Wawona and Glacier Point roads were improved. The ski
potential of the Chinquapin and Badger areas were each carefully
studied, with the eventual decision made to develop the Badger area.
A lodge was built, the wonderfully named Queen Mary up-ski was
installed, and Badger Pass opened in 1935, the first resort in the country to be directed exclusively to alpine—downhill—skiing.[1] The
Queen Mary was long gone by 1950 but people regaled us with de-
scriptions. The lift was composed of two platforms balanced in such
a manner that as one went up the other came down. The skier took
off his skis to stand on the platform for the ride up, tightly holding
skis in one hand, the railing with the other. The first Constam (T-
bar) lift was installed in 1947 on the main hill, and two years later
another was built on Badger hill. Twenty years later, a Riblet chair
lift replaced the T-bar on the main hill. We were moving up in the
world—and faster!

Charley Proctor and Luggi Foeger both came to Yosemite in the
fall of 1935. Charley came west from New England to be the Winter Sports Director, and Luggi from Austria to run the ski school.
Charley had been one of the first American skiers to compete in the
Olympics, at St. Moritz in 1928. Yosemite appealed to the Proctors
and they stayed for thirty-five years. Charley became head of the
YPCC Commercial Division. In the early seventies the Proctors retired to the Santa Cruz area where they continued to indulge their
love of golf for many years. Somewhere along the way, Charley was
elected to the Far West Ski Association's Ski Hall of Fame, and in the
early nineties another honor came his way. The North American Ski
Journalist Association/West now gives an award annually in his

name. The Charley Proctor Award is presented to an individual for outstanding contribution to the sport of skiing.

In 1932, Yosemite made a bid for the Winter Olympics, with the blessing of the National Park Service. Unfortunately, the bid was turned down in favor of New York's Lake Placid. There must have been a bit of local gloating, however, when Olympic time rolled around. Snow had fallen in abundance in Yosemite, while a dearth in the east necessitated much snow redistribution and straw scattering. Years later, when the 1960 Olympics came to Squaw Valley, Park personnel became very actively involved. Many, including Avery Sturm, who was appointed Olympic team physician, went to Squaw to give assistance to the undertaking. Yosemite was able to contribute personnel well versed in resort management, food handling, ski techniques, and race management.

When we arrived on the scene in the fifties, Badger had an outstanding bunch of instructors. They were capable, great fun, and part of the life of the community. I sorely needed the expertise of an understanding ski instructor. Ross Moore and part-timer Dale Devine became the two long-suffering steps to my plateau.

Luggi remained Ski School Director until the mid-fifties, then moved on to other challenges in the Tahoe area. Nic Fiore took over the directorship. Other instructors included Jim McConkey (from Canada), family man Bob Brelesford, Tony Freitas, Ross Moore, and Bob Heeter (who often came back for the Ancient Jock race in later years). Ray Patten soon arrived, as did seasonal park ranger Jack Morehead in 1954. Jack was later to come back for a tour of duty in the early seventies as chief ranger and again in the mid-eighties as park superintendent.

By 1961, the Ski School had three women on the staff: Char Spranger Lockwood, Patty Walker Anderson, and Martha Miller.

In the late fifties and early sixties, Charlie and I had close Park Service friends stationed at Badger Pass, living in the small house just across from the lodge. The Betts and Browns each offered us the warmth and pleasure of their open-door hospitality. It was handy to have a place to hang out until the traffic thinned, a place to talk over the events and gossip of the day. Ski-fashion watching became one of the favorite off-hill activities. The advent of Bogner stretch ski pants was a true milestone. No more baggy pants. That ski instructor Max Goode's wife had over a dozen pair in various shades was absolutely mind boggling to our frugal budgets. If we had one pair, we considered ourselves style-setters. The coming of Head skis and, later, buckle boots left their marks as well, but not in the same manner as Bogner outfits. Girl-watching had taken on new interest.

THE YOSEMITE WINTER CLUB

The Yosemite Winter Club (YWC), organized in 1928, became an important factor in the history of early skiing in the Park. Not only did the club promote interest in Yosemite skiing, it had the added appeal of being a social entity. Our Winter Club was the first such organization west of the Mississippi and has continued actively into the new century.

By the time we arrived in 1951, many of the races formerly sponsored by the club were glories of the past: among them the Intercollegiate Winter Games, the Far West Kandahar, and the special Gold and Silver races. These races were phased out in deference to the Park Service's wish to minimize spectator sports in the Park. Continuing, however, were the Sunday slaloms, the various Junior races, the North/South race (until the early sixties), and the infamous Flying Fifty.

The Flying Fifty was first held in the early forties. It had a very uncomplicated racecourse. One started in the gate at the top of the main hill and ended in a finish gate at the bottom. How many checks—quick slowing turns—the racer took on the way down was self-determined. Many ran the course as a straight schuss. A permanent listing, in the form of a ladder, hung prominently on the ski lodge wall. The names and race times of the top twenty-five men and the top twenty-five women were entered thereon, and anyone could be bumped down at any time. The race was run on Friday afternoon, just prior to lift closing. Prime running spot was as close to last as possible, the theory being that the later the hour, the icier (faster) the course.

When our kids were well into racing, we let them skip school one Friday afternoon each winter to head for Badger and give the Flying Fifty a try. Chuckie made it onto the board once—for a brief stay. For the good or the bad of it, the race was stopped in the late sixties for reasons of safety and liability, and because Doug Coe, the official timer, was tired of leaping aside for out-of-control finishers.

In the post-war forties, Yosemite and Badger Pass became the holiday destination for many Bay Area ski buffs. (Sugar Bowl, at Tahoe, was about the only other place to ski in northern California.) Quite an ongoing social scene evolved. The Winter Club drew members from the southern part of the state as well. Although club membership was open to all for a two-dollar fee, when we first became involved, it seemed rather an exclusive social appendage of the Yosemite Park and Curry Company—a club more in the closed sense. The presidency rotated yearly among a small group of YPCC executives, Stuart Cross and John Curry among them, with Henry Berrey as executive secretary. Byron Nishkian, of San Francisco (and Wawona) was president in 1960. We felt honored to occasionally be invited to a pre-Ski dinner cocktail party given by the club for various selected hotel guests. We were to represent the local community. This exclusiveness dwindled as more locals became actively involved in both skiing and the club. Roger Hendrickson and Charlie each served as president in the early seventies.

Easter week at Badger was quite special in those early years. Many families came from outside the Park to participate in the fun. The Badger Pass management and the Winter Club sponsored a weeklong series of organized activities and fun for all ages, culminating in the Easter Bonnet contest and the YWC Junior Ski Race on Easter Sunday. Traditionally, this closed the Badger season.

In the fifties, the Winter Club sponsored the Junior Race Team and the local races. By the sixties, Junior racing had become much more serious in nature and the local Lions Club took on a share of the funding and responsibility. Members of the community, race parents in particular, became more involved in the operation of the club with the result that it became much more race-oriented and a bit less social. Over the years, however, I came to miss the kick-off-the-ski-season dinners as they used to be and lament the crush they became. To dress up in a long skirt, to go to the Ahwahnee for a beautifully appointed buffet in the underlounge, to have, perhaps, a ski-fashion show or a good ski movie after dinner was quite appealing. The Yosemite Park and Curry Company did things with considerable class in those days.

In the seventies and eighties, the Winter Club branched out to sponsor activities in other areas of the Park. These included Hans Brinker Night at the Curry ice rink, evening cross-country ski and fondue gatherings at Crane Flat, overnight cross-country ski trips into Ostrander Lake, Christmas caroling for Valley residents, and eventually the always upbeat August Tenaya Lake picnic, with volley ball, sailing, and all. Later, the challenging annual trans-Sierra cross-country ski trip was added to the list of endeavors.

Nic Fiore became Ski School Director in 1957, and at this writing continues in the job. One year he was appointed Winter Sports Director, with another man directing the Ski School, but that proved a short-lived experiment. Nic and his wife, Midge, have both been active in the Professional Ski Instructors Association (PSIA). In 1982, Midge was presented the Tommy Tyndall Memorial Award, an award given by the PSIA for outstanding service to the organization. She had been the working secretary for years. To generations of Yosemite skiers, Nic Fiore is Mr. Badger Pass. Their daughter, Cindy, made her mark with the Junior Race Team in our Betsy's era. Now Nic often skies the Badger slopes with grandchildren. In January of 1998, he celebrated the fiftieth anniversary of his arrival in Yosemite—and at Badger Pass—with a gala weekend hosted by the Yosemite Concessions Services, successors to the YPCC. Friends and admirers came from near and far to gather in Nic's honor.

SKI-DAY

One of the most unique and long-standing events in the ski world of Yosemite is the Wednesday Ski-day program for the local school children. This activity was begun in the forties, again underwritten by the Yosemite Park and Curry Company. Every Wednesday during the ski season, children from the Yosemite and El Portal schools who choose to participate leave school at noon, eat a quick bite, then ride a Company bus to Badger for a two-hour ski lesson. In our day, a mere eighty-five cents covered the cost of the bus ride, lesson, and rental of skis, poles, and boots. The instructors were volunteers, usually parents, who had been given a "how-to" clinic by members of the regular ski school. At the first session each winter, a youngster was assigned to a class of his ability and stayed with that class for the duration of the season, the class advancing as a unit. Porch mothers were solicited to control things on the porch, bus mothers on the bus. When we first became involved, the volunteer instructors were given a season ski-pass. Later, when the program enlarged and surrounding areas started their programs, the remuneration lessened to one free day for each day of helping.

Charlie and I were closely involved in the Ski-day program for years. He closed the dental office at noon on Wednesday; we picked up our kids for the drive to Badger, then tried to get in a run or two before the bus rolled in. Charlie taught an advanced class. I was more often involved in the running of things. Long after our own were out of the nest, I wound down my last involved years by teaching a just-above-beginner class. For a tall person, riding the beginners T-bar with an eight-year-old was a labor of love. The backs of my knees screamed by the end of the day. What a reward it was, however, to watch those little people shed their fear of the lift and begin to take to skiing. *They* plateaued far more rapidly than I had.

Our own were for years involved in this challenging Wednesday program. Due to the extra curricular skiing they had done, it didn't take any of them long to reach Coach Rusty Rust's class. His Wednesday class was composed of the race team members and a few other good young skiers who just didn't choose to race. When the chips were down and a race was coming up, however, Wednesday could be an extension of the weekend training sessions. Rusty not only taught skiing to these kids, he taught ski manners as well—and this reputation followed the youngsters throughout their racing careers. To him, they may have been his beloved "crappy kids," but he'd better not ever see that kind of behavior on the hill.

During the winter of 1959, I was pregnant with Betsy, not skiing, but still wanted to be in on the action. I jumped into the fray by volunteering to run the Ski-day program. In those days that meant doing *everything:* collecting the money at school, making the stormy day decisions (didn't automatically mean a cancel, but that only the top classes would go), riding the bus, being sure that enough instructors turned up, checking kids into classes (and hoping they stayed), wiping noses and warming hands for those who didn't stay in class. Then came the task of getting everyone back onto the bus for the ride home. El Portal was still under our wing, our bus meeting their group at the Bridalveil junction to take them aboard. The last-of-the-season Ski-day was Carnival Day with races, testing, and then a barbecue dinner on the ski lodge porch. Awards were made for passed ski tests, and certificates were given for advancement. It was a fitting climax to the wonderful season of winter.

I had a great crew of helpers on hand; I couldn't have done it without them. And I made a special friend that year. Just as I rode the ski-bus every Wednesday that winter, so, too, Louis DeSandres drove that bus every Wednesday. The developed rapport between us lasted until he died a few years ago. His calm manner helped keep the noise level down, the excitement under control—and neither of us would tolerate "Ninety-nine Bottles of Beer on the Wall!" His one-year-old Tracy and my yet-to-be-born Betsy eventually went to high school together and will also be friends for life.

In 1966, I co-chaired the Ski-day program with Bill Jones—and we were organized! Bill was great to work with and could tactfully handle any disgruntled parent at the end of the day. He improved the caliber of instruction. There was no more "just follow me down the hill" sort of thing. Bill was a perfectionist in his own skiing, and it showed in what was accomplished that year. He also took seriously the testing program. Many of our students took the Class 3 and 4 tests, a few Class 2. If a student passed and received a certificate, that skier knew it was deserved. By then the Ski-day program had its own large, wooden trophy skis on the walls of the Yosemite Elementary School hallway. The names of qualifying students were importantly engraved on the appropriate Class ski for all to see.

The names of people unfailingly involved with the Ski-day program in my time are engraved on my heart. Among them are: Eileen Berrey, Mary Proctor, Nancy Maynard, Lenore Cross, Glenn Mapes, Gary and Pat Brown, the Betts, Dotty Power, Connie Metherell, Del and Donna Armstrong, Ralph and Julia Parker, Dee and Dick McLaren, Darla and Bill Jones, Bryan Harry, Cindy Worthington, Gail and Bill Thompson, Donna Mackie, Jan and Margene van Wagtendonk, Lou Carter, Gayle Sleznick, Fran Scoble, Diana Abrell, Don and Jo Ann Rees, Steve and Janice Hickman, Don Baldwin, Margrith Raspotnik and, of course, Rusty. Those I have neglected to mention are in my heart, just not in my mind at the moment.

A nice tradition to culminate a great Wednesday at Badger was that of heading over to the lodge cafeteria to join other families for dinner. No cooking that night! This, for our own, was also an exercise in dining out manners. In those days of thirty per cent off for locals at the cafeteria, it was manageable for even the six of us to do this weekly. Of those evenings out, Anne remembers best the treats of Jell-O in cubes and ice cream wrapped in paper. We had good times—and many of the cafeteria servers became great family favorites.

CROSS-COUNTRY SKIING RETURNS

The seventies saw a definite resurgence of what, in the days of the Tresidders, had been called *ski-touring.* Although our children didn't get into cross-country skiing until they were almost out of college, Anne's memories do include the following, "I remember the one or two times a year in late winter when we got to ski down the Rail Creek run. It really was exciting for me to *ski off-piste* (as the French say). In fact, that's where I first got my taste and longing for real backcountry skiing and ski mountaineering. It was so exhilarating to take off downhill from the top of the number one lift, not the regular way back down to the lodge we'd done thousands of times before, but off into the untracked powder."

When Wayne Merry returned to the Park to organize the Yosemite Mountaineering School in 1969, he also envisioned a cross-country ski school as a winter offshoot. The following year YPCC's Bob Maynard agreed to give it a try. Ned Gillette and Jim Speck, members of the U.S. Nordic Combined Olympic team, were hired to run the Yosemite Cross-Country Ski School—and it was soon in operation.[2] Gradually, with more modern equipment and groomed trails, an avid interest in the sport took hold. The areas around Crane Flat and Badger Pass became hubs for new cross-country trails. The fact that alpine skiing had become so costly also attributed to the growing popularity of the sport. By the eighties, Bruce Brosman was in charge of the operation and its base was moved from the Mountaineering Shop in Curry Village to Badger Pass.

The snow-covered Glacier Point Road became the main artery for cross-country skiing out of Badger and, later, a very popular area for track skiing and skating. Offshoot ski trails from this route include the two-mile trip to Dewey Point with its fine overview of the western end of Yosemite Valley, the Bridal Veil Campground loop back to Badger on the old Glacier Point Road, the longer trip into Ostrander Lake, the highly rewarding ski to Taft Point for a different Valley overview, and the steep climb of Sentinel Dome. The main trail culminated in the descent past the incredible winter panorama of Washburn Point to the breathtaking spectacle of Glacier Point itself.

With pre-booking, overnight accommodations at both Glacier Point (through the Company) and Ostrander (through the Yosemite Association) are available. Howard Weamer has been the capable winter caretaker/guardian/host of Ostrander Ski hut for years. While Anne and Chas were Tuolumne Meadows winter rangers in the early eighties, they had regular radio contact with Howard at Ostrander to compare snow conditions and avalanche dangers.

The Nordic Holiday weekend was added to the Badger agenda in the early seventies and its popularity mushroomed. Cross-country ski races were a major part of the weekend activities. The decade also saw the addition of a cross-country class to the Wednesday Ski-day program. It drew a small, but eager, group of devotees.

With cross-country skiing came an increase in winter visitation to Tuolumne Meadows. By the mid-seventies the Park Service felt the need to hire a winter backcountry ranger to be posted at the Meadows, the job Anne and Chas later filled for five winters. Snow-mobile encroachment into the pristine backcountry was becoming a threat. The Macquaries tell amusing stories of occasionally hearing the quiet-shattering noise of snowmobiles in the distance and making a ski-dash to the bridge over the Tuolumne River to waylay and turn back the culprits. The struggle to keep these machines out of the Park is a continuing—and, so far, successful—one.

There are two routes to Tuolumne in the winter. One travels east, the other west. The former, the more strenuous, follows the path of the earlier mentioned ranger snow surveyors. This route starts from the Valley at Mirror Lake, climbs the Tenaya zigzags, to continue on past the old Snow Creek cabin. Further uphill the trail intersects the Tioga Road. Here one has a choice: to continue on the road past Olmsted Point to drop down across Tenaya Lake—now frozen—and continue on the road to the Meadows, or to ski on the old Tioga Road past the Snow Flat cabin, the May Lake Junction, and then drop down to join the trail at Tenaya Lake.

The western route was the more popular and was the one used by the Winter Club's Trans-Sierra cross-country ski trips. These trips started in the late seventies and were efficiently organized by Don and Kay Pitts, cross-country aficionados. Usually consisting of a dozen or so people, the group flew over the Sierra in a small charter plane. They started from Lee Vining, skied up and over Tioga Pass, and on to Tuolumne Meadows where food and fuel had been cached in a cabin during the accessible fall months. After a few days of exploring the Meadows in its winter grandeur, the group continued on to the Snow Flat cabin where additional supplies had been cached, then on down past Snow Creek to descend the zigzags into the Valley. These trips have continued for well over two decades. Shorter overnight excursions, again under the auspices of the Winter Club, were made into Ostrander Lake and to Glacier Point.

Charlie and I skied in to Tuolumne from the Lee Vining side in 1982. It was a multipurpose trip: We wanted to see Anne and Chas, I had never seen Tuolumne in its winter splendor, and we needed some good conditioning for our upcoming spring trek in Nepal. We drove over Carson Pass and south to Lee Vining where we parked the truck near the winter gate at the foot of the Tioga Road. The first few miles we did on foot, skis strapped to our packs. When we reached the curve at Warren Creek, snow dictated that we put on our skis for the continued climb to the Pass. Anne and Chas met us there to urge us on to Tuolumne and to the warmth of their winter home in the old mess hall/present Visitor Center building. We spent three nights enjoying their hospitality and two days exploring the Meadows to our heart's content. One day we all skied across the Meadow to Soda Springs and Parsons Lodge. We were sitting on the steps of the lodge enjoying our sandwiches and the incredible Tuolumne panorama surrounding us when Anne's park radio began crackling out the news of the attempt on President Reagan's life. In just that moment, the real world came crashing in.

THE ANCIENT JOCKS

Another creation of Rusty's, with added ideas and help from a number of us, was the Ancient Jocks Annual Slalom, kicked off in 1973. It turned into a wonderful, nostalgic gathering of old- and new-timers. Everyone brought a picnic lunch to share on the deck above the Badger ski-rental room. Conviviality reigned, and then came the race. Entrants were to be thirty years and older, categories by age bracket, no racing experience necessary. Charlie always entered, and I when coerced. All the officiating, timing, gatekeeping, and penalizing were done by members of the ski team—and did they love that. The only job that legally couldn't be handled by team members was the beer-stop set up halfway down the giant slalom course. Here, the racer had to come to a full stop, swill a paper cup of beer or coke (spilling added penalty seconds to one's time) then head for the finish gate. With the advent of camcorders came some hilarious tapes. At five o'clock, a no-host happy hour in the Badger Lodge began, followed by a barbecue steak dinner and awards.

In its hey-day, the Ancient Jock Slalom was a great gathering place for all ages of Badger buffs. Four FWSA Ski Hall of Famers were in attendance one notable year: Albert Sigal, Byron Nishkian, Charley Proctor, and Luggi Foeger. Each had strong Badger Pass ties. Unfortunately, the ebullient spirit of this congenial race ebbed following Rusty's death, although it is still held most years. Badger Pass didn't open in the flood year of 1997, but the race was again held in 1998. Charlie and I, however, had skied our last Ancient Jocks a few years earlier.

THE BEAT GOES ON

Both Chuck and Rob took advantage of UC Davis's "stop-out" program while in college, taking a year off between their sophomore and junior years. And where did they head? To ski areas. Chuck, in 1972, used his year to teach skiing at Aspen Highlands in Colorado. Rob, in 1975, chose Sun Valley, to work for Dillon Giles at The Ram restaurant and ski every chance he could get. Each of the boys met his future wife while pursuing the love of skiing. All four offspring have used skiing as a vocation somewhere along the line: Chuck in his Aspen era and ski patrol work in Bolton Valley, Vermont; Anne in her winter rangering in Tuolumne; Rob in his ski patrolling at both Badger and Keystone, Colorado; and Betsy in her ski patrolling at Badger. All now live in or near ski areas, and Charlie and I have skied with each in his/her own wonderland. I must add, however, that I'll take the powder of Colorado or even the Sierra cement of California over the blue ice of Vermont any day.

Skiing has remained so much a part of Charlie's and my life. We now share the joy of watching grandkids take to the sport, and wonder how many of them will go on to snowboarding. I don't think I could ever plateau in that sport. Perhaps even the 'boarders will keep a pair of skis honed and handy for when the grandparents join them on their mountains.

15. Junior Ski Racing

I would have won if I hadn't missed that gate!
—many a disappointed ski racer

THE SKI TEAM

The Junior Ski Racing program in Yosemite was always Rusty Rust's baby. It was established in 1949 and was underwritten by the YPCC through the Yosemite Winter Club. Henry Berrey, the spokesperson for the YWC, was very much involved with the logistics, but Rusty chose the team members. He looked for ability and eagerness. In the early days it wasn't as essential that parents be involved; that came later when by necessity ski racing became more of a business.

Because our children were on skis at least a year before starting kindergarten, once in school they soon reached their goal: Rusty's race team. Sometimes the skiing ability came more quickly than the growing up. We have a wonderful snapshot of Anne running the Sunday Slalom gates with her thumb in her mouth. So much for keeping that pole behind her!

The entire team skied and trained together, the little guys and the big guys. There always seemed to be more boys than girls in those years. Initially, team members resided either in the Valley or in El Portal. Early ski team members included the Proctors, the Sturms, Frankie Carter, Dennis Parrish, Malcolm McGregor, the older Berrey boys, Toni Culver and Jeanne Evans (both of whom went to the Junior Olympics), the Ouimets, and Randy Rust. One year Danny Sturm, then in the eighth grade, had the misfortune to break both legs in a ski accident. He was confined to a wheelchair for several months, under the caring and watchful eye of his dad, Dr. Avery Sturm. There wasn't a dry eye in the auditorium on graduation night that June as Dan arose from the wheelchair and walked to the podium to receive his diploma.

By the sixties, eligible youngsters from outside the Park whose dedicated families got them to Badger for weekend practice sessions joined the team. The Tamms, Kip Ferguson, the Wagners, and our nephew Steve Polhemus came from Fresno. The Carlisles came from Merced, and our most distant racers, the Davisson-Hellands, came faithfully from Southern California. Debbie Wall joined the team when her family lived in Oakhurst, then continued for a year after moving to Sacramento. Team members were enthralled by the fact that Debbie's mother was a former Roller Derby star. Bert and Bobbi Wall were great help on race days and a lot of fun. We were sorry to lose them when the commute became too difficult. There was a special camaraderie in the ongoing group. All the parents helped, be it officiating, gate keeping, handling a stop-watch, making and delivering lunches, giving rides, or just being the "go-fer."

By the time our own came onto the team (Chuck, in 1961), they were racing with the younger Berrey boys, Tom Cross, Rick McElligott, the Powers and Parkers, the Armstrongs, Leslie Rust, the McLaren girls, the Ihlenfeldts, and the Betts and Sharp boys. Ric Sharp was a fine young skier but lacked the weight to really attack the course. Rusty loaded Ric's pockets with silver dollars one race day, with the result that Ric cut several seconds off his overall time. In 1966, we were all extremely proud of Danny Armstrong's earned place in the Junior Nationals. True, the Armstrongs had recently transferred to Zion National Park in Utah, but we still considered him one of our own.

Kathy Metherell, Cindy Fiore, Debra and Russ Jones, Tom and Annie Harry, Lannette Bagley, Lynn Cross, Tom Wolfe and Clark Kraus each left a mark on Badger racing. After our older three were off and away, Betsy continued for a few years, racing with the Thompsons—Chris and Heidi, the Hendrickson boys, The Birchill girls, Jim Shackelton, the Reeses and Conways, the Mackie twins, Andy Garza, Clark Hardy, Jan Jones and others. Then Betsy—and we—retired from Junior racing leaving it to the next bunch: Jessica Rust, Eric Abbott, the Littles, Smiths and Hinsons, Miguel Soria, the Elchlepps, Mazzaglias, Evans, Rothells, and others to come.

THE MODUS OPERANDI

When we entered into Junior racing, it was a whole-family adventure. All age groupings—1, 2, 3, 4, and 5—raced at the same area on the same weekend, usually on the same racecourse. Later, when the entire race picture became much more sophisticated, the older 1, 2, and 3 groups and the younger 4 and 5 groups raced at separate areas, often on the same weekend. This could cause considerable logistical problems for those parents with youngsters in more than one group. Ours, fortunately, grew out of racing before this became a problem. For us, it was a family trip to a single area, and everyone skied.

The ski race trips, although strenuous and often hectic, were great fun. We all stayed wherever Rusty could make suitable reservations, and always with a kitchen facility or two. The mothers planned and purchased ahead for the dinner and breakfast meals. No going out on the town for this group. While the parents prepared dinner, Rusty, the kids and knowledgeable fathers stripped and re-waxed the skis for the next day's race. Rusty unfailingly brought along an old electric iron for smoothing on the applied wax. I'm sure the smell of hot wax mingled with the aroma of simmering spaghetti sauce would bring back fond memories to a number of the parents of our generation.

It was early to bed, up at dawn, breakfast, then off to the slopes. In the earlier days, a snowfall the night before could mean a session of foot packing the racecourse before the forerunner could be out of the starting gate. But once the forerunner okayed the course, the race was on—and would continue until the last racer went through the gates. Lunches were often delivered and consumed on the hill. The award presentation came at the close of the day, after all the facts had been calculated by hand. As timing became more sophisticated, the lag time between the end of the race and the presentation of awards lessened. But in the early days winning an award and waiting for it to be presented could mean the long drive home was delayed by an hour or two.

In later years at Badger, Rusty arranged for a spaghetti feed for the racers and their families on the Saturday night of a two-day meet. This became a gala award dinner for the first day's race and was much appreciated by all. The YPCC was most hospitable in all of this. And who but Rusty would think to put together an Olympic-like set of platforms of differing heights for the presentation of awards?

Among our away-from-home meets were those at Alpine Meadows, Squaw Valley, Heavenly Valley, Homewood, and Sierra Ski Ranch—all in the Tahoe area. Our first experience at a Heavenly Valley meet came in 1962, with both Anne and Chuckie, ages eight and ten, competing. There is nothing quite as daunting to the spirits of a beginning racer—and her mother—than to arrive at Heavenly for the first time and see slalom gates set up on the snow-covered cliff called The Gunbarrel. I have blocked out the race, can't remember any results, but can still feel the relief of having everyone on the team in one piece at the end of the day.

Other away meets were held at China Peak (now Sierra Summit) above Fresno, Dodge Ridge out of Sonora, and Bear Valley below Ebbett's Pass. The furthest afield we traveled was the long trip to Mammoth, via Bakersfield, the most direct winter route. How frustrating it was to have to drive thirteen long hours to reach a place only fifty miles from home as the crow flies. On that particular trip we celebrated Mike Power's sixteenth birthday on the way home. On another occasion, we carried a birthday cake over the snow and through the woods to a rustic house near China Peak to celebrate Tom Berrey's birthday. We were one large, extended ski racing family in those days.

SKI RACE OFFICIATING

No successful ski race could be pulled off without the dedicated efforts of a group of trained officials. Over the years, Badger gained— and kept—the reputation for running a good race, just as Rusty's racers gained a reputation for being a mannerly bunch of kids. It was a point of honor to all of us. Let's face it: If you haven't much of a ski mountain to attract racing families, you certainly better have the ability to put on a well-organized race. Of course, having the grandeur of Yosemite to back us up was also a plus. It worked for years.

We were fortunate to have some committed, knowledgeable people whose only connection with racing was the love of skiing and devotion to Badger Pass. People such as Doug Coe and Don Pearson gave unstintingly of their time to further good, trained race officiating.

Doug Coe was a delightful character. I still miss him. He had a long history of skiing in Yosemite. He was an avid ski-tourer in the forties, and after the YPCC's Ostrander ski hut was built, he visited the area many times. By the time we knew Doug, he had retired and was living with his wife Ora near Oakhurst. He was the official timer for the Flying Fifty and the Sunday Slaloms, so it was by natural progression that he evolved into a timer of Junior races as well. He became widely known for the huge hourglass displayed on a heavy cord around his neck. He would get it out and make a great pretense of using it when things got a little too serious around the timers' table.

Doug was unfailing in his help to Rusty and to the integrity of our race staff. He could be as feisty as they come, but he gained the greatest respect from racers, coaches, and parents. More than once I witnessed his verbal chastisement of a racer skiing with bare arms, especially when the snow was icy. He was a true Badger institution and the deserving recipient of the 1976 Stan Walton Award for outstanding work as a Certified Ski Race Official.

In 1978, Don Pearson was also presented this Award, again much deserved. Don's forte was in the race-timing mechanism field. He was with the U. S. Forest Service as a telecommunications expert. He brought that expertise to Badger, helped immeasurably with the start-finish gate communication, and developed a system that was quite unique and very accurate. Don was asked to take his highly developed timing apparatus to other race areas and did so for several years before retiring from officiating. The Yosemite Junior Racing Team owed a great debt of gratitude to these two men.

In the late sixties and early seventies, Junior ski racing became more sophisticated in every way. Equipment greatly improved, more youngsters became involved, and the whole coaching set-up became more serious—and more costly. The program itself was becoming big business. In Yosemite, the Winter and Lions Clubs still underwrote most of the expenses of the team, which now included uniform sweaters and racing helmets. Rusty still donated his services to the team. The one area in which we had to get serious in order to stay competitive in attracting ski meets to Badger Pass was in the upgrading and training of our staff of officials. Charlie and I, with the help of Doug Coe, organized race clinics for interested residents in the Valley. We had several who worked diligently to become certified referees and others who became well-qualified timers, starters, and gatekeepers. The latter were most essential in that it was not an easy matter to disqualify any racer, and even harder if that racer was in contention for the top spot. We all learned to know what we were doing, and to have any disqualification verified by both the gatekeeper above and the one below our own station. We knew the current ilk of coach would challenge any disqualification and we had better have the facts at hand. Anne Hendrickson became a capable, dedicated referee—later technical delegate—and continued to contribute many hours to officiating after their move to the Tahoe area.

CLOSE TO ROB'S HEART

Skiing was our life in the wintertime. Unfortunately, during Rob's years at Mariposa High School, some of the coaches would not permit their team members to also be on the ski team. Rob would love to have gone out for basketball, but opted for the ski team every winter. Skiing was his love and he, too, credits Rusty for the success of the Yosemite ski team.

From his Colorado Rocky Mountain home, where he lives with a family of his own, our second son wrote:

> If anyone other than family had an influence on my life it was Rusty. Skiing was, is, and will continue to be the most enjoyable sport in my life. Despite the fact that all we had to ski was Badger Pass, the friendships, fun, training, and victories were the highlight of my adolescence. I have done— and achieved—a lot in my lifetime, but the excitement and success of my skiing is by far the most memorable accomplishment. (Let me add special thanks, Mom and Dad, for encouraging us and making it possible.) After all these years in the great Rocky Mountains—with their steep, long, powder-covered slopes—I still remember the days at Badger: wallowing through the "Sierra cement" with Tom and Allan Berrey, foot-packing a course with Lucy Parker and Lannette Bagley, posing for the Fresno Bee photographer with Annie Carlisle when we won the Silver Ski Race—and I remember a *ski area!* In this modern era of mega resorts and ski area mergers, it is sad to think that probably Badger's days are numbered. I am proud to know that we were all a part of it and that I can walk through the Ahwahnee Hotel with my girls and show them, in the Winter Club Room, my name engraved on that special trophy in the case. They were days from a time gone by, a good time, a fun time, a time that every kid should have the opportunity to experience.

Rusty was awarded the FWSA Coaches Award for his longevity in the field of Junior Ski Racing. In 1983, the community, spearheaded by a committee of race parents, sponsored a "Rusty Roast" at Curry. As well as providing a rollicking good time, the evening was highlighted by the presentation of a coveted and much deserved ski trip to the Bugaboo Mountains in Canada for Rusty and son Randy.

Rusty was later honored with the Charley Proctor Award for his outstanding contribution to the sport of skiing—and, we all agreed, to the kids of Yosemite and beyond. His was a career spread over fifty years. He was much loved by his crappy kids, and left his mark on a number of young lives. Many of Rusty's racers turned up for his retirement party in March 1991. The gala was held in the Curry dining room, with snow falling steadily outside. Our four came from all over the country: Chuck from Vermont, Rob from Colorado, Betsy from Wyoming, and Anne from Nevada. When all the people who had raced under Rusty's tutelage stood in recognition of their coach, eyes misted and heart strings tugged. It was thrilling.

Rusty died the following January in his home on our shared Wawona hillside. It was most fitting that his memorial service be held on the porch of Badger Pass that following July day. The decks were again filled with Rusty's kids and their families, there to give him the kind of send-off he so richly deserved from the place he loved.

Randy Rust was his dad's good right arm in later years. He could be seen on the Badger slopes carrying armloads of slalom poles, setting racecourses, or putting the racers through their paces. It was by natural progression that the coach's mantle passed to Randy upon his father's death. Randy, in turn, enlisted his daughter Jessica to be his assistant coach, a job she filled until her eventual move from the Park. This was in essence a ski-coaching dynasty dedicated to the kids of Yosemite. Those who had the privilege of being involved with the Junior Ski Racing program over the years reaped the rewards of this dedication.

16. Hats Off to Kids

There's a time when you have to explain to your children why they're born and it's a marvelous thing if you know the reason by then.

—Hazel Scoll

"What do you mean you were born in Yosemite?" "Wow, how lucky can you be?" "What was it like to be a kid in Yosemite?" These are the reactions our four often receive when the "Where were you born?" question comes up. To the last of the three questions, Rob answers, "It was the same, but much different." Tales of growing up in the Valley are best told by Charlie's and my offspring in their own words, recorded here with just a few asides from mom.

It was the 1950s, and like most families, activities for our small ones were family or mom-oriented until the onset of school years. There were no pre-school or day-care situations. It was family on the weekends, moms and kids on the weekdays. One graduated to big kid status only when old enough to venture out into the neighborhood world alone, but when Mom blew that whistle it meant head home pronto. There was a pecking order with those whistle blasts. With longevity, we finally made top spot and just a single blast echoing through the neighborhood called all Woessners home. We kept that position for years—until ours were well out of the nest.

Rob reminisces:

There must have been a couple dozen kids at any given period in our neighborhood. There was always someone around with whom to do something and always something to do. My earlier recollections, preschool age, were of groups of kids, seemingly always down in the Hubbards' yard, playing great games of hide-and-seek, kick-the-can, sardines—or maybe just lolling around talking about how time goes by. As we grew older, the games changed: anny-anny-over (the Cottrells' house was best for that), homemade go-carts down the hill by the Metherells', and deeper ventures into the woods behind the Clarks' house. The infamous tree fort shared with Tom Harry and Bobbie Clark was a constantly evolving architectural masterpiece just up the hill behind our house (speaking of things kids probably wouldn't get away with in a National Park in this day and age). In a few more years we moved on to fishing, backpacking, skiing, golf lessons on the Wawona green, then climbing, and sailing.

Growing up in Yosemite had its Huck Finn side: create and explore. From the realm of creating/making came log rafts on Tenaya, tree houses in the woods, a canvas-covered kayak, and a crate go-cart put together in the backyard. One fall the masterpieces were lovingly sanded hunks of scrap wood with skate wheels attached—the Valley's first skateboards. These actually held together long enough to carry the boys all the way from the Foresta turn-off (where Highway 120 was closed in those earlier wintertimes), through the three tunnels, and on down to the dam at the west end of the Valley, a distance of about five miles.

The exploring began in the neighborhood, the nearby woods and rivulets, Dog Cave, Rain Falls, and Dirt Slide (all kid-given names for special spots along the horse trail above us). As ages and curiosities grew, Spider Cave, Sunnyside Bench, Devil's Bathtub, and the inviting granite slabs were added to the list. When water skills were proven, the reaches of the Merced River as it meandered through the Valley were added to the summer's adventures. These children's dad encouraged them in any venture they proved capable of attempting.

Even public buildings were subject to scrutiny from the curious young. The elevator at the Ahwahnee—the only one in the Park, perhaps in the county—was without a doubt the biggest draw of the man-made creations. Many a sneaked ride was taken in that wonder, but only after one passed through the solarium to toss a penny or two into the wishing fountain. The under-construction Valley Visitors' Center was of great interest to many a curious young sidewalk superintendent, and, we later learned, the scene of some fascinating after-hours nosing around, some perhaps not entirely well thought-out. When serious mischief occurred and the youngster was confronted, a parent appreciated having our good friend Rick Anderson as the official ranger voice. Rick had a great understanding of kids and monkey business. He could do more straightening out with one calm, serious lecture than any ranger I've ever known. It was a real knack—and the kids respected and appreciated him. We all missed him when he and Patty moved to Sequoia National Park.

My move to Yosemite, as a young adult, gave me my first exposure to true seasons. In addition to seasonal weather, I discovered seasonal flora and fauna, seasonal activities, and seasonal "openings," as well as seasonal tourist influxes. Our children, on the other hand, grew up in a world of seasonal changes from the beginning. Anne has described her seasons in this manner:

> In the spring Yosemite Creek, below the Falls Bridge, jumped its banks and ran all over the place. The little wilderness (not far from our home) was full of small, rocky islands covered with blooming white azaleas, separated by temporary streams of various sizes—some so small you could jump over them, some almost as big as the main channel—and all of them *very cold*. We claimed islands, built forts on them, built log-and-stick bridges across to them, rolled up our pants and waded across the frigid little streams. It was a good way to play in the water before the main river was warm enough for swimming.

It was an idyllic time. When our children were into these activities, the Park was still ours in the springtime. There were no tourists wandering through the woods who might wonder and worry about eager stream-hopping youngsters. These kids were already at home with the elements and creatively adapted them into their fun.

The other three also mentioned this wilderness-of-their-own in their reminiscences. Chuck and his buddies stomped trails in the spring frazil-iced rivulets[1] where, some years later, Betsy and her pals would don Al Garza's old waders in order to leave no sign of a trail as they sneaked up the middle of the creek, Indian-fashion. All groups professed to eventually ending their wanders at "Mr. Muir's Bench,"[2] to rest awhile, to contemplate the meaning of life, and to drink in the beauty of Yosemite Falls.

To Anne, summer was water: swimming lessons at the lodge, picnics at the river, and "floating-down." It was swimming the river astride her horse on a warm day—joined by Ginnie Harders and Katy Maynard. It was the high country, made even more magical in those early years by the difficulty of getting there via the old Tioga Road. It was going barefoot, and playing outside 'til dark. Then came fall with its exodus of Park visitors. To quote Anne:

> We had the Valley to ourselves—and could enjoy the delicious contrast between the warm, sunny, yellow meadows and the cold blue shade of the cliffs. I loved picking apples in the wonderful abandoned orchards near the school, over at Curry Village, and behind the stables—then coming home to bake a pie. School was just a moderately boring interruption to real life.

Anne's cherished memories of the winter season include, of course, skiing at Badger and skating, both at the ice rink[3] and on Mirror Lake in those rare winters when the lake froze before the snow fell to roughen the ice. Everyone agreed the ice rink at Curry was the preteen social hangout. Her memories of Christmas: "You know there's a Santa Claus when he actually comes to Curry Village and brings you just what you asked for wrapped in paper your mom would never use."

Anne is our reader-of-books. Like her mother, she had teasing brothers. Unlike her mother, Anne would not rise to their bait. She became very adept at stepping around the field of combat and dissolving into a book. Sibling recollections of Anne as a youngster all have her with her nose in a book. This tendency led to an unusual friendship with classmate Sonja Hoie:

> We read together. We fell into the habit of going to the library together once a week or so after school. We each checked out the maximum six books, took them home to Sonja's house, and read. Then we'd exchange the books each had finished and I'd go home, often a little after dark. We talked, of course, on the way to the library and on the way back, but the rest of the time we just quietly read. I don't remember thinking it was unsociable that we spent so much time together with noses buried in books. On the contrary it was warm and intimate—and quiet.

Sonja and her mother, Ruby Hoie, came into our lives and neighborhood in the early fifties. They were, to my knowledge, our first single-parent family. Ruby continued in her National Park Service career until retirement from Yosemite in the eighties. When Sonja was little and her mom was at work, she stayed with Bea Abbott, just down the street from us. Bea, an NPS wife, had raised a large brood of her own and was a comfortably round, motherly (albeit strict) sort of person. Guidelines for Sonja's after-school perimeters were laid down and definitely adhered to. There was no wandering out of that yard in the early years. I've always suspected, however, that Sonja partook of some of the neighborhood's tastiest after-school snacks. Bea Abbott was a renowned cook. Long after grammar school days, Anne and Sonja were housemates for a year while in college at UC Santa Cruz and tent mates at Tuolumne while working for the NPS. Sonja went on to make a career for herself in the U.S. Forest Service.

The favorite hangout spots varied with age, gender, time of year, and interest. The ice rink, schoolyard, and Sentinel Bridge (i.e., the river) were on everyone's list. Anne and Betsy added the Curry stables, the lodge pool, and the cozy Ahwahnee Hotel lounge. There, occasionally, if one was polite and looked presentable, a cup of afternoon tea might be had. The boys veered more toward tree houses, forts, and caves. Each child grew up with a bike, and used it daily unless snow covered the ground.

Betsy reminisces about the new basketball court built at the school, with picnic tables tucked into the trees to separate it from the football field:

> That became the great meeting place. We could sit and talk, and watch the guys play basketball (then, Randy Beck, Phillip Downing, and Tom Wolfe were the ones to watch) or ride our bikes around and around the court. Randy once figured out how many times around equaled a mile. I never tried that one—there were many more interesting places in Yosemite Valley to ride your bike for a mile.

Anne recalls:

> One of the best hangouts of all was the Village Store. In our days you walked in the front entrance and met the candy counter head on, with the magazine rack to one side. There was a space between that was paradise for kids—candy on one side, comic books on the other. We didn't hang out there much in the summer because it was too crowded with tourists, but in the other seasons, especially winter, it was an important part of our rounds. We'd buy candy, sit cross-legged on the floor and eat it while reading comics or *True Confessions*. Funny, I don't *ever* remember any store employee or manager telling us to leave!

AN INVOLVED COMMUNITY

Because it does take a village, and we had one, there were other influential adults in the children's growing lives. Among them were dedicated scout leaders, effective swimming instructors, enthusiastic football coaches, involved clergy (both resident and seasonal), and the very important schoolteachers.

Charlie did a stint as Boy Scout leader before ours were even of the cub scouting age. This proved to be a great idea, in that it gave him the opportunity to get out on the trail with earlier Scouts (and out of the house), then retire by the time ours were eligible. In this way, each of ours had his own admired scoutmaster, and could hike with Dad independently. Charlie's co-leaders, at different times, included Dale Devine, George White, and John Earle. They had some great outings, and managed to produce two Eagle Scouts out of the bunch: Bruce Fladmark and Hoppy Hubbard. Chuck and Rob each remember their scoutmasters Doug Hubbard and Bryan Harry with a great sense of camaraderie. Rob also gives top marks to his Cub Scout den mother, Lee Fleming. With four sons of her own, Lee was a natural. Long after ours were grown and gone, in the eighties and nineties, Jan van Wagtendonk became a very involved, active, and challenging scout leader for the El Portal/Yosemite area.

There was also an active Girl Scout troop in the Valley. Barbara Morris was the pillar of the organization in the early sixties, with Nancy Maynard active as a Brownie Scout leader. Bonnie Bagley was Anne's scout leader; Paula Krisko, Betsy's. I assisted at several points along the way. When we moved from the Valley in 1987, Girl Scouting was in the capable hands of Linda McKenzie.

All four of ours had group camping experiences of one form or another. Since there wasn't a Boy Scout camp connection yet for the Yosemite troop, Chuckie joined Shirley Conner's son Sherrill at a session of the Alameda Boys Club camp at Mendocino. Rob went along the second year. They met all kinds of inner-city boys on these ventures—a true exposure. And I well remember flippantly asking Rob (last minute Mom-talk) if he knew the facts of life—and his quick comeback: "I sure do, Mom. When I'm sixteen, I can get my driver's license!" And off he went to camp at age nine.

Anne's first away-from-home camping adventure was in a very rustic Girl Scout camp somewhere on the old Wawona/Chowchilla Mountain road. It was *so* rustic and dusty I hated leaving her there, but she survived quite nicely. Betsy and Annie Harry went off to the YWCA Camp Merrimack out of Fresno, and later to a Girl Scout camp at Green Meadows near Fishcamp. For our gang, organized group camping soon gave way to family camping adventures.

WATER FUN

Red Cross swimming lessons were given at the Yosemite Lodge pool during the first two weeks of summer vacation, and always before the official pool opening at 10:00. It was *cold*. The pool was unheated in the earlier days. The more proficient one became, the earlier one's lesson. Junior Life Saving, the most advanced group, was at a chilly 8:00. The hardy instructors included Joann Gill Cross, Jan Haag, Connie Metherell, Paula Krisko, Babs Albert, Ruth Harry, and, later, Anne Hendrickson and others. Rob remembers swimming

> ...back and forth, lap after lap, "Sarge" blowing her whistle and yelling instructions at us. What swimmers we became, not racers or hot divers, but more than capable of holding our own in any water activity. This led to the river. Hour after hour we'd float down the river with fins and snorkel, frog gigs for spearing suckers. We dove under in search of lures and other trinkets. Always a stop was made at the sand-piles below Housekeeping Camp, then a jump off Sentinel Bridge, a swing on the rope tied to that ancient oak, then back into the water to shoot the riffle under Redfoot Bridge.[4] The riverbank at the site of the old Sentinel Hotel dump would often give up an old bottle or two. [Rob and Rod Whitfield were avid searchers.] The river was the best water world a kid could ask for—and it was free.

No wonder they all paid attention to their swimming instructors.

Our older children had an occasional private lesson from Ferdinand Castillo when he was stationed in the Valley, the youngers from Larry "Rabbit" Rojas, one of the lodge lifeguards. With all the running water, lake swimming, sailing, and eventual rafting available, Charlie and I placed great importance on water safety. Anne recalls the long air mattress floats. We would put in by the company stables and float all the way to either Sentinel Beach or, if the current still had its early summer vigor, to Devil's Elbow. It was a peaceful water meander of two or three hours and presented views of the Valley and surrounding cliffs not noticed from trail or road. Always there was a car stashed at the far end—and food. This was long before the era of commercial rafting on the river. The sport was still for the innovative.

We had a number of favorite beaches: Sugar Pine, until the road was closed; El Cap Bend, our secret beach when we had babies; Sentinel, perfect for supper picnics and gorgeous views; Yellow Pine, when more challenge was needed; Cascades, if we had time for the longer drive. This latter was a great place to swim when the kids were older. It is where we first met Shirley Sargent, who came down the old Coulterville road from Foresta with some of her extended family. The beach has also seen rendezvous with the Sturms and, later, the Harders after both families had moved from the Valley. We rarely went to Muscle Beach (Devil's Elbow), unless it was the get-out point of a rafting excursion. It was usually far too crowded. Cathedral Beach always seemed too dirty. In the eighties we found another secret beach—and so it shall remain.

OTHER INFLUENCES

Football brings to mind a photo in *National Geographic* magazine in the early sixties. It pictured our school playing field with the granite cliffs and a majestic, pounding Yosemite Falls in the background. The caption said something like, "Could anyone ask for a lovelier setting for a football game?" During our first couple of decades in the Valley, the grammar school could field a full football squad of eleven with a full bench of substitutes. The coach in that first decade was Sterling Cramer of YPCC connection. In the sixties, came NPS ranger Jake Metherell, assisted later by Tommy Thomas. When Chuck was in the seventh grade, the team had depth—and was good. Our adversaries consisted of three disparate teams: Mariposa Elementary, a school in Lodi, and Menlo Preparatory School in the Bay Area. The trip to the latter game was an undertaking. The boys rode to Menlo in a YPCC bus, coaches in charge. Jake Metherell was an absolute stickler for the dress code. This meant each boy traveled in dress shirt and tie, which made great sense, as good deportment seemed in direct proportion to pride of appearance. The team spent the night before the game in the Menlo School gym. Parents provided their own transportation, and many of us turned up. Yosemite Elementary School had its own cheerleaders: red skirts, white blouses, pompoms, and all. It was good fun.

By the time Rob was in the seventh and eighth grades, a lowered number in school enrollment meant fewer team members. Being trounced became commonplace due to lack of manpower. Track and field sports were introduced at this juncture and soon came into their own—and girls could get involved. Weren't we proud parents the year that Rob came home from the Atwater track meet with a huge high point trophy? These were the beginning years of the Yosemite track meet, which is still held each spring. All the county schools participated in this event. The Lions Club, in cooperation with the Parent's Group, did the organizing—lining up manpower to fill the gopher holes, stripe the field, and to serve as officials and timers. In a nutshell, involved community cooperation made the event happen. And the sun shone down gloriously on that "playing field beneath the falls."[5]

The Church Community was very much involved with the young of Yosemite. For our own, the childhood years meant Sunday School, Vacation Bible School for two summer weeks, and the annual Christmas pageant. The activities were traditional in preacher Al Glass' time and continued on with Dr. Woodruff, Duane Murphy, and Bill Henning. Bill and Mary Alice Henning came to the Park in 1961 and soon Bill had a very active teen club up and running. Ours, however, were still too young to participate. Don Baldwin succeeded Bill in 1965 and brought with him a genuine interest in the youth of the Park. He kept them active. The first major undertaking that winter was to organize and film the movie *Goldtoe,* a take-off on the rage-of-the-moment *Goldfinger.* Chuck, Ken Metherell, Rob Johnson, and Eric Oster all had starring roles in this classic, Anne, a more minor one. I remember Chuck being filmed skiing hellbent down a Badger slope, red cape flowing behind him, in one chase scene. The Hubbard's wonderful black Model A was borrowed for other chase scenes—Joan Hubbard at the wheel. Don did all the filming and splicing, using some trick photography occasionally. Imagination ran wild. There were many showings of this masterpiece.

Don was also instrumental in involving the summer student ministers in the youth program. One summer, the YPCC hired student minister Art Cunningham solely to coordinate the Youth Activity Program, and provided the group with a small building behind the Curry Firehouse. It was dubbed The Shack and Anne recalls the kids' delight in being able to paint the interior in any manner and colors they chose. That was a true high point summer for local kids. In the next couple of summers, volunteer parents took over, with Lenore Cross and Midge Fiore spearheading the project.

After Chuck and Anne had gone off to boarding school, Rob remained our involvee. He joined a Baldwin-organized Youth Group trip to the Sea Ranch home of Don's parents that fall of 1967. Sea Ranch lies on the coast just north of Marin County. These mountain kids relished being at the ocean, and a lot of beach was minutely exploring. A visit to historic Fort Ross, formerly a Russian outpost, was on the agenda for the next morning, and then came the long drive home. Henry Berrey, Don, Peggy, and I served as driver/chaperones for the venture.

Inevitably the Baldwins left the Park, in the very early seventies, for an assignment in Lawrence, Kansas. They had added two born-in-Yosemite daughters to the family—Eve and Joy. Once again, we had gained close family friends, only to see them move away. The ties that bind, however, brought them back to the Park on many occasions. Don later performed the marriage rites for both Anne and Betsy in the glorious outdoor setting that is Yosemite.

John Davis followed Don Baldwin as resident minister, to remain until the late eighties. With John came wife Paula and children, Lance and Camille. Student minister Melinda Greeley was active with our youngest, Betsy's, age group during the summers.

In the world of music, Thelma Warnock filled the role of piano teacher for Anne. When Wes and Dotty Conner offered to leave their piano with us for storage, we jumped at the opportunity. A decade later, Sylvia Robinson was on hand with guitar lessons for Betsy. Both offered appreciated adult involvement in local children's lives.

THE ALL-IMPORTANT
YOSEMITE ELEMENTARY SCHOOL

The Yosemite Elementary School (YES) sat to the south of our residential loop, just around one set of houses. From home it was a three-minute dash through the neighbors' yards or a six-minute walk via the less intrusive route. By the time ours entered kindergarten, the new school (dedicated in 1956) was well established. All four of the children were under Miss Trabucco's tutelage for that beginning experience, and off they all had gone, resting mats in hand. Principals and other teachers would come and go, but Pauline Trabucco reigned, lovingly, for some thirty years. Pauline and Jane Rust are sisters, so Pauline was extended Valley family from the beginning. In later years, when the classes were combined, she covered the local kindergarten needs from El Portal. I'm not sure Pauline was quite prepared for the fourth Woessner. After three quiet, mannerly Woessner children, Betsy was another cup of tea entirely—a bustly, busy, social number. We still love to remind Bets of her grade of *minus* in "ability to relax during rest period." Since this was before the days of preschool, kindergarten was the first step out of the nest and the first exposure to group interaction. Betsy just happened to be one who thrived on the interaction.

Jean Leedy, an excellent teacher and good friend, had our older three for the first and second grades. They received a fine basic foundation of learning from Jean, however strict they may have deemed her. As they sailed through their academic careers, Charlie and I remained forever appreciative of Jean Leedy's instillation of good study habits. Next in the line of progression was Thelma McGregor, with the third and fourth grades. Anne professes that Mrs. McGregor was her favorite teacher. "She had the perfect combination of intelligence, dignity, firmness and kindness that makes a memorable teacher. I didn't feel intimate with her—she wasn't the kind of teacher who would encourage that—but I liked her and respected her." Chuck echoed these words. Thelma was to retire before Rob and Bets reached grade three. Rob moved through the grades, rocking no boats, but acknowledged respecting ski coach Rust above all others. Betsy put Isie Tinning and John Chavez at the top of her list of favorites.

Judy Degen, wife of NPS employee John, was the school's first full-time secretary. Things in that office hummed along smoothly for years under her capable guidance. The principalship was always a short-term stand in our school. The combination of school administrator and two-class teacher was a daunting task, and a couple of years seemed to be the average tenure of most principals. Several turned the challenge into a rewarding learning experience and advanced onward in the school administration profession. Other teachers who influenced our youngsters were Marilyn Huson, Mrs. Hart, Mrs. Stark, Cornelius Kuhn, Hazel Cavanaugh, Mr. Hafner, Erik Bruun, Cecil Stalvey, Jack McLaughlin, Derry Kirschman—and the infamous Mrs. Moore.

In what was to be the only year all four of ours were together at YES (Chuck in the eighth grade, Anne in seventh, Rob in fifth, and Betsy in kindergarten), up from the heart of Texas came Mary Margaret Moore to take over the principalship. In light of ensuing events, one might safely say to take over the *school.* A large, formidable-looking, no-nonsense woman, she brought with her the need to run a tight ship. It was soon evident that she would brook no interference from the likes of parents. She wanted no other adults around. Scout groups and all others were denied the traditional use of the multipurpose room for meetings and activities. Volunteer help in the school library or classrooms was discontinued or highly restricted. I think I caused the exodus of what remained of the volunteers. I had checked out *The Decline and Fall of the Roman Empire* to a curious student Mrs. Moore deemed far too immature to tackle such a tome. I knew he was intrigued by the book's impressive size and would soon be returning it, curiosity fulfilled, but she lit into me for "condoning his inappropriate choice." Out we library aides went. The school was tightly locked upon the cessation of each school day. It was Mrs. Moore's domain. Needless to say, concerns rose and a counter-Moore-culture took shape. On the plus side, she taught well and did care about her students. Before leaving for her Christmas break in Texas, she presented each of her students (which included both Chuck and Anne) with a small, faux-Tiffany kerosene lamp, stating that she "wanted to add a little beauty to the lives of these children."

Mrs. Moore then committed her fatal transgression. She returned from her Christmas break with more special gifts—just for the boys in her class this time. Each was presented with a wooden slingshot, rubber sling in place, upon which the words "genuine Texas nigger-shooter" were engraved. The hue and cry went up all over the Valley when *these* gifts were carried home that afternoon. "Miz Mo's" days were numbered. The year was 1965, before the era of political correctness, but well after the beginning of civil rights awareness.

The Parent Group chairman that year was Bill Jones, a most articulate, unflappable young man who took the lead in gaining control of a disintegrating relationship between school and community. By this time most parents were understandably irate. Bill appointed Stuart Cross to chair a fact-finding committee, resulting in the involvement of both county and state educators. Meetings and interviews with parents were held. Mrs. Moore was allowed to finish the school year, but was to be out of the Valley, large white Cadillac and all, the day after graduation. It may not have been the best eighth grade experience for Chuck's class, but the memories of that year will linger long in the lore of Yosemite Elementary School. With a great feeling of relief, we all enjoyed the traditional after-graduation party on our patio that evening. And with an earned sense of freedom, the first thing Chuck and fellow graduates Mike, Ken, and Rob did was to slap our extension ladder against the side of the Knowles next-door house, climb to the second level, and nail a heavy blanket over Valerie's bedroom window. No nosy seventh-grader was going to spy on their festivities!

Any mention of school year endings brings back fond memories of the traditional school picnic, usually held on the Monday of the last week of school. It was one huge potluck and one great good time. The scene changed a few times during our years, from El Capitan beach, to one or other of the campgrounds, to the school field. Tricycles and bikes were decorated grandly for a parade around the housing areas, ending wherever the picnic was to be held. Games and races had been planned, and the gala was underway.

The fall of 1966 launched us into our first off-to-boarding-school experience. We had put much thought and effort into choosing what we deemed the right place for our young. In those years many of the local high schoolers went off to boarding schools rather than attend Mariposa High School (MHS), forty-five winding miles away. A combination of reasons led to this decision, among them the long daily bus ride, the lack of a late bus to make after-school activities a possibility, and the marginal curriculum offerings for college-oriented youngsters. Many students went to the Wasatch Academy in Utah, others to Menlo Prep School in the Bay Area, a few to Chadwick in Southern California, or to San Joaquin Memorial in Fresno. For ours, we sought a non-religious, non-military, coeducational boarding school in the west. These were few and far between in the sixties. We discovered the Colorado Rocky Mountain School (CRMS) through information gleaned from David McKean, then working in Aspen. Our trip to look it over and our trip to deliver Chuck for the first time were made in connection with Betsy's birthdays.

For many years thereafter, on several of our late summer picnics at Tenaya, a stack of teen clothes and linens, and rolls of appropriate nametapes would accompany me. There I would sit, basking in the sunshine and beauty of the place, sewing on labels like mad—with that sinking almost good-bye time feeling in the pit of my stomach. Fall, traditionally the goodbye season as summer seasonal friends left, now became even more poignant with the peeling off of our own. It was the beginning of the breaking away, eventually to be followed by the college and out-into-the-world leave-takings. It is still a very nostalgic time of year for me.

Each of ours did the high school years differently. Chuck was three years away, then home to Mariposa High School for his senior year. Anne attended CRMS all of her four secondary school years. Rob had two years at MHS, then went to CRMS for his last two years. Unfortunately, he was not there during Anne's years, as she had just graduated. Betsy attended MHS only, it having by then a much more college-oriented curriculum and a bus schedule that accommodated extra-curricular activities. We thoroughly enjoyed not giving her up as soon.

HIKING WITH DAD

There wasn't a summer, after the boys were capable, without some kind of backpack with Dad, be it a weekend or a week. I don't know that Anne was invited along, but I don't remember any hue and cry about discrimination, either. She really came into her own in the outdoor world of challenge during her CRMS boarding school years. The boys, meanwhile, covered the Park backcountry with their dad. They picked up backpacking and mountaineering skills as they went along, and developed a lasting appreciation for the outdoor environment. Often another lad or two were included on the trip. Sherrill Conner went with them on several occasions. One was a trip to Ottoway Lakes, remembers Rob. As they were crossing Red Peak Pass, they took a side jog to climb the peak. They conquered the summit—and Rob had "bagged his first peak." At seven, he was the youngest name in the Sierra Club register "in recent history."

Over ensuing years successful climbs of Mt. Lyell, Cathedral Peak, Mt. Gibbs, Merced Peak, and Tuolumne Peak out of the Tuolumne Meadows basin gave way to adventures further afield in the Sierra. Among these later feats were the climbs of Mt. Humphrey, Bear Creek Spire and Clyde Minaret in the Southern Sierra. Often, Charlie's good friend and fellow outdoorsman, Wes Conner, was along, occasionally Wes's son Terry. With this as his background, plus some gained climbing skill and knowledge, Chuck offers:

One of *my* favorite things-to-do memories of growing up in the Valley combined trout fishing with rock climbing, always with good results. There weren't a lot of places to find this combination. But with and without my dad's help, I found three, the most arduous being the legendary pool at the base of Pywiack falls in Tenaya Canyon. This venture involved an overnight, lots of bushwhacking—and a little bit of climbing. Because few people ventured into this trailless canyon and even fewer carried fishing gear along, these fish hadn't got smart because the pool hadn't been fished. Usually had a fish on the minute your lure hit the water. The second spot was along Bridalveil Creek, just above the falls into the Valley. The creek is accessible via The Gunsight, a notch between lower and middle Cathedral Rocks. Climbing The Gunsight from the Valley floor involves a scramble up the increasingly steep and narrow gully, and requires an easy roped pitch near the top. We used to fish a series of six or seven pools within a quarter mile of the top of the falls. Each pool was good for two or three successful casts into the unsuspecting trout before they got wise.

Charlie, out for a hike with Chuck one day, had first introduced him to these two spots. Chuck saw their great potential and challenge, and later returned with a friend and fishing gear. He had the bug:

Those two trips and the lessons learned about *quality fishing* in seldom-fished areas led to my (our) discovery of the third special place. That spot was along Sunnyside Bench in the middle Yosemite Falls cascades. Getting there involved either a class 3 scramble along the bench or taking the more direct (and exposed) easy class 5 route up a "book" nearer the falls. Sunnyside Bench, while literally in our back yard, was off limits when we were little, but as our confidence and ability grew it got to be okay.

As confidence and expertise continued to grow, the middle cascades were explored, and fished successfully. Chuck remembers catching a fifteen-inch trout in one of the pools. He and a friend successfully made the middle gorge traverse on óne occasion. These are feats a mother likes to hear about only much later. One fishing hole he never had the time or opportunity to tackle was the pool at the base of Vernal Falls, the one behind the mist. He muses:

> If the theory is true, it's got big, hungry fish that have lived their lives there, never been fished, and never known fishermen. With the mist, you'd have to time it just so—and probably end up soaked anyway. While I've never been there, I do keep wondering...?

A factor Charlie and I have always considered a great plus in regard to raising children in Yosemite was the natural progression into a summer job, made possible by the YPCC. For ours, sixteen was the earliest employment age (since, lowered to fourteen). Chuck entered the work force at the Yosemite Lodge Chevron station, with Dick Beverlin as his boss. Rob's first job was in the vending machine operation under the tutelage of Dave Downing. We were pleased that their introductions to job ethics were under men each held in great regard. The local teenagers could work at the early age because they lived at home. Jobs involving Company accommodations necessitated being at least eighteen. The girls' first non-dad jobs were at Best

Studio/Ansel Adams Gallery, then on to the Tuolumne Meadows Lodge for Anne, to the Village Store curio/clothing for Betsy. A job was the normal summer pattern for local youth—with all the only-in-Yosemite fun crammed into the off-hours and days.

Betsy's extra Valley years, made possible by her not going away to boarding school, gave her even stronger Yosemite ties than her siblings. She and her close group of friends have carried these ties into adulthood. Together with contemporaries Julie Harders, Mary Lee Shackelton, Kitty Donohoe, Mary Lou Garza, Sandy Degen, and later arrivals Polly Hardy and Lisa Abbott, Betsy feels the *Yosemite Magic*—possibly she and Julie the most strongly. She puts it this way:

It's more than just love-of-place. It's more than just respect. It even goes deeper than intense admiration for an awe-inspiring place God created on one of His *best* days. It is something so deep-rooted in our souls that it is as much a part of us as our births, our families, and our loved ones. And, truly, you can't understand it if you haven't felt it.

As Rob puts it:

Perhaps it is all of the memories, or perhaps the anticipation of seeing some of the most beautiful trees and rock formations and waterfalls on the face of the earth. Regardless of the reason, there is just that special, magical feeling of being in Yosemite. To feel that closeness, that awareness, that knowledge of the region one can only know from living there and experiencing it in all of its seasons and all of its grandeur is to truly know the *Yosemite Experience.* That experience has been mine!

17. The Turbulent Years

*One of the oldest human needs is having someone to wonder
where you are when you don't come home at night.*
                                                —*Margaret Mead*

And yet, by the late sixties, many young people were walking away
from the homes that had provided the solace for this need. They
came to makeshift homes in remote, natural places—and found like-
minded youth. A generation was on the move. Our Park became a
favorite destination.

When did it begin? When did the unrest of the younger generation slowly seep into Yosemite Valley? Charlie and I were busy trying to keep abreast of events in Vietnam and of the growing unrest
in the nation as a whole. Chuck went off to boarding school in the
fall of 1966 and came home at Christmas with long hair and new
ideas. Had he been a more loquacious young man at this point, our
understanding of the younger generation of the era might have presented less of a dilemma. These were not easy times for parents of
our generation, not easy times to write about these thirty years later.
Certain happenings—the now-rare waft of patchouli oil, certain
melodies of the sixties reappearing occasionally on radio stations, a
whiff of marijuana from anywhere—momentarily affect me like a
kick in the stomach. Back flood the thoughts, the uncertainties, the
pain of seeing one's own youngsters dealing with the choices, temp-
tations, and differing mores of the cultures and countercultures of
the times.

At the same time, the Park Service was going through the uncertainties and concerns of how to handle the droves of young people who flowed into the Valley, to gather together, to commune with nature, to groove on the simple life. The events of the next few years, as the situation headed toward the confrontation of July 4, 1970, were to culminate in a drastic and lasting change in NPS policy and image.

The resulting turmoil and criticism heaped upon the Park had far too lasting an effect to leave to hearsay. What follows is often told in the words of those who were eyewitnesses. Once again we see that there can be two sides to every story.

THE BUILD-UP

My awareness of a change in Valley demographics came in the summer of 1967, when I perceived an increasing number of idle youth hanging out in front of the post office, Degnan's, and the Village Store. What caught my attention first, puzzled me, then annoyed me was the extent of panhandling, especially in the vicinity of the Village Store. I had been raised by a father whose credo was "a day's wage for a day's work" and was strongly indoctrinated with the principle that to beg—to ask for money—was to have reached an all-time low in ability and self esteem. These youths looked like anyone's teenagers. Why weren't they working somewhere? I soon lost patience with their actions. Likewise I deplored the actions of those who stood at the produce case in the rear of the store helping themselves to samples of this and that. Surveillance cameras were not long in coming, nor was an increased YPCC security force.

Having little occasion to visit the Valley campgrounds, we were not aware of the increase in numbers of young people clustered in large groups. By 1967 the Park policy was to discourage these large, organized camps. That spring, Rangers Darryl Steele and Russ Cahill were sent to San Francisco to attend a conference offering training in the handling of two growing Park problems: runaway juveniles and drug abuse.[1] Important, too, was the instruction in how to keep constant pressure on offending groups without harassing. Recommendations were made to incorporate training in the handling of peaceful sit-in demonstrations into the Albright Training Center program for intake NPS trainees. In the campgrounds at this time, the major cited violations were overtime camping, underage drinking, furnishing alcohol to minors, and various drug violations. Nearby Stoneman Meadow became the social gathering spot, and the ten o'clock quiet hour decree became more difficult to enforce as the numbers grew. More and more nonpaying campers shared other's sites, there was more sleeping in undesignated areas, and Stoneman Meadow was being trashed and trampled.

Cars loaded with young adults were stopped at Park entrances and underwent a thorough scrutiny for mechanical malfunctions. They were turned back if any could be found. The turn-backs felt discriminated against and often used other means to gain Park access. Why did so many keep coming in spite of professed dissatisfaction with the campgrounds and with their reception? Answers varied: the magnificence of the area, to meet other young people, to commune with, and be reaffirmed by, their like-minded peers. Some of the troublemakers really didn't know the regulations: some manipulated the rules. The smarter ones learned to keep a low profile to avoid eviction from the Park. Individuals were found to be better about complying with the rules if the reasons for the rules were explained. However, the explanations that Stoneman Meadow should be closed for ecological reasons or that all cars entering the Park received the same type of safety inspection were met with suspicious doubt.

The Beatnik sub-culture of the mid-sixties with its "stop the world, I want to get off" was evolving into the middle-class hippie movement with its "stop the world, I want to complain about it." In the outside world, sit-ins and group protests were growing in number and violence. "Power to the people" became the motto of choice. The Vietnam War controversy was heating up. The wave of white, somewhat affluent expatriates from suburbia continued to pour into the Valley over the next three years.

By 1968, the Park Service delineated designated camping sites in the Valley campgrounds, eliminating a few and limiting the number of campers in each. The requirement to register campers to specific sites was instigated, and eventually a campground fee schedule was added. The one-way road system in the east end of the Valley was also established in 1968, bringing more ease to congestion. A free shuttle-bus program in the busy east end of the Valley was put in place, and the clampdown on hitchhiking in the Park was enforced. NPS ranger law enforcement training received strong emphasis. I have strong recollections of a group of mounted rangers being instructed in crowd control at the government stables near our home. There was tenseness in the air, and we knew our ranger friends were under considerable stress.

By the next summer our eldest and some of his peers decided to forego the local kid-hangout on Sentinel Bridge in favor of checking out the action in Stoneman Meadow. He later recalls:

> I perceived it more as a hippie gathering, flower child, peace, love, and groovy thing. We found that more to our liking than the heretofore-usual Stoneman Bridge black leather, macho, greaser, motorcycle scene we had shunned for years. Here, now, was a bunch of young people too cool to have to look cool—something to associate with, even peripherally. Here were young people sitting around in a meadow, some strumming guitars, beating drums, singing together—and, yes, the wineskin and occasional joint being passed—but mostly just talking and laughing together, enjoying each other's company. It was a scene but it wasn't a bad scene, other than to the extent that the meadow was getting trampled, the crowds were getting larger, there was some drug use and probably some selling. The rangers decided it couldn't be tolerated.

In the meantime, life in the Park community moved on. We viewed the firefall for the last time, I served a grand jury year, and our young peeled off to boarding school. The YPCC put into use the tramcar for guided Valley tours, and installed its first computer, an IBM 360-20, making the leap into technology. The Yosemite Master Plan made its first appearance, and the Valley Singers, under Glen Willard's able direction, continued to provide fine summer entertainment. The Shasta Corporation took over the Yosemite Park and Curry Company. The Ahwahnee changed to European Plan, and the Mountaineering School, under Wayne Merry's able guidance, was established. Russ Olsen arrived to replace Ted Thompson as assistant superintendent of the Park. The Glacier Point Hotel burned to the ground and Chuck's birthdate drew number 312 in the military draft lottery. Neil Armstrong stepped on the moon, and the following year Chuck graduated from high school.

Over in the Stoneman Meadow section of the Valley tensions continued to build. Possibly both factions foresaw a confrontation in the offing. Easter vacation in April 1970 brought warm sunny days and many young people to a park with insufficient ranger manpower. This was the first stage of a situation that would culminate on July 4. Both during that Easter week and again over the three-day Memorial weekend (always crowded in the Valley by nature of the high country's not being open to campers yet) the undermanned ranger force lost control of Stoneman Meadow.[2] In the face of complaints from the traditional campground users regarding drinking and narcotic parties, theft, loud music, abusive language, fighting, and sexual orgies, the available ranger staff was ineffectual in bringing things under control. In anticipation of the traditionally rowdy July 4 crowd, combined with the growing numbers appearing daily in Stoneman Meadow, training of rangers intensified, men were borrowed from other parks, and reinforcements were alerted in the surrounding towns. It was a happening just waiting to happen.

The following is excerpted from an account of the gradually deteriorating situation in the Park sent by Dr. Robert Craycroft, then of Los Gatos, California, to Secretary of the Interior Walter Hickel. It was offered to provide background for events leading to the 1970 incident and to defend the rangers' actions on that later date.[3]

My family, which consists of my wife and three minor daughters, have had the privilege of visiting the Park and staying in the Valley as campers annually for the past six years...we have witnessed the gradual increase of undesirable young men and women with their dirty, unkempt appearance, hostile social attitude, and at times outright lawlessness. I can no longer distinguish by appearance between so-called hippies, hard-core hoodlums, drug addicts, ordinary thieves and social anarchists.... One thing is clear, however, none of them are in Yosemite to experience its natural wonders or to learn about its history or anything else concerning the park. Instead they come because it has been cheap, supervision or regulation of their activities is difficult or impossible, and their objectionable behavior and use of drugs can often go on with minimal chance of detection or prosecution by authorities.... For the past six years I have had to step over their sprawling legs as they sat on the pavement in front of the village store.... I witnessed innumerable instances of their illegal camping in prohibited sites in the valley and the litter and destruction they leave behind them. I have smelled the unmistakable odor of marijuana in their gatherings, and finally I have witnessed the disintegration of the entire fabric of law and order at times such as last July 4, 1969.

THE CONFRONTATION

A Park Service report issued in defense of the July 4 1970 confrontation states:[4]

Those who were directly involved in the vicious mob action of July 4 were, beyond question, members of the "tuned-out, turned-on" subculture among the young generation who hit the road in California in burgeoning hundreds during the summer months.... Stoneman Meadow is the favorite gathering place for the group.... By midafternoon hundreds collect to puff grass and drop pills, beat bongo drums and hurl

Frisbees and to drink quantities of wine into the night. The scene is at least annoying to neighboring campers if not disgusting as the action increases.

By this time, the quiet hour policy had been changed. The new rules stated that the meadow be cleared by 7:00 P.M. rather than the traditional curfew of 10:00 P.M. The report continues:

During the afternoon of July 4 from approximately 3 to 7 P.M., rangers from the Valley District force patrolled the meadow on foot and on horseback advising that the meadow was to be cleared by 7 P.M., explaining the reasons for the controls. At 7:00, a loud speaker announced that the meadow was to be cleared. After an interval of ten or fifteen minutes, with no response, the ranger force comprising 21 footmen and 16 horse patrol men entered the meadow with the intent to break the crowd into smaller groups capable of easier handling and dispersal.

The rangers were met with a barrage of thrown rocks and wine bottles, and assaults on individual ranger and horsemen.... They were forced to leave the meadow. One ranger patrol vehicle was damaged and put out of action.... At about 7:40, all ranger personnel were ordered out of the immediate area of the meadow. Roadblocks were established at major intersections.... to isolate the action and prevent the innocent movement of park visitors into the area.

At about 7:45 P.M., the Park called for assistance from neighboring law enforcement agencies.... 107 officers responded from the outlying areas and were on the scene by 11:30 P.M. During the remainder of the night and early morning hours constant patrols were made of campgrounds in the Stoneman Meadow area—and order restored primarily through a constant succession of arrests on a variety of charges. For the entire holiday weekend, July 2 through 5, a total of 174 arrests were made...133 adults, 41 juveniles...

narcotics violations totaling 37 comprised the largest single category of arrest charge. Other arrests were made for drunkenness, disorderly conduct, resisting arrest, illegal camping and 11 for assault on a Federal Officer. The offenders were sent the next day to the Fresno Juvenile Hall or to the Fresno County Jail. The majority of them came from the East Bay/San Jose/San Francisco area.

An additional Park Service report put forth the information that the rocks thrown, each nearly the size of a coffee mug, came from pre-gathered piles. The wine bottles thrown were water-filled for added clout.

AS WE EXPERIENCED IT

Fourth of July had dawned calmly in our neighborhood across the Valley. We looked forward to joining the Berrey family and friends for their traditional Fourth of July al fresco supper. One of the after-dinner traditions involved the good old art of oration. A speech in honor of the historic occasion, brief or wordy, was the order of the day. As Tim Berrey presented his offering at the improvised lectern, I became aware that the males in the audience were quietly slipping out the gate. A call had come to YPCC's Bob Maynard with the news that an uprising was in progress in Stoneman Meadow. Charlie went along with the YPCC men to wherever forces were being mustered for back-up help. The rest of us stayed awhile longer with Eileen then dispersed for our homes with a great sense of unease.

From Chuck's recollections of the night:

> I left the Berrey's when Dad left and hooked up with a good friend whose dad was Park Service and who was also aware of what was going on. We wandered over to see what was up in the meadow. The crowd was large and in a largely celebratory mood. After all, they'd been minding their own business, partying harmlessly, when the "pigs" had attacked

and tried to drive them out. They'd retaliated, the pigs were gone and the meadow was theirs. Power to the people, and party on! Little did they know....

I can honestly say that except for being somewhat larger and more celebrating than usual, the mood among the people in the meadow was not unlike other times we had been there. Yet there was an irony, because as we mingled among the crowd, we knew the rangers were marshaling their forces. We didn't know how much time we had, but we were a little scared about what we felt might soon be swooping down on us, so we decided to leave. Rather than head home, we decided to go by the Visitor Center (Park Headquarters) to see what was going on.

Well, reinforcements were arriving: every available protection and interpretive ranger (seasonal and permanent) from the entire Park was on hand, along with several NPS maintenance and administrative people pressed into service; sheriff's officers and deputies from surrounding counties; and U.S. Marshals from who knows where. I don't know whom we ran into—some ranger acquaintance—and we mentioned we'd just come from the meadow. Well, oh boy, that was akin to instant celebrity status since we now could offer first hand information from the scene.... We were ushered into somebody's office and "debriefed" as we described the crowd scene and mood.... Finally…we were taken into the Visitor Center auditorium—which was chock full of rangers, deputies, and various other pressed-into-service wannabes about to be briefed on how to take the meadow. The strategy was not to be a direct group assault, as had been the earlier failed attempt, but one of massive individual arrests from the periphery. Working in teams of two, three, or more, authorities were to work the edges and stragglers from the main group, listening for obscenities or any other minor infraction and to arrest the offender for whatever reason was good enough to get him or her into jail for the night (or out of the Park) until the crowd was thinned and those fearing arrest returned to their campsites. And then before heading out to take the meadow, the entire assemblage was asked to stand, and we were sworn in, en masse, as Deputy U.S. Marshals.

I suppose my friend and I could have gone back and participated in the cleanup, but we were still somewhat scared—and our loyalties, quite frankly, were split.... We wanted no part of it and so we just went home, secure in the knowledge, if nothing else, that we were both Deputy U.S. Marshals. We never did get badges, and I've never used it on my résumé, but I was there.

In the meantime, Charlie had been assigned, with a group of four, to stand guard in front of one of the YPCC establishments. He observed no action and later came home. So ended the infamous July 4, 1970.

THE AFTERMATH

In the ensuing weeks, Dr. John J. Fisher of Jacksonville, Florida sent an open letter to then President Richard M. Nixon, with copies to widely scattered senators, congressmen, and newspapers, to National Park Service Director George Hartzog and to the Office of the Superintendent in Yosemite.[5] The letter read, in part:

> On our way...we stopped to spend a week at Yosemite National Park...the week preceding the July 4 weekend... dismayed to find ourselves assigned to a site in which we were surrounded by those youths whom we have, in our American way, labeled "hippies." Apprehension was soon dispelled, however, as we found these long-haired, oddly-dressed children to be more polite than most of my youngsters' college friends.... The campground was neat and orderly.... Curfew was observed and we were very impressed indeed by the spirit of brotherhood that abounded in this youthful movement...

the grassy clearing provided a beautiful natural gathering place for the youngsters...tossing Frisbees, running footraces and singing songs in small groups around a guitar.

On Friday, July 3, I heard that the meadow was to be closed at 7 P.M., two hours before darkness comes at Yosemite and three before the park curfew. No reason for such action was given, but there were rumors that the concessioners, such as the Curry Co., were fearful of the young people congregating. This held some ring of plausibility to me since I had observed that the stores employ uniform guards to keep barefoot children out of their establishments.

At 7 P.M., I was taking a predinner stroll with my 21 year-old daughter...when it happened. First came the trucks from one side, with bullhorns ordering all off the meadow and back to their campsites. Before one could comply with this order, mounted troops wearing helmets and brandishing clubs...rode in from the other direction. Before my very eyes we watched these children being stampeded, several being clubbed, and two thrown to the ground, handcuffed and led off to jail....

The next evening, July 4th, promptly at seven the public address warning sounded. Helmeted rangers grouped at one side, clubs and mace at ready. A string of armed horsemen filed in from a new direction into the area between the meadow and the campground and were relatively screened from view.... The young people in the meadow did not see them. Moreover, they had decided that their intentions would appear more peaceful if they sat, and had formed a huge circle of several hundred on the grass.

Without any warning, the horsemen suddenly burst forth in a pack, riding...directly into the midst of the seated assembly...scattering those who were fortunate enough not to be run over.... The foot troops then moved in with their clubs, while the horsemen circled about and returned swinging lariats and belts. In one moment the peaceful meadow had been changed into a sickening spectacle by these "peace officers".... Their escape route purposely cut off, the young people did the only thing they could, they fought back. I found myself cheering as with their bare hands and the few missiles they were able to find in the field, they drove the rangers from the meadow.... The Park Service and the rangers had the riot they wanted at last.... Fireworks were set off and a celebration party ensued.... I was awakened in the middle of the night, 3 or 4 o'clock, by the blood-chilling scream of a human being beaten....

A short time later the nearest raiding party came into view...they moved quietly from campsite to campsite, waking the sleeping occupants up, thrusting them against trees for search, scattering their belongings. If any objected, even verbally, he was beaten. I subsequently learned there were ten to fifteen in these patrols, some rangers, some highway patrolmen, and some U.S. Marshals. They carried riot guns, sidearms and clubs. Now they enjoyed superiority in numbers as well as weapons, as they singled out each campsite.... We left the following morning....

Dr. Fisher's letter was picked up by the news media and appeared widely in newspapers around the country. Responses poured in to our Park and to Director Hartzog. Yes, responses poured in—pro and con NPS—but the most credible came from those who had also been in the Park on that fateful weekend.

From a parent in Maryland:

Like Dr. Fisher, my family embarked on a trip around the U.S. this summer.... Dr. Fisher's account of the event in Yosemite was almost unbelievable.... We, too, were there.... Never have I read such a flagrant untrue account of an event as related by Dr. Fisher. In view of Dr. Fisher's story, my family joins with me in responding.... The events which followed our arrival resulted in a night of anxiety for our safety, and the safety of our trailer and car, coupled with complete disgust at the conduct of those who profess membership in the human race, whose conduct would have put animals at a superior level. Dr. Fisher calls them innocent children? I would say the hippie nomenclature "pig," directed at law officers, is grossly misdirected…it was not the rangers who provoked the events, but rather the other way around.

My reaction to Dr. Fisher's account is complete disbelief that anyone could have been in Yosemite Valley on the weekend of July 4 and attempt to condone or justify the behavior of a lawless, filthy mob.

And from Northern California:

We were in Yosemite Park on July 4th. Entering the Park that morning, we marveled at the tremendous number of hippies coming in too—so many on foot with only a bedroll on their backs.… We had occasion to drive through the meadow referred to five times during the day—it is the only public access to a grand tour of the Park, the kennels, the stables, the beauty spots and the trails at the east end of the valley. It was quite obvious to us that the hippies flowing into the Park in such numbers were heading for that meadow for a purpose. The dozens turned into hundreds, and by evening thousands. Before the melee started, my husband estimated four thousand—the next morning's news said five thousand.

From a YPCC employee living and working in the Park:

I am deeply incensed at the lengthy Sunday article in the *Fresno* (California) *Bee* by Dr. John J. Fisher regarding his five day stay in Yosemite National Park during the July 4 period.… Where was Dr. Fisher when these "dear children" were stealing food, gifts, etc. from all the retail outlets?… Where was Dr. Fisher when these "lovely children" were gathering rocks on the Merced River bed all day—for that carefully planned encounter with the rangers.... Where was Dr. Fisher when 70-year-old Mr. Johnson, a local resident trying to get to his car from the Curry Village restaurant was hit on the head by one of those carefully gathered rocks and spent 9 days in the local hospital?...

And more from Dr. Craycroft of Los Gatos:

It is my deep attachment to the park and to the men who helped establish it and who currently administer it which prompted this letter. The final impetus came when I learned of the letter of Dr. John Fisher...in which he criticized the manner of handling the July fourth riot by the authorities. My comments spring from years of intimate association with the park and from close annual observation of the problems of law enforcement in the last six years. I can readily understand the difficulty of assessing a riot situation by an individual such as Dr. Fisher even though he was present at the time. Unless an individual is part of the enforcement personnel and has access to their information channels he can witness only a small segment of what is occurring and will not readily understand even that small portion. Being from Florida I doubt that Dr. Fisher had much knowledge of the years of turmoil which underlay the riot. What may have seemed to be peremptory action by the U.S. Marshals to Dr. Fisher was not that at all. I am certain that he was not aware of the months and years of defiance, which the hippy [sic] meetings in Stoneman Meadow represented.

This letter was also widely distributed. Who was in the right, who was wrong? Certainly there were no winners in that night's confrontation. The repercussions of July 4, 1970, were to change our Park in many ways. To Dr. Fisher went an answering letter from the office of NPS Director George Hartzog[6] in which he wrote:

Secretary (of the Interior) Hickel has asked us to thank you for your courtesy in providing him with a copy of your letter to the President in which you described…and we appreciate this opportunity to provide you with some additional information. First, you should know that a thorough investigation is now under way to establish the facts surrounding these events so that we can analyze both the cause of the disturbances and the validity of the emergency control methods used to restore the public peace.

As you might imagine, we have received a great deal of mail on the affair from visitors who were in the park at the time, not all of whom saw the same things. Some like you, expressed concern over the degree of force utilized. Others who had been offended, and in some cases terrorized, by the actions of some of the young people present earlier in the day, expressed strong support for what transpired.

As you know, the events of the Fourth of July weekend did not take place in a vacuum, nor were the events preceding the arrests isolated incidents. For some three years now we have been troubled by the fact that Stoneman Meadow in Yosemite Valley has become a popular assembly point for young people who gather to smoke marijuana, partake of other drugs and indulge in excessive drinking. In addition, we have had many complaints from families or campers that they have been bothered by panhandling youngsters and by loud noises that keep them awake at night.

It was in this context that we received information from law enforcement agencies and other intelligence sources that an organized "confrontation" with the Yosemite Park authorities was being planned for the Fourth of July weekend.

Despite what you may have personally observed, Dr. Fisher, our own Park Rangers and other visitors reported widespread violations of narcotics laws and park regulations regarding drunkenness and other types of misconduct.…

When the Park Rangers attempted to disperse the assembled crowd about 7:15 P.M., they were driven from the meadow by a barrage of rocks, wine bottles, and other missiles. Following this, park authorities were forced to seek help from law enforcement officials in surrounding communities to restore order and protect law-abiding visitors....

Following the July incident the reaction of the Park Service was two-fold: immediate measures and long-range recommendations. The former involved increased entrance station surveillance, and controls on entering traffic, to forestall a build-up within the Park of the kind of population that precipitated the action of Stoneman Meadow. By the fall of 1970 the following recommendations were made:

1. To keep a separate image for the traditional ranger. If major law enforcement is needed, bring in the Park Police, with their distinctive uniform.
2. To instigate a massive public relations program between the Park Service and all visitors, with Park rules explained clearly, in a friendly manner, and applied indiscriminately, and along this line to make the rangers visible in more casual surroundings.
3. To present additional evening programs of a sort to appeal to young people.
4. To put in place Park personnel orientation training programs to familiarize rangers with other life styles.

The following are excerpts from "A Park Administrator's Viewpoint of Social Change." Assistant Superintendent Russell Olsen presented the paper to a Fresno group soon after the July 4 incident.[7] To me, it succinctly expresses a great deal. After an explanatory lead-in to the riot and a description of NPS actions and reactions, Mr. Olsen goes on to say:

This incident...has caused many different kinds of reactions.

TV coverage had one viewpoint, two letter writers had distinct differing viewpoints and newspapers plain raised hell.... People read newspapers as fact, then get upset and write their congressmen and others, who react in their traditional way.

Who was right? Was Yosemite right? Would we react differently? We paid a terrible price in monetary value, public opinion and personal anguish for our actions. Yet the summers preceding the 4th of July 1970 also caused adverse public opinion from many for lack of action. The summer after the 4th was, however, pleasant and had a traditional atmosphere.

This is a time of great social change in America. All facets of our culture are being questioned, some modified. Many people are impatient with questions that are by-passed, but they cannot agree on which questions are vital or which answers are acceptable. Collectively, I presume we are all sure that change is needed. Individually and in our groupings we have specific ideas, yet we are often intolerant of others' ideas. Parks now have become enforced participants in this process of questioning tradition and change.... Without question a park experience is a heavily regulated experience in many senses. Only certain kinds of use are encouraged but more are discouraged. We like fishermen, but not hunters; we like folk singing around the campfire, but not in the middle of a meadow or in the wee hours of the morning. We like shuttle buses but not noisy motorcycles.... For years we have been saying that "Parks are for the People," which of course they are, without stopping to realize that although we welcomed all, we wanted only those who would enjoy the experience we were attempting to provide. For a long time only those with an enthusiasm for the park idea came.... Perhaps a longhaired youth in the meadow with his guitar and marijuana is not really so different from the suited gent at the grand piano with his drink at the Ahwahnee. Who is having the most appropriate park experience?

And so we have in the 1970's a new factor in park management to contend with.... We have today a new question being asked by a society with strong individual beliefs, and that is whether the park idea is in itself worthy of sacrificing some personal freedoms, and whether there really is value to saving part of our heritage for future generations when it is so pleasurable to use it up now. To those of us devoted to the park idea, there can only be one answer to this question, yet ultimately society will be served in the way it demands.

Certainly it would be unreasonable to expect the National Parks to be left out of the social revolution of today. I can't help but feel that if they were, parks would be the worse for it....

Thus our Park entered a new decade, licking its wounds and suffering from the kind of notoriety that can come from headlines such as this one in the *Fresno Bee*: "Riot Echo—Smokey Dons His Police Helmet, Grabs Weapons."[8] Scapegoats were designated—good men and close friends of ours among them. They were soon transferred from the Park. These were capable men who happened to be in the right Park at the wrong time. It hurt us all. The Yosemite mystique dimmed.

18. The Seventies:
No Quarter Untouched

Things are more like they are today than they have ever been.
—Author Unknown

The seventies blew in on the winds of change, and before the decade was over every facet of our community felt the effects. The Yosemite Park and Curry Company changed ownership three times. The National Park Service underwent changes in policy, image, direction, and management style under the leadership of four different superintendents. The medical facility changed from our all-inclusive, all-caring Lewis Memorial Hospital into the Yosemite Medical Clinic, a 24-hour emergency care facility. The medical and dental administrators were tossed into the insurance melee, with all of the accompanying paper work and worry. The simpler life was blown out the window.

The Kent State tragedy had preceded our July 4, 1970 riot by a few weeks. The nation was reeling from the actions and reactions to the war in Vietnam. Even while we were concerned for the safety of young friends involved directly in the war, our doubts grew about our military force's right to be involved. Nationwide, the debate was growing and tearing the country apart. So much changed for so many. Historically, much can be said for the good of change and its inevitability, but people can be hurt, traditions trampled, and community strengths weakened in the process of absorbing the changes.

So it was in Yosemite.

The chance to delve into the background and politics of these various changes, after a hiatus of twenty-five years, proves fascinating. At the time, we were busy living our own lives, seeing children off to college and into lives of their own. Things happened all around us: abrupt personnel changes, policy changes, road and traffic pattern changes. If we approved the changes, we applauded, if we didn't, we complained. But life moved on, and eventually the changes were absorbed. When you are in the middle of the change, the magnitude of the impact is often only perceived from the distance of time.

THE PARK SERVICE REACTS

The riot of July 1970 left the Yosemite National Park administration in a shaken state. With the departure of Superintendent Lawrence Hadley at the end of July, Wayne Cone came to take over the reins. Criticism of the handling of the riot still ran strong. Law enforcement training soon became an integral part of the ranger intake trainee program at the Albright training center in Grand Canyon. Although the plan to keep the ranger in his kindly, helpful, protector-of-the-parks image, while using the U.S. Park Police[1] for the messy law enforcement work, was suggested, it was not implemented.

By 1971, we became used to the Valley's one-way road system and to the closure of the east end of the Valley to private cars, which continues to provide a fine bike path in the Happy Isles and Mirror Lake areas. The free shuttle buses made excellent sense and were hailed as a sign of progress. Director George Hartzog wanted the shuttle buses to be "free, frequent and fun." They were—almost too much fun in some cases. The double-decker buses became moving party scenes for the hip generation on balmy summer evenings, and a ranger presence was occasionally needed to restore peace. As soon as feasible, the double-deckers were phased out, to be replaced by a single level model. As transportation, however, the shuttle buses were excellent and are still going strong.

One small area of the road change was sensibly short-lived, when the one-way section between Yosemite Village and Yosemite Lodge proved impractical. A Bailey bridge[2] was proposed across the Merced River behind the lodge to circumvent the annoying five-mile loop back to the village. This brought a hue and cry from the newly formed "Friends of Leidig Meadow," with much accompanying publicity. The new road, with its invasive traffic, would have desecrated Leidig Meadow, a meadow that was the scene of Indian games in the early part of the twentieth century. From high on the cliff trails one can still see, faintly, the circle outline of one of the meadow's foot games. The Bailey bridge proposal was scrapped and the stretch of drive over the hump bridge crossing of Yosemite Creek again became two-way.

In the summer of 1971, another change made itself felt. We were losing friends right and left. Before fall, the purge, as we came to call it, had swept out the remaining six riot-tainted Park administrators: Superintendent Wayne Cone (not even in the Park during the riot), administrators Roland Johnson and Larry Quist, and Park area managers Bryan Harry, Bill Stephenson and Claude McClain. This move, politically motivated, was a blow to the community. In addition, Russ Olsen had transferred earlier in the year. Dick Marks left in October. Two of these men left with such bitterness that they have not returned to the Park since. We lost very close friends and neighbors. Annie and Tom Harry had been school/ski/mischief pals of our Betsy and Rob; Rob Johnson was a long time school/hiking/fishing buddy of young Chuck's; the four Marks kids were extended family to all of us. We shared many good times with the senior Marks, Harrys, and Johnsons. We bemoaned their leaving and their hurts.[3]

Into the superintendency-vacuum that November came bachelor Lynn Thompson. Hartzog picked Lynn to cool things in Yosemite, to turn the Park Service image from "repressive to responsive."[4] Lynn brought with him three associate superintendents—a concept new to this Park—in the persons of Bill Whalen, John Good and Jim Wolfe, each with his designated area of expertise. Jack Morehead returned for a second tour of Yosemite NPS duty, this time as chief ranger. Because the ranger force in the lower grade levels had also been purged, eight young rangers transferred to the Park that summer/fall. Several were just out of the Grand Canyon Training Center. All had been schooled in the new law enforcement/ crowd-handling/low-key confrontational tactics. The idea was to present a lower profile ranger, but one possessed of law enforcement skills to be used when needed. The ranger's hair was allowed to be longer, the atmosphere and approach more relaxed.

The influx of single rangers added considerable interest for the female population of the Park, but as far as benefiting the community and school population, they were not families. Families, per se, nurture a community and are essential. These men, however,— Roger Rudolph, Paul Henry, Rick Smith, Mark Forbes, Tim Setnicka, Ross Rice, Walt Dabney, and Butch Farabee—became our *young* friends. Their tours of duty in Yosemite ranged from four to eight years. All but two left with met-in-Yosemite wives. Just as fashion watching had become sport at Badger with the arrival of Bogner stretch pants, so date watching became the great diversion in the Valley in the early seventies. They were a great bunch of young men, and in positive ways added a dash of pizzaz to a community coming out of a few disconcerting years.

Several of these men weren't much older than our oldest, Chuck, now well into college at UC Davis. Our generation was no longer the young guys. In fact, for the past few years we'd been older than our chief ranger, and we soon became older than the medical doctors, with Avery's retirement. We were now middle aged—and were well reminded of it when this group came roaring in.

Things quieted down considerably in the Valley with the low-key approach to confrontation. The establishment of a minimal-fee, walk-in campground near Yellow Pine beach, further to the west along the Merced River, also aided in calming the atmosphere. Yellow Pine was far removed from the family-oriented campgrounds and it appealed to young wanderers. Later renamed Muir Tree, it eventually had its own low-key resident ranger.

Meanwhile, the hippier hips moved up the trail to Little Yosemite Valley, above Nevada Falls, where a mountain commune soon thrived. In 1971, H.A. Worthington was dispatched to become Little Yosemite's first resident ranger: the need for "guidelines" becoming apparent.[5] He found "It was getting so bad there the hippies had the place to themselves. It was just turning into one hell of a big sin bin." H.A. was assigned to rap with the campers and to bring a low-profile authority figure to the backcountry. Little Yosemite traditionally had been a first night's stopover for Valley hikers heading into the backcountry.[6] It was discouraging for weary backpackers to find the campground already crowded with often-zonked settlers.

H.A. credits Ron Mackie, then supervisory ranger of the backcountry horse patrol, with the success of the Little Yosemite clean-up program. At Ron's behest, a mounted ranger came through the camp often, and had quite a stabilizing effect.

H.A. spent two summers in Little Yosemite, joined the second by ranger Meredith Alpert. The situation had improved greatly by the summer of 1973, when Little Yosemite became Chuck's first NPS seasonal ranger assignment. He and George Durkee shared the responsibilities that summer. In June of the next year, Chuck and Dana Stevens were married, had a short honeymoon, and then took up residence as a seasonal ranger couple in Little Yosemite Valley.

That Yosemite Valley had calmed somewhat can be seen by these excerpts from the Superintendent's 1973 report.[7] "Yosemite is no longer a place trapped somewhere between Smokey the Bear and Buck Rogers. It is an area where professional park managers are as proficient in human relations as in resource conservation and law enforcement...the low-profile attitude of rangers provides an open flow of communication." Referring to other positive steps in the Park, the report states the year "saw women make strides in the fight for equal opportunity, and the area's Indian people take an active interest in reviving and strengthening the customs and crafts of the Valley's first residents." The construction of an authentic Indian roundhouse had been completed that year in the Indian garden behind the Yosemite Village Visitor Center.

The National Park Service Public Information Officer (Lew Albert in 1971, later Jim Sleznick) became adept at getting positive news to the media and in keeping lines open for the positive flow of media/Park communication. In 1971, with advance publicity, Park entrance fees were raised to $3 per day or $10 per year. The following year saw the introduction of the Golden Age (free entrance over 62 years of age) and Golden Eagle ($10 per year) Passport programs, which were instigated in all national parks. The public responded most favorably to these programs. They are still in use today, although all fees have increased considerably.

Meanwhile, in Washington, NPS Director George Hartzog was "hanging on by his fingernails."[8] He barely survived Nixon's 1968 narrow-margin election. Nixon wanted control over all government agencies. He got it by firing many careerists and placing his White House loyalists in key positions. Excerpts later heard on the Haldeman tape, in Nixon's voice, "Knock them the hell out of there.... Clean the bastards out." Following his 1972 reelection victory, Nixon personally fired George Hartzog. In the fifty-six years since the agency had been established there had been seven NPS Directors. This was the first firing. Three more directors were precipitously dismissed by the end of the decade. They were Ron Walker (a Nixon man who proved a mismatch for the job), Gary Everhardt, and Bill Whalen (aforementioned associate superintendent in Yosemite under Lynn Thompson). Russ Dickinson, the decade's fifth director, lasted into the eighties. Park historian/writer Bill Everhart states:

> There is a consensus that George Hartzog presided over the last—and some might say best—years of the old Park Service and that the old Park Service came to an end when he was dismissed by Nixon. His firing began the politicizing of the Park Service and broke a tradition as old as the agency.

Another change attributed to the Nixon Administration was a ban on government employees accepting discounts from concessioners. Thus our NPS friends could no longer take advantage of the YPCC's community-wide privilege card program. The program offered all

Valley residents a ten percent discount on merchandise, groceries, and other items, and an even greater discount on ski activities and meals in certain establishments. In the years that followed, the change was often misconstrued to have been YPCC instigated. It was simply not so. But I believe it to be one of the factors that led to the we/they (NPS/YPCC) syndrome that gradually developed in the community. Being a resort area, local prices were high. Without the discounts, more and more Park Service people tended to shop outside the Park. Loss of discounts also meant fewer Park Service families could afford to ski at Badger or to eat out with family and friends in the Park establishments. As the YPCC evolved into eventual ownership by Music Corporation of America (MCA), with even more generous meal perquisites for its employees, this schism became increasingly more noticeable. Gone was the all-community camaraderie at Ski-dinners and similar events.

CONCESSIONER CHANGES

Stephen Mather, during his tenure as the first Director of the National Park Service, had occasion to critically assess the hodgepodge "serve the tourist" situation in Yellowstone National Park. There, any and all entrepreneurs could vie for tourist dollars, with the situation at times becoming chaotic. Mather came to the conclusion that the parks "were no place for a free enterprise system."[9] The "Mather solution," which still survives, was that each park would have a single franchise holder who would supply all tourist services. The park concession became a monopoly controlled by the U.S. government. The NPS, agent for the government, sets the rules, approves the rates, protects the concessioner from competition, and looks out for the public interest. Whether this arrangement works as well as it sounds has at times been the basis for much critical discussion.

For years the Yosemite Park and Curry Company was *the* concessioner in our Park, with Best's Studio/Ansel Adams Gallery, Degnan's, and the medical and dental operations as smaller, special interest concessions. It is worth noting—in the bus-oriented era of today's Park—that until the 1980s all private bus tours were transferred to YPCC buses when traveling inside Yosemite.

In the late sixties, the YPCC was catapulted into its own world of change. While we were visiting Mickey and John Curry, then with the Disney Corporation in Southern California, John told of becoming aware of offers quietly being made by a group interested in acquiring YPCC stock. Although no longer with YPCC, John had great loyalty to the Park operation. He felt the powers-that-be in the Park perhaps were not heeding these rumors of a stock buy-up. The upshot: By the end of the sixties the Shasta Corporation had purchased 38% of Curry Company stock.[10] In so doing, however, the Shasta Corporation had overextended financially, and was in turn acquired by U.S. Natural Resources, a miniconglomerate chaired by Robert Katz, which also controlled concessions in Lassen and Mt. McKinley National Parks.

By 1971, a former USNR executive, Alan Coleman, had been elected chairman of the YPCC board. By year's end Coleman had switched titles with Stuart Cross, to become YPCC President and CEO. The battle for stock buy-up by USNR—meaning board control—intensified. Cross and eleven board members fought the takeover.[11] USNR made a tender offer, in the spring of 1972, for 115,000 shares of YPCC stock. It was an agonizing decision for employees and YPCC friends: to hang on loyally to YPCC stock or accept the monetary incentive to sell. If successful, USNR's ownership of 50.4% of the stock would control the Yosemite Park and Curry Company and its concession contract, which would be in effect until 1993.

USNR was successful in the takeover bid, and was in control of YPCC by the end of 1972. The old guard began to be replaced, and the Curry family company was no more. Mary Curry Tresidder was spared the final two years of the takeover battle, having quietly passed away in October of 1970. Gone was the patriarchal/matriarchal feeling of the Yosemite Park and Curry Company—although the name, per se, was retained until the mid-nineties.

Thus it was that in both significant community groups—NPS and YPCC—the early seventies brought the exodus of much of our Yosemite family. To our NPS-connected, departing friends were added those of the YPCC: the Berreys, Crosses and Robinsons, as well as the Proctors and Maynards.

Only a few months later, in the summer of 1973, YPCC was purchased by Music Corporation of America (MCA). With USNR, then MCA, the era of big business came to Yosemite. From 1972 on, the ultimate bosses lived elsewhere, with corporate headquarters in Menlo Park, California, then Los Angeles, and eventually Buffalo, New York. There was little in the brief period between board takeover by USNR and YPCC's purchase by MCA that affected us personally. Don Hummel followed Alan Coleman as president and CEO of YPCC. With MCA's arrival from Hollywood, however, came far-reaching changes. This company was far from a mini-conglomerate.

A LEARNING VENTURE

The Yosemite Institute (YI), a new educational entity and one that is still thriving, established itself in the Park in 1971.[12] The program was hatched with collective planning. The planners included YPCC Vice President Robert Maynard and Public Relations Manager Jan Studebaker, NPS Superintendent Lynn Thompson and Assistant Superintendent John Good (with input from the Park interpretive division), and Donald Rees. Don was then teaching at a college prep school in Santa Barbara and developing a program to bring students to the Park for a week of environmental and scientific hands-on learning. He had brought just such a group to the Valley that March of 1971, with the aid of Will Neely, long-time summer naturalist in Tuolumne Meadows. The week of outdoor education was deemed highly successful. By the end of that summer, after much discussion and more planning, Don was given the okay and the start-up funds to set the concept in motion—and the Yosemite Institute was on its way.[13]

The essence of the YI program was to provide groups of students with a week of outdoor science, history, rock climbing, hiking, and cross-country skiing in the Park's off-season. It was not to be a vacation; it was to be a week of serious learning in the Park setting.

Since the YI groups would be seasonally oriented to the spring and fall, it was noted that the participants would help fill otherwise empty beds at Yosemite Lodge. There was much local speculation, pro and con, about the new venture.[14]

The first YI group arrived in the Valley October 1971, with the program still in the formative stage. A board of directors was named in November, curriculum expanded, full staff hired and the institute, as we know it, was established. Staffing brought another group of enthusiastic young people into our community. They were college graduates well versed in appropriate scientific and environmental fields. They were young, laid back enough to appeal to teenage students of the seventies, yet able to relate to the accompanying classroom teachers by involving them in several of the activities. We met and came to know many from that seventies contingent.[15] We also became very used to seeing eagerly interested groups of young people walking or sitting with their YI instructors here and there around the Valley.

In 1973, the institute was granted the use of the old blister rust/summer fire camp at Crane Flat. Following considerable refurbishing, the facility was opened as a secondary campus. The idea of using it as a summer youth hostel was briefly explored but scrapped because of the distance from the Valley. The Crane Flat location, however, became very popular with YI's California schools and with college alumni clubs when adult participation was added to the program. Eventually, a partial scholarship program was set up for the institute's distribution to appropriate applicants.

The Rees family consisted of Don and Jo Ann, Chris, Carol, and Ann. They entered into all facets of Valley school, community, and ski life. Later in the decade, they moved to Squaw Valley where, in 1978, Jo Ann and Don founded the Squaw Valley Academy, a traditional, college preparatory school near Lake Tahoe.

When Don Rees left Yosemite, Bob Hansen took over the YI directorship, later followed by Dennis Hansen, Vince Kehoe, and others. In the years since its inception, thousands of young people have gained from exposure to the Yosemite Institute's Park program. One hopes that many have carried an awareness of and concern for the environment into their adult lives.

CHANGES HIT HOME

The decade of the seventies brought more change to the Park medical/dental sphere than any other period during our thirty-seven years in the Valley. Like Ave Sturm, Roger Hendrickson, and Jim Wurgler at the other end of the hospital, Charlie tended to treat every type of case that walked into his office. If new procedures came along, he went outside the Park to take a course of instruction in the procedure. A case in point involved a two-day seminar in Southern California. The subject: a breakthrough in the dreaded root canal treatment. Two days after returning to the Park with the necessary new instruments in hand, Charlie received an emergency toothache call. Returning from the office sometime later, he announced with great enthusiasm the completion of the first in-his-own-office root canal procedure. The tooth had been saved—and Charlie went on to master a new technique. So it went, with Charlie doing all but the most intricate dental surgery. He handled the less complicated orthodontia cases and performed periodontal procedures and considerable crown and bridge work, as well as routine general dentistry. It was an interesting, varied, and challenging practice.

With the early seventies came the concern about drugs—the protection of the office supply and the need to dispense all drugs with care. It was a druggy time in the Park. Some users thought any source was fair game. Going back to the office alone at night in response to an unknown toothache call took on a sense of risk. Several times I went along with Charlie. If I didn't go, the on-duty person in the medical area was alerted to Charlie's presence in his office.

Often, before the era of dental insurance and preventive dentistry, transients in the Park lacked the means to cover the cost of emergency procedures. Not being of a mind to dispense too much charity work (with four of his own in various schools and colleges), Charlie often held a bicycle, camera, or even a driver's license as collateral. The hat would be passed at Camp 4 or Muir Tree, perhaps a parent was contacted for a bailout, and then the article was redeemed.

It was also during this time that Charlie taught me the basics of chairside-assisting so I could fill in should Jeannette be absent. We were into the pattern of making do with who or what was available—in all facets of our Park life. And I was available. At least I knew instrument nomenclature and the importance of meticulous sterilization from my former dental medicine job at UC San Francisco. Charlie was patient and tolerant of my occasional ineptness. We still chuckle about the time I inadvertently dropped a tiny, costly diamond stone from the tip of the handpiece directly into the ample cleavage of the patient. What a gracious lady she was. Charlie stepped out while she disrobed down to her bra to recover my loss.

Because the practice included almost every phase of dentistry, and because Charlie could work in less than opulent, state-of-the-art surroundings, he and Clark Burton, who had a similar country practice in Murphys, California, were naturals to offer help to Third World countries in setting up dental clinics in remote areas. In the early seventies, Charlie went twice to the remote Mexican village of Ajoya, high in the hills above Mazatlan—to work and to train the locals. Later a young man from Ajoya came to the Park to stay with us and work in the dental office for a couple of weeks. Clark went along on the second Ajoyan trip. In 1992 they went together to Namche Bazaar in the Sherpa country of Nepal to work for several weeks on a similar project.

In the spring of 1975 Charlie was struck down—literally—by the extremely debilitating hepatitis B, *serum* hepatitis. He awoke one morning with yellow skin and a desire to die: He was miserable. Treatment: bed rest and diet restrictions. Prognosis: out of the office for three months. Betsy, a Mariposa High student, was the only one still at home with us. The other three were in California colleges, but came home when they could to cheer us on. It was a difficult few weeks in that Charlie, usually a stoic, groaned and ached, and suffered and groaned some more. Friends were the daily support system for Betsy and me. As for the dental office, Clark Burton drove over from his practice in Murphys every Wednesday to work on the patients left mid-treatment. Others were put on hold. Jeannette literally ran the practice. Charlie was able to narrow the probable infection source to two patients—and made the required report to the County Health Department. Because he had been in such good physical shape when stricken, Charlie was back in the office in six weeks' time. His first real outing was a trip to UC Davis to see our Chuck receive his college degree. It was an excellent tonic: one down, three to go.

As the seventies moved forward, other changes came with the increased number of patients having good dental insurance coverage. A different kind of dentistry evolved. Payment was eased by insurance, preventive procedures became more accessible, techniques honed, teeth saved rather than pulled. The benefits of fluoride treatment became evident. The end of the decade brought far fewer emergency calls. By that time, the toothaches interrupting a scheduled day or a night's sleep were much more apt to come from the build-up of pressure caused by change in elevation and not from rot or neglect. Good dentistry was getting better.

The emergency interruptions did still come occasionally, however. Charlie and I were celebrating our twenty-fifth anniversary in January 1976, with a group of good friends in our home, when a call came. Back to the office went Charlie, to repair a mouth on the receiving end of a fist. The tooth replanted successfully, the party went on.

With every program comes accountability. Insurance programs are no exception. Some would say this intrusion took the fun out of our kind of practice. Paper work mushroomed as the decade wound down. OSHA[16] was born (with all of its dos and don'ts and must dos), and from Southern California came the influx of MCA employees steeped in the specialist-only mind set. The nature of the Park dental and medical practices changed—and something was lost along the way.

AT THE OTHER END OF THE HALL

December 31, 1970 was a milestone in the medical history of our Yosemite. Avery Sturm retired. It was truly the end of an era. After a memorable retirement gala, Ave and Pat moved to The Ranch. Looking back Charlie and I appreciate the fact that Ave and Pat did not have to cope with the changes that came to Lewis Memorial Hospital in the next decade. Ave retired at exactly the right time. But it took him a while to fully recognize that the changes that came to the practice were inevitable, not just because he was no longer at the helm. The outside world had imposed itself, with new rules, new regulations, and higher costs.

Ave left the practice in the capable hands of Roger Hendrickson and Jim Wurgler. Dr. Wallace LeBourdais, recently retired from the army, joined them in 1972. Roger and Wally had practiced together in Germany prior to the Hendricksons return to the Park in 1963. Wally and Bettye were another welcome addition to the community.

The medical services carried on much as they had, patient-wise, but the business end became more complicated and red tape riddled. As with the dental practice, medical insurance had become the norm for patients, and it resulted in the same burgeoning paper work. A factor unique to the medical practice in Yosemite was the extremely diverse range of that practice. It covered local and transient patients; it provided general medicine; it handled obstetrics, orthopedic and emergency surgery, and an occasional cardiac case. It covered a myriad of medical needs for a myriad of people. The malpractice ogre was raising its head. Malpractice insurance had begun to sky-rocket throughout the state, a fact soon brought forcibly home to Yosemite. LMH had some of the highest insurance risk factors in the book. The words *transient patients* raised a red flag. Adding *transient* to the procedures of obstetrics, emergency surgery, and orthopedics sent the LMH malpractice insurance premiums through the roof. Our small medical group simply couldn't handle these cost increases. After much anguish and many hours of seeking a viable solution, the financial reality of the situation forced the closing of the inpatient facility in October 1975. Lewis Memorial Hospital disappeared from maps, directional signs, and letterheads. The Yosemite Medical Clinic was born.

The clinic became a 24-hour outpatient facility with a small bed and board capacity for the stabilization of emergency cases before sending the patients on to hospitals in Mariposa, Merced, or Fresno. Even local obstetric cases were referred out. This was a difficult adjustment for both the local mothers-to-be and the doctors. Having a baby in Lewis Memorial Hospital had been a coveted event. Referrals to specialists in other fields also became commonplace. Helicopters were heard more often as the number of medical evacuations grew.

The recently refurbished patient rooms were put to other uses. The hospital insurance plan with YPCC, which had covered 80% of a hospital stay, was discontinued. Private plans took over. Additional employees were hired to cover the paper work. The three doctors made an effort to keep the same staff when the change came, a point of honor. That staff—including Inky Ringrose, Chris Becker, Dick Ditton, Lois Smith, Kathy Knierierman, Kathy Loucks, Gin Watson, and Alice Schmidt—pitched in to make the transition successful. It evolved into an efficient clinic.

During the latter part of the decade, the LeBourdais retired and returned to the Bay Area. Dr. Jeff Folkens came into the practice and brought his family into the community. In 1979, Roger Hendrickson decided he wanted his own general medicine practice. He set it up in the Auburn area, and the family left the Valley, after sixteen years. With this move, not only did the Valley lose a fine doctor, but the ski team lost an excellent referee, in Anne, and two eager racers, in Vik and Mitch. Jim Wurgler and Jeff Folkens carried on, and shorter-term medical help came and went.

MOVIES AND THE LAW

The new YPCC/MCA group arrived in Yosemite in 1973 with some grandiose ideas, among them to build a cable car to Glacier Point and to keep the Tioga Road open year-round for the development of winter sports at Tuolumne Meadows. Fortunately, common sense and the NPS prevailed in both cases. In the mid-seventies the ire of the NPS Director's office was provoked by the Universal Studio—a division of MCA—filming of the television series *Sierra* in the Park. The series was the saga of a couple of park rangers and was blatant drivel. Many of our friends were hired as extras and advisors to the project and loved the action. What led to the demise of the venture was media discovery that some of the Park's sacrosanct granite had been painted—to cut down on the glare from filming lights. By NPS decree the production was halted.

Concurrently, the new company was widely criticized for allegedly gouging the public. This action, the television fiasco, and the increased advertising campaign aimed at pulling more conventions to Yosemite in the peak summer tourist months focused NPS attention on our Park. Gary Everhardt, then NPS director, saw the need for added control of concession obligations and limits.[17] The NPS establishment of a professional concessions management program for the parks, with a handbook outlining procedures, policies and regulations was the result. A Concessions Management Office was added to the Yosemite NPS hierarchy. Almost immediately, Yosemite was off-limits to convention groups between mid-May and mid-September, and stricter guidelines were set for outsider uses of the Park year-round. The Concessions Management Office became the communicator between the concessioners and the National Park Service.

The mid-seventies saw the addition of a second new division to the local NPS framework, that of the Law Enforcement Office (LEO). By 1975, with a heightened crime rate in the Park, this separate unit was needed to handle the increasing workload and to move law enforcement out of the Valley District Ranger office. Valley crime was now likened to that of a small city. The prevalence of this more urban-like crime was related to the proximity of growing nearby city populations coupled with the increased ease and speed of transportation into the Park. Lee Shackelton was appointed to head the new LEO endeavor, a position he would hold until his retirement in 1992.

Another change in 1975, this one to the office of the U. S. Magistrate, came with the retirement of our long time friend Gene Ottonello. Gene had served as U. S. Commissioner in the Park since 1943. In 1971 his title and duties were increased to U. S. Magistrate, although still designated a part-time position. That Gene could hold this part-time appointment as well as manage the local credit union points up the fact that law enforcement cases, with the attendant court proceedings, were still relatively few in number during his tenure. After thirty-two years as the judicial presence in the Park, this respected man and his wife Adrienne retired to Wawona.

The magistrate vacancy was filled with the appointment of Fresno Judge Donald Pitts. The position was still nominally part-time when Don and his family moved to the Valley. During this time, the growing increases in case numbers and gravity of the crime necessitated the construction of a sixteen-prisoner jail in the government maintenance area. By 1981 the year's caseload topped one thousand,[18] and Pitts' position evolved into a full-time appointment bringing the additional need for court aides. The mid-eighties saw construction of a separate court facility. Crime had become a major concern in the Park—a trend that had not abated when we left the area in 1998.

In retrospect, Yosemite was a microcosm of what was happening in the rest of the nation during those turbulent years. Changes were coming thick and fast. The second half of the decade was no exception and continued to bring new ways, new thoughts and new activities to our Park and community. There was no going back, and so we move on in the spirit of adventure.

19. The Changes Keep Coming

If change is inevitable, have it be for the better.
—*Anonymous*

YMP EVOLVES INTO GMP

Throughout the decade of the seventies, the Yosemite Master Plan process moved along, first in its formative stages, then in the development of more practical and possible solutions to the Valley's congestion problems. Through media publicity and advertised public meetings it became an ongoing project. In 1974, a first Master Plan was put forth, and then rejected because the results appeared to have too little public input and too much YPCC/MCA influence. Many balked at the idea of big business moving into the Park.[1]

In 1975, the process began anew and was retitled the General Master Plan (GMP). The order of procedure this time included workshops and workbooks.[2] Using the gathered material, a tentative plan and alternatives were formulated. The public was then asked to review the plan. A draft GMP and Environmental Impact Statement (EIS) were developed. Following more public review, the final GMP and EIS documents were presented and distributed. We, along with hundreds of others, did our homework, pondering over practical and possible solutions to congestion and other Valley problems. We spent the three or more hours necessary to fill out the workbooks, submitted them, then awaited results.

When the draft plan came out, we wondered if we had been heard. Criticism arose from many sides. How had the workbook answers been compiled? Were NPS computers sophisticated enough for this huge task? The results showed an orientation toward profit. Had the YPCC/MCA managed to stuff the ballot box during the workbook stage? Many of the participating locals, ourselves included, were disappointed with the results.

The GMP came out in its finished form in 1978—and the Taft Toe issue made its debut. Taft Toe is the name given to an area of pristine forest lying at the base of Taft Point in the west end of the Valley. A group of Park planners envisioned this as a potential parking area for tourist cars and busses. The Sierra Club Tehipite Chapter Newsletter stated Taft Toe "might be acceptable provided the NPS will regard this facility as an interim measure while studying the feasibility of removing the main bulk of cars to parking areas away from the Valley—such as El Portal or Wawona."[3] Somewhere along the line, the idea of a day-use entry reservation system had also been presented. Then, as now, the idea was not something the NPS wanted to address. With environmental cries of "deurbanize the Park" on the one hand, YPCC/MCA calling the plan unworkable on the other, and various critics saying deurbanization of Yosemite would be too costly, the GMP faded from the limelight and was put on the shelf.

FAMILY AND FRIENDS

What of our own family during this decade? *Major* changes. The onset of the seventies found Chuck a UC Davis freshman, Anne about to graduate from CRMS to enter UC Santa Cruz, Rob soon off to CRMS, and Betsy in the sixth grade at home. By the end of the decade, Chuck and Dana Stevens, whom he met in Aspen, Colorado during his stop-out year from Davis, had been married six years. Theirs was a lovely, traditional wedding in the tiny village of Tisbury, on Martha's Vineyard off the coast of Massachusetts. They settled in Vermont where he worked with the Vermont State Parks System, and they were the parents of four-year-old Heidi. Anne, now a UC Santa Cruz graduate, was two years married to Chas Macquarie. They summered in the Tetons and wintered at Tuolumne Meadows—and visions of Everest captured their imaginations. Rob had graduated from UC Davis and settled in the Keystone area of Colorado, where he ski patrolled and was about to meet his future wife, Amy Riesman, of Pittsford, New York. He would soon move into a career with the Mountain Bell/U.S.West Telephone Company. Betsy was now a class of 1978 Mariposa High School graduate and a sophomore at Humboldt State University in Arcata. Her move to the Northern California coast gave us a new chunk of California scenery to explore.

The community changed with the times. A Wells Fargo Bank branch opened in 1970 in an attractive new building in the Village Store complex. Roland Ely and his delightful Barbara came in with the bank. In 1975, when Roland retired, Dick and Dru Ehrhardt came on the scene. Many pleasant faces smiled across those bank counters—Merrie Hinson, Marsha Lee, Ginger Springer, and Linda Krieger among them. Banking facilities in the Valley proved an appreciated convenience.

Old friends moved on, new friends came. The Bill Jones family left the Valley in 1972. The Shackelton and Morehead families each returned for another Yosemite assignment. The community welcomed the Hardys, Goertzens, Grahams, Abbotts, Bill Thompsons, and Scobles into the concessioner field. We became acquainted with Betty and Hank Johnston—living in their unique setting at the end of Henness Ridge, well beyond Chinquapin. From their deck on a clear day one could count seven ranges of mountains off to the west. Into Park Service ranks came the Karrakers, Sholleys, Abrells, Bradys, Lees, Hinsons, Tony Andersens, Alberts, van Wagtendonks, Mackies, Wendts—and the Sleznicks, host and hostess par excellence. Jim and Gayle Sleznick and friends instigated the clever—and tasty—"Briceburg Dinner," a progressive dinner event set in the El Portal community. Many interesting, enthusiastic people became a part of our world in that decade.

Les Arnberger succeeded bachelor Lynn Thompson in the superintendency in 1975, and Residence 1 with its magnificent meadow setting, once again had a gracious hostess in the person of Gayle

Arnberger. Residence 1 was the scene of many gatherings for the entertainment and introduction of visiting NPS and other dignitaries. Superintendent wives were still the Park Service on-the-spot hostesses. There was no supplemental entertainment allowance and this hosting could prove a thankless job. We were sorry to have the Arnbergers leave for Santa Fe after a brief four years. We'd shared some good times, including an exhilarating raft trip down the Stanislaus River one spring. Les Arnberger was to be the last superintendent to live in the stately Residence 1, henceforth to go down in local history as "the superintendent's old house."

Bob and Midge Binnewies succeeded the Arnbergers in the superintendency. Midge played down the NPS hostess roll, choosing to pursue her own career in the Mariposa area. The Binnewieses made the decision to live outside the Valley, first in Park housing in El Portal, then in their own home beyond Mariposa. This was a less than ideal situation for the Park. Subsequent superintendents came back into the Valley to live in the residence formerly assigned to assistant superintendents. Unfortunately, Residence 1 had been permanently converted to NPS offices in the interim.

In the annals of new-to-the-Park activities, 1975 was a busy year. Hang-gliding was introduced to the Park. Soon after Superintendent Arnberger's arrival, the situation was brought to the attention of NPS Director Everhardt, who came to the Park to find out more about this new recreational venture. Discussions on whether to ban the sport from the Park became intense. Arnberger argued for allowing it, citing the strict guidelines set up by the hang-gliding community itself. One of these guidelines was the mandatory early morning flight hours, a time that created no spectator congestion on the Valley floor. Arnberger further cited other in-Park sports—skiing, climbing, golf—as more intrusive and possibly more dangerous. With a near perfect safety record, the hang-gliders made their case. Chief Ranger Bill Wendt appointed Dean Paschall as the first Yosemite hang-gliding ranger. Rich Romero later held the job. From our point of view, it was breathtaking to watch the gliders float quietly down from Glacier Point on an early morning breeze. Even more of a heart-in-the-mouth thrill was being atop Glacier Point to watch the steep, running launch. Contrasting the hang-gliding decision with another stand taken that year is to contrast grace and beauty with noise and speed. The latter was turned down when snowmobiles were banned from the Park, a ruling still in effect. A group based in Wawona had lobbied long and hard for inclusion of snowmobile use in Yosemite.

THE HISTORIAN

In October 1975, Charlie and I were invited to a dinner at the Ahwahnee to honor the publication of Shirley Sargent's new book *Yosemite and Its Innkeepers—The Story of a Great Park and Its Chief Concessionaires.* It was a gala occasion, complete with speeches, book signing, and the works. It was announced during the evening that the old Degnan's sign would go back up on the family restaurant building in Yosemite Village. The tacky Great Yosemite Food and Beverage Company sign[4] would come off the wall to go into oblivion. The Degnan/Donohoe family, upon retirement the year before, had sold the facility to YPCC/MCA. With typical Hollywood flourish, the building's name had been jazzed up. It was indeed a coup for Shirley Sargent and her perseverance that this unpopular name-change had been reversed. History had triumphed!

We first met Shirley in the early sixties on the sands of the Park's Cascade Beach, we with our four, she in the midst of some exuberant teenage nieces and pals. They had dropped down to Cascades from Shirley's home at Flying Spur in Foresta via the old Coulterville Road. Shirley, we learned, had been confined to a wheelchair since the age of fourteen. Her arrival at the beach with her chair, supported by laughing young people, was eye-catching indeed. Into the water she went—and her undaunted spirit captured us.

Shirley spent much of her childhood in the Park, the earliest phase in Tuolumne Meadows when her engineer father worked on stretches of the Big Oak Flat and Tioga Roads in the thirties.[5] Living in and out of the Valley, she eventually settled at Flying Spur in 1963, and went on to become a resident Park historian/writer, one who makes history come alive between her book covers. An autographed copy of *Pioneers in Petticoats*, published in 1966, was the first of an ongoing Sargent collection in our home library. For years Shirley and Hank Johnston joined forces in the "Flying Spur Press." Shirley, the Ahwahnee Hotel, and I share the same birth month and year—quite distinguished company, I've always felt.

The devastating fire of 1990, with its sweep up the mountainside from El Portal, didn't spare Flying Spur. Shirley and friends made a valiant attempt to ride out the approaching conflagration, but nothing could stop the onslaught. She finally agreed to evacuation. We saw the site soon afterward. It was heartbreaking, as were the rest of the Foresta losses. With spirit lowered but not daunted, Shirley soon had trees planted and a new home built on the original site. Her writing, too, continued. At this juncture, a new book has been published, *Protectors of Paradise*. Yes, it is on our bookshelf, too.

HODGEPODGE

Other additions to our lives in the mid-seventies were recycling, dumpsters, and a cat. The YPCC/MCA initiated the very successful recycling program early in its Park career. Both the public and the locals were ready for this kind of an environmental statement and the program immediately took hold. The NPS was busy installing bear-proof dumpsters—ugly, large, brown metal boxes placed strategically and conspicuously around the neighborhoods. They worked, so we learned to accept the aesthetic blight.

The third addition came with the reversal in the traditional "no pets" Park policy. Each household was allowed one cat or one dog, and there was a stringent leash law. Although our gang had owned hamsters, white mice and an occasional turtle, they had grown up in surroundings where animals moving around the Park freely on four legs had been wild. Occasionally in the outside world I found a child of mine cowering behind me, even shinnying up my leg, when approached by a dog. The change took some getting used to, then we finally settled for a cat. In retrospect, I'm sure many a law enforcement ranger rued that change of policy. It was so often abused.

When another crazy decided to have a unique Yosemite experience and performed a successful tightrope walk across the top of Yosemite Falls, we knew another summer was upon us. The summer of 1976 brought the beginning of a new tradition: the gathering of friends on the deck at Badger Pass. These events became known as our "almost full moon picnics," as we congregated at Badger on the third evening before the actual full moon of each summer month. Betty Johnston and Rusty were the spearheads. Often the Badger meadow was awash with wild flowers. It was a potluck sort of thing, libations and food, then we welcomed the rising moon with song—every moon song anyone could remember and some we couldn't. There were several excellent voices in that group, Betty and Hank Johnston and Donna Mackie among them. Who could ever forget Jack Saulsbury's rendition of "Me and Bobbie McGee"?

THE BASKET WEAVER

The Indian Cultural Museum opened in the original wing of the Visitor Center in 1976. All things relating to Indian culture and its preservation immediately bring to mind one outstanding person: Julia Parker. Julia is a gatherer: of acorns and basket-making reeds in the tradition of her people; of four generations of family into her nurturing home; and of people, clustered around her in the Valley's Indian Cultural Museum as she demonstrates her basket weaving artistry and talks of her heritage.

Julia arrived in Yosemite three years before I did, in 1948. She came, the wife of Ralph Parker, and they made their home in the Indian Village just west of the Yosemite Lodge. Chronologically, it would be more appropriate to say the Yosemite Lodge was just to the east of the Indian Village. Julia and Ralph met while attending the Stewart Indian School in Carson City, Nevada.[6] Julia's heritage is Kashaya Pomo/Coast Miwok, Ralph's Yosemite Miwok/Pauite. At that time it was the policy of Indian schools to teach "don't be Indian." At the Stewart School, students were forbidden to speak their native language or to follow the other customs of their people, including sitting on the floor. Knowing Julia as I have come to know her, seeing her firm will and determination, I strongly suspect this counter-culture schooling may have had just the opposite effect. It may have become the seed of her great sense of loyalty to her people and of her ongoing determination to keep their traditions alive. This challenge has dominated her life's work—along with the nurturing of four generations of her own family.

On coming to the Valley, Julia found a perfect mentor in Ralph's grandmother, Lucy Telles, basket maker of note. Lucy taught Julia much about traditional Miwok culture, including basket weaving and acorn techniques. Julia was a willing, apt, and creative student. Her baskets are treasured acquisitions, as were Lucy's in earlier days. I, along with Elizabeth II, am lucky enough to have one—a "burden basket" won in a fund-raising raffle some years ago. Queen Elizabeth was presented with hers during her visit to the Park in 1983.

The Parkers lived in Indian Village with two of their to-be-four children when I arrived to join Charlie in 1951 so we have known them all of our Yosemite-lifetime. Their son Allen and our Chuck were classmates. The younger daughter Lucy was tucked into the grade between Rob and Anne. We were all with them in spirit and heart when Allen had his life-changing automobile accident in the later high school years.

The most important of the activities we shared with the Parker family were the Wednesday afternoon ski-days and Rusty's ski team, kids and parents alike. We were all there and we all helped. For Ralph and Julia, the helping continued into grandchildren years when oldest son Louie and daughter Lucy each produced some fine young racers.

Indian Village ceased to be a residential area sometime in the mid-sixties, with families absorbed into other residential areas. The Indian Village homes were razed. This was not an easy giving up of tradition for Julia.

In 1960, the Park Service hired Julia to demonstrate various facets of her Indian artistry in the garden behind the Visitor Center.[7] She was the first Indian demonstrator hired since the demise of Chief

LeeMee and his colorful dances in 1953. Julia reintroduced Indian tradition to the Park with her own manner of artistry. In the summer of 1972, her son Allen joined her in program presentations. Daughter Lucy later followed suit. In 1975-76, two federal grants were given the interpretive branch of the Yosemite NPS to honor the upcoming United States Bicentennial. The grants were used to create the Indian Cultural Museum, as we know it today.[8] Julia was involved in the discussion of plans and then moved into the demonstration phase. Her demonstrations are still a major attraction of the program.

One of the main trans-Sierra trails used by earlier-day Indians was the Mono Trail, which comes from the east over Mono Pass, drops to Tuolumne Meadows, then continues down to the Valley. This "walk" was reestablished in 1990 and has become a yearly event. Julia and various members and generations of her family have done the walk many times, including one within days of the loss of daughter Virginia. This woman is a traditionalist in the deepest sense of the word. She has traveled throughout the country giving talks and demonstrating, with intrinsic dignity, the artistry of her people. Her very being speaks to the best of her people's traditions.

HIGH JINX

A fascinating adventure befell the Park in the winter of 1976-1977, in later years referred to by some as "the great Yosemite gold rush." Snowshoers touring in the southern end of the Park over Christmas vacation came upon bits of airplane wreckage in the area around Lower Merced Pass Lake. The identification number from the one visible wing piece matched that of a plane reported missing the preceding month. A Lockheed Lodestar twin-engined plane carrying a 5,000-pound cargo of Colombian marijuana had taken off from Baja California, filed no flight plan, and headed north. Ten days later the plane was reported missing, and it was learned that the destination had been a clandestine airstrip in the desert north of Reno, Nevada.[9] California and Nevada Civil Air Patrols had conducted an air/sea search, to no avail. With discovery of the plane's wreckage by the snowshoers, it was deemed to have crashed in the mountain terrain, a mere ten linear miles from the Valley floor. To get to the crash site in winter, however, is to hike ten miles up the snow-covered Glacier Point road beyond the winter closure point at Badger Pass to the Mono Meadow trailhead, then along an additional twelve miles of twisting snow-covered trail.

The NPS investigated the site, and found metallic debris and minor scraps of wreckage. A nose cone was sitting upright on the frozen lake, and snow-covered humps were scattered around. Upon inspection, these humps proved to be bales of marijuana. The rest of the plane, and the bodies, were assumed to be under the lake ice. The Federal agencies involved helicoptered out seventeen 160-pound bales before a late January blizzard closed down the recovery operation until the coming of spring and snow-free roads. As it turned out, this was a major miscalculation on the part of the Park Service. In early February, the *Los Angeles Times* published the pot story, and TV crews even cited the exact location of the downed plane.[10] The rush was on. Reportedly, by late March there could be as many as twenty people on hand at the lake "working the claim." By the time NPS got there to close off the area and post guards, it was pretty much too late.

Meanwhile, we at home heard more and more about the caper. Camp 4 saw much coming and going, and the action spot was Lower Merced Pass Lake. Tales came later of ingoing gear (chainsaws, scuba gear, sleeping bags, etc.) being jettisoned lakeside as backpacks were loaded with marijuana for the carryout. Some adventurers even crossed the winter passes to emerge more safely at the remote roadheads on the eastside of the Sierra. It wasn't long until visible signs of a new affluence began to appear around the Valley: upgraded cars, top-grade climbing and camping gear, talk of grandiose plans for climbing trips abroad. Rumor had it that the smokeable pot brought a retail value of $400 per pound. Nicknamed Lodestar Lightning, it was potent stuff. When the Park Service got a handle on the situation the rush was over. By mid-June, the bodies and wreckage had been salvaged—to the tune of some $20,000 in expenses. Financially, there was something very one-sided about this adventure. Thus, another chapter was added to the lore of Yosemite.

IN THE COMMUNITY

July 1977 brought the fiftieth anniversary of the Ahwahnee Hotel. The occasion was marked with a gala gathering of invited guests at the hotel for cake, champagne, and speeches. Soon thereafter the hotel was placed on the National Registry of Historic Places—and the chain-link fence around its periphery was removed. This fence had been put up in the forties when the hotel had been under the care of the navy, and served as accommodations for personnel undergoing rest and rehabilitation. These men were not always at liberty to wander around the Valley—hence, the chain-link. Now it was fortunately a thing of the past.

In 1975, Merced Community College expanded its extension program to include Yosemite. Diana Abrell was local coordinator, a role I took over in 1977 when the Abrells transferred from the Park. The instructors were drawn primarily from the local intelligence pool. It was up to the coordinator to decide on qualification and organizational ability of each potential instructor, as well as what subject matter might appeal to the community. The schedule was set, courses advertised, and the first session called. The magic number was fifteen. If, in the first two sessions, that number of participants hadn't signed up, the college would not underwrite the expense. The number fifteen came to haunt me until I passed the job of coordinator on to Mary Gess in the early eighties. During my reign, we presented such varied courses as Emergency Medical Training, Advanced First Aid, Spanish, Real Estate, Learning the Stock Market, Auto Mechanics, Drawing and Composition, Basic Law, a Book Group, and even Planning Your Future. It was an excellent program for our community, and was eventually taken over by the YPCC Employee Activities Dept.

The gradual settling-in of the new YPCC/MCA Company and its management people was interesting to observe. Those of us with longevity in the Park were not accustomed to people coming to live in the community because they were sent—or for the financial re-wards.[11] Some of those coming from the southland were basic urban-ites who could never fully understand what had drawn many of us to this place. As time passed, however, more and more of the new-comers were caught up in the mystique of Yosemite.[12] Their children couldn't resist the pull to the outdoors, to the ice rink, to Badger Pass—especially if they could look forward to skiing with Rusty someday.

By the end of the 1970s, the Yosemite Winter Club, like the Ahwahnee, had celebrated its fiftieth anniversary. The Wawona Ho-tel and the Yosemite Chapel had each celebrated a centennial. All of these events were greeted with proper respect and much fanfare. Throughout this crowded decade, the celebrations of long-estab-lished institutions were blended with the arrival of so much that was new. These traditional institutions remained our touchstones with the past as we continued our passage into the future.

20. Fire, Flood, and Other Disasters

Fate keeps on happening.
                    —Anita Loos

So much about our Yosemite was positive: the beauty of the Park, the magnificence of seasonal changes, the just plain enjoyment that could be found by visitor and resident alike. Every once in a while, however, negative aspects entered in the guise of fire, flood, rockslide, or other "act of God." These difficult times brought about community cohesiveness and some interesting experiences.

FIRE

The ominous crescendo of the NPS fire alarm was exactly what it was meant to be, an attention-grabbing, ear-splitting call to action. In the silence of the night, it could be momentarily heart stopping. Our rush to the window to check the surroundings and sky for the glow of fire was followed by the slamming of doors and the quick footfalls of our NPS neighbors hurrying to the firehouse and the waiting tanker truck. There was a point of honor in being among the first to hop aboard.

Several of the more famous, or infamous, structural fires occurred during our first two decades in the Park. First was the razing of the old Yosemite Lodge by fire in the winter of 1955–1956. That the new lodge structure was well under way gave rise to many a raised-eyebrow, knowing wink of "oh, yeah, spontaneous." But the ashes of the old were cleared away, and the new doors were open and welcoming by the following June.

On a winter night in 1964, the fire siren awakened us, followed by a quick phone call from our good friend Gary Brown, then winter ranger at Badger. The main Badger Pass lodge was afire and Gary was evacuating skis from the locker room as fast as he could. Our minds snapped awake and we shot our locker combination back to him, then awaited further news. Lee Shackelton was acting fire control officer on that blaze, a heavy-smoke affair centered in the north wall and upper passageway of the main lodge. Tons of water and much human perseverance saved the building, as the Browns provided a warming fire, hot coffee, and dry socks to the exhausted, chilled men. Repair crews jumped in the next morning, and the ski area was back in operation by the following weekend.

July 9, 1969 brought us one of the most spectacular structural fires, that of the old Glacier Point Hotel and Mountain House. The conflagration began about 9:30 P.M. The first responder was a fire crew stationed at Badger that summer[1], soon followed by engines from the Valley. It proved an exercise in futility, however, as the old tinderbox-buildings were gone in minutes. Fortunately, all of the employees escaped harm and very few trees in the surrounding area were burned. But a great chunk of Yosemite history became a mere pile of ashes that night. The fiery sky and soaring sparks made a spectacular post-July Fourth show from our front yard. Then we sped to Mirror Lake to look up at the actual blaze. The cause was later determined to be a mechanical malfunction in the hotel, with the fire spreading rapidly to the Mountain House. Those special dinners with our children on the wonderful old deck, seemingly suspended over the edge of the world, came swiftly to an end.

Temporary buildings—gift shop, snack bar, and restrooms—thrown up to get on with serving the growing number of visitors stood for nearly three decades. It was not until 1998 that the temporary buildings were replaced by handsome stone structures that blend so well into the magnificence that is Glacier Point. These works of art and the spectacular amphitheater were built with the combined funding of the NPS, the Yosemite Concession Services, the Yosemite

Fund, and a private donation from Ambassador and Mrs. Bill Lane. They are not yet steeped with history, as were the wonderful old buildings lost to the fire of 1969, but their history is in the making.

The latter part of July 1972 brought us our physically closest, and easily most frightening fire—that of the government barn not two hundred and fifty yards from our house and just across the street from the Shackeltons. Again the howl of the siren crashed into our night. This time we were aware of a bright red glow the minute we opened our eyes. Chuck and Anne were working at Tuolumne; Rob and Bets were at home. Charlie was quickly out the door to see where he was needed. Rob gathered hoses and joined Dave Shackelton to hose down neighborhood roofs threatened by flying sparks. Ti Shackelton and I grabbed our purses and any important papers we could think of to throw into our Jeep Wagoneer. We parked the younger kids with Kay Arenguena down the street. Then we waited. Since the fire had cut our neighborhood off from road access, Charlie had advised me to throw the Jeep into 4-wheel drive and cut through the schoolyard, should the need to evacuate arise. We were all cognizant of the very large propane tank in the government maintenance area not far from the blazing barn. Adrenalin pumped, as did tons of water. YPCC and NPS firefighters, together with many volunteers, joined the battle. At long last the blaze was overcome.

No one present that night will ever forget the worst nightmare of that holocaust: the screams of pain emanating from the horses and mules trapped in the burning barn. By the time they could be extricated, fourteen head of stock were beyond saving. Among them were several of the prized Morgan horses used by the NPS horse patrol. There was a deep sense of loss among the NPS rangers whose mounts did not make it through the night. That it was later deemed arson, the work of a disgruntled former employee, enraged the community. Much of the government trail stock carried the scars of that fire a lifetime. Local legend tells of the continued regard given these animals by the government packers. Although the propane tank did not blow, the damages were still around $500,000. A new barn was built and life carried on, but that night remains deeply etched on the minds of the many who were there.

There were other more routine fires—if a fire can ever be routine. Curry Village lost an old garage to arson. Its dining room and mountain shop were scarred by other fires, as was the employee dorm at the Wawona Hotel. But as newer buildings replaced the old, and as equipment and fire safety checks became more sophisticated, we seemed to hear the scream of the siren less often.

WILDFIRE

The other variety of fire seen in the Park is classified as wildfire. This type could by caused by lightning strike or be the result of human carelessness. The NPS maintained several fire crews throughout the Park during the designated fire season months. Rob was a fire crew member for several college summers. When the need arose, personnel from other divisions, even other parks, joined these crews. In our earlier years, being called out on a fire meant overtime pay—and men jumped at the opportunity. Yes, fire fighting was still a man's world. A needed appliance, new skis, even a vacation might result from this good boost to that month's paycheck. One neighbor had a clothes dryer named Rancheria, after the huge fifties conflagration in the Hetch-Hetchy region. Fire fighting was hard work—hot, dirty and grueling. Those extra dollars were dearly come by.

Using fire to fight fire, the backburning procedure, had been part of the wildfire-fighting practice for years, but using fire to prevent fire, "prescribed burning," didn't enter the Park until the early seventies. Yosemite had evolved from no fire management, pre-1886, to complete suppression of all fires with the coming of the U.S. Army. When the newly formed National Park Service took over in the twenties, "all-fire suppression" became the official policy. The NPS and the Forest Service worked cooperatively in those beginning years; then, with the formation of the Civilian Conservation Corps in 1933, the NPS gained the manpower to establish its own professional fire camps. The end of WWII brought the introduction of the helicopter and airplane to join the bulldozer as routine fire control tools. The full-suppression policy marched on.[2]

—— In 1959, the voice of Dr. Harold Biswell, of the University of California at Berkeley, began to be heard.[3] He pioneered the concept of the benefits of prescribed burning. The philosophy evolved from an analysis of fires set by early Native Americans and by lightning strikes. The Aldo Leopold Report, commissioned in 1963 to advise on wildlife management in the National Parks, mentioned the benefits of "control burning." The basic tenets of prescribed (control) burning are to have "fires in selected places, at selected times and under selected conditions of fuel moisture content, air temperature, relative humidity, wind direction and velocity, atmospheric stability and weather predictions." The basic purpose of prescribed fire is to be "in harmony with nature to reduce debris and modify plant communities to make vegetation more resistant to wildfires, thereby also helping to prevent damage and to reduce costs of fire suppression."

One of Dr. Biswell's students at UC Berkeley was Jan van Wagtendonk who, in the early seventies, came to Yosemite to be the Park's research scientist. He also became our admired friend. Jan worked to promote a prescribed natural fire program for Yosemite and was involved in years of experimentation and refinement of policy in regard to these prescribed burns. By 1988, Park policy stated "prescribed fires include fires deliberately set by managers (prescribed burns) or fires of natural origins permitted to burn under prescribed conditions (prescribed natural fires, sometimes called let-burns) to achieve predetermined resource management objectives. All fires that do not meet the criteria for prescribed fires are wildfires and will be suppressed."[4] The hue and cry arising from the huge Yellowstone National Park conflagration of 1988 brought about further study and some modification of the prescribed burn/let-burn policy.

Knowledge of this forward-thinking policy helps one understand why we often have a pall of smoke over the Valley at otherwise pristine times, why Park roads can pass through smoldering verges and smoky forests, and what is meant by the oft-posted signs "management fire—do not report." The myriad of conditions has been met and a control burn is in progress.

One of the Park's more devastating—and largest—front country wild fires occurred in August of 1990 while we were vacationing in Montana. Lightning strikes on both sides of the Merced River in the El Portal/Arch Rock area set the hillsides ablaze, and flames climbed rapidly up the slopes on both sides of the river. Again "Yosemite" screamed at us from passing newspaper headlines. We headed for a phone—and Rusty. Who else could tell us more about the state of Wawona and the Park? The amazing part, we heard later, was that our call went through. It was one of the last to do so. Rusty told us the Valley and Wawona were safe, and the Wawona Redwoods had opened its cabins to evacuees from Yosemite West. From news broadcasts along our route, we followed the devastation. On the north side of the river, the fire swept up the mountain to engulf Foresta, then jumped Highway 120 as it snakes its way along the hillside toward Crane Flat. The Arch Rock fire swept up the mountain south of the Merced River, jumped Highway 41, and then climbed until it reached the Glacier Point Road turn-off to Badger Pass. Fortunately, the road acted as a firebreak, thereby saving the Badger Pass operation. No one entering the Park since 1990 can miss seeing the scars and skeleton trees from these blazes.

We reentered Yosemite that late August through the Tioga Pass east entrance, traveled the spectacular route to Crane Flat, then held our breath as we turned down into the Valley. By the time we reached the Foresta viewpoint, we could have been on the moon. Thick gray ash everywhere, black sticks of trees, even the roadway was burned to a gray sponge. It was eerie. With hope, we looked down and found Big Meadow and its historic barn still intact, then spotted a bit of a green patch off to the southwest. Over the crest of the hill, we later heard, Shirley Sargent's Flying Spur home had been wiped out. This raging fire scarred not only trees and landscapes. Many homes were destroyed, many lives changed. Such is the power of wildfire and wind.

WIND

Wind, even without a fire to aggravate, left its mark in the chronicled dilemmas of the Valley. When severe Mono winds—the same ones that had earlier hit the children and me while camped at Tenaya—come roaring over the passes and down the canyons, falling trees often lie in the wake. Those cozy campgrounds nestled in the trees were necessarily evacuated. On a few occasions *all* Valley visitors were requested to leave. The cabins at the Yosemite Lodge were particularly vulnerable to falling trees. One guest who ducked authority to go back inside for a forgotten article was crushed when a tree hit that cabin squarely. Badger Pass, especially in its earlier, more forested days, was very vulnerable to wind-caused tree falls. In 1971, *The Yosemite Sentinel* reported that over three hundred trees blew down in the path of "an icy Mono wind." Two of the four ski lifts were damaged in the tree fall, yet the area was closed for a mere few days.

These forceful winds had much to do with the demise of Camp 6 as a summer seasonal residence area. By the late seventies most of Camp 6 was abandoned due to damage inflicted by various wind blow-downs and the swirling high water of spring run-off. The YPCC moved some of its tents to the higher ground at the east end of the camp. The rest of the area gradually became a dumping ground for chunks of asphalt and concrete. In recent years this has become the overflow parking spot for the Village Store and environs. Then came the inundation of high, rushing water in the January 1997 flood to complete the destruction of the tent city.

On a calm September day in the early eighties, a tree near the Yosemite Lodge hump bridge dropped with no warning onto one of the Company's open tramcars. There were many injuries and a call went out to all units for medically trained personnel. What could be deemed more "an act of God" than this tragedy—yet it adds a second line to my chapter subtitle: "Fate keeps on happening—*and then someone sues.*" Someone did.

WATER

One cannot live in Yosemite Valley without gaining a tremendous respect for the power of water. Falls thunder, spewing clouds of mist, rattling windows, pounding down into the streams below. Rock-grinding streams rush blindly to the Merced River. The river roars and crashes in its sweep through the Valley. This is spring run-off, a yearly happening in the Park as the snows of winter melt. This is normal. Some years see the river topping its banks with fingers reaching out into the meadows. These are the years small boys paddle through meadow pools in homemade kayaks and photographers excel at reflection shots.

What isn't normal is the set of conditions leading up to the destructive floods we have experienced in our years in the Park: those of 1955, 1964 and, indirectly, 1997. Each of these floods climaxed between December 23 and January 2—and interfered with quite a few holiday plans, as described in earlier chapters. The basic requirements for a major flood include: a fairly substantial snowpack already in place above 5,000 feet, a warming temperature, and a couple of days of heavy, constant rain. A snowpack can absorb just so much water. When the rain continues beyond the saturation point, the whole mass gives way—to slide down the sloping granite walls, as in Tenaya Canyon, or to wash into streams as in the Tuolumne and Merced Canyons. In the Valley, the tumbling creeks join the fast-rising river and the flood is on.

It was our experience while living in the Valley that knowledgeable Park personnel recognized the signs, and when the situation became ominous the river gauges were monitored religiously. Store merchandise, chapel prayer books and carpeting, personal possessions, even furniture were moved or elevated above the water's reach on the occasions when flood stage threatened. A tremendous community work-effort arose on these occasions. When the January 1, 1997, flood hit we were living in Wawona.[5] We were aware of the snowpack/warm rain conditions in the Park, and were intent on watching our own South Fork of the Merced River rise. We sensed a flood in the offing. We have since wondered what happened in the

Valley. Where was the community leadership and cohesiveness as the damage was being done? Was it missing because it was a holiday weekend? Was it missing because many of those counted on to pitch in with knowledge no longer lived in the Valley? Was it that old-timers' opinions were neither sought nor deemed important? And why did the rubble from the destruction remain blight on the land for so many months after the Park finally reopened? Where was the spirit of picking up the pieces and getting on with things so prevalent in the earlier years? Was there a plan just waiting for a catastrophe to happen? Indeed there was. The GMP soon came off the shelf and into its next phase.

SNOW

The other form of water—snow—can also become a concern on occasion. Living near a ski area as we did, the coming of the first snowstorm was heralded with glee. If Badger could be up and running by Thanksgiving, great. If it still couldn't operate by the Christmas holidays, gloom. On two occasions in our forty-eight years it opened not at all, disaster. Fortunately, the Park is not dependent upon the ski business. The state of California, however, is crucially dependent upon the water run-off from the melting Sierra snowpack. The depth of that snowpack, as well as its water content, is carefully monitored at the gauging stations in the high country. As noted earlier, Charlie had the pleasure of going along on some of these snow surveys in the early years. The information so gained has great effect on the handling of the annual run-off and its storage in the various reservoirs. The local and state water situations can become a very real dilemma when snow is sparse.

On the flip side, too much snow causes inconvenience rather than real damage in the Valley. Roads may be temporarily closed, roofs and paths may demand heavy shoveling, plans may change, isolation may temporarily set in, but it is a time of slow-down, never of real danger. In the early summer when we could again drive to Tuolumne we often saw swaths of trees swept down by a winter snow avalanche in the Tenaya Lake region. One spectacular slide swept many new snags-to-be into the southeast end of the lake. We learned to give that area a wide berth for years when out in our sailboat. Cross-country skiers in the backcountry were pre-warned during avalanche-danger times, and knew to look out for themselves.

In the springtime, when the snows are melting and the impatience of people wanting to open the Tioga Road is mounting, the area at Olmsted Point again becomes the center of controversy. That same scarred, glacially polished granite face Sierra Clubbers bemoaned is the reason this section is most critical in determining when the road can be safely opened. Granite is slick, and melting snow slides. One end-of-May opening day, Charlie and I drove toward Tuolumne to check that winter's effect on the high country. We arrived at Olmsted Point in our yellow VW bug, sunroof open to the sky, waited until the ranger signaled us through the plowed snowbank, then proceeded. No sooner had we started than we heard an ominous rumble and glanced up to see chunks of snow barreling down. We both snapped to, Charlie slammed the car into reverse, and I ground the sunroof closed as quickly as I could. A large chunk bounced off the front of the VW as we madly backed up. There was a good-sized dent in the hood and we lost a headlight, but that was the extent of it. *We* were not buried under a pile of snow. Earlier that month a snowplow working on that stretch of road had been pushed over the side by loose, sliding snow. The driver, fortunately, jumped clear.

Years later, Barry Hance was not as lucky. In the push to get the Tioga Road open, Barry and his snowplow were fatally pushed over the side of the road by a snow slide at Olmsted Point. A great sadness came from his death—and the hope that greed to get on with business would no longer get in the way of safety. Nature still rules in many cases.

ROCK

There is another, more dangerous, falling element: rock. Easily, falling rock and rock avalanches caused more deaths than any other act of nature during our Park residency. My first contact with this type of accident came in 1954. Our across-the-loop neighbor, Assistant Chief Ranger Chuck Scarborough, was killed in a rock avalanche on the John Muir section of the Nevada Falls trail. He and ranger Herb Ewing were enroute to Merced Lake that June when rocks suddenly crashed down from above. Scarborough and his horse were swept over the trail's edge. He left a wife and three daughters, one a mere baby. Our neighborhood was stunned, the whole Valley profoundly affected. Certainly Herb was left with a great sense of his own mortality.

The sound of a rockslide can be like the approach of a freight train. It can be the thunder of a jet or the shot of a cannon—or simply the muffled ping, ping of a rock or two bouncing downward. In any case, it means some degree of physical harm to anyone in its path. In many places, the walls of the Valley are susceptible to the loosening of rock and the inevitable slides. Major slides have occurred on the Yosemite Falls trail (some with fatalities), along northside drive in the Rocky Point area, on the stretch before the Highway 120 junction, and on down the road toward El Portal. The Merced River Canyon highway has been closed by slides on numerous occasions. Some of these rock-falls have closed Park roads for days, even weeks. In the early eighties, the Mammoth earthquake loosened rock on the Sierra Point trail, a lesser-used climb veering off from the Vernal Falls trail as it leaves Happy Isles. The resulting slide closed the trail permanently, with the loss of a good hike that culminated in a rewarding view. It became our habit, after a good quake-jolt, to listen for ensuing sounds of falling rock. We felt many earthquake tremors in the Valley over the years and never lost that eerie sense of "What comes next?"

We were living in Wawona when the Loma Prieta quake hit the Bay Area in October 1989. I was watching a Bay Area news broadcast on television when our kitchen cupboards began that ominous rattle. On the screen the background draperies were weaving back and forth, and then the broadcasters' explanations began. We knew it was a big one. Though the quake was felt in the Park, no damage was reported.

One of the more recent severe rock-falls occurred on July 10, 1996. Two huge blocks, sections of an arch, broke off from the cliffside just below Glacier Point, free-falling the seventeen hundred feet to the Valley floor. They landed a hundred feet out from the base of the cliff, just to the southwest of Happy Isles. The tremendous air blast created by the rocks' free fall and crash landing felled hundreds of trees, one of which killed a lingering employee. Almost immediately, the area became enveloped in a huge, widening dust cloud that resulted from the disintegration of the massive blocks. Two additional smaller blocks fell the following day. It was estimated that a total of eighty thousand tons of rock crashed into the Happy Isles forest on those two consecutive days.[6] With hundreds of downed trees, broken bridges, and a heavy, heavy cover of dust, Happy Isles was designated a disaster area and was cordoned off for many months of clean up and repair. That the rock fall happened as late as seven o'clock in the evening saved untold numbers of lives. Traditionally, hordes of people mill around that popular area during the daytime hours. It is quite sobering to contemplate the difference a few hours can make. Major rock fall has continued in this Glacier Apron/Curry Village area as the new century opens. The NPS and U.S. Geological Service are very much on an active alert.

Recently, I was enjoying one of my frequent telephone chats with grandson Jacob of Jackson Hole, Wyoming. Knowing he had just finished watching a favorite television program, I asked, "Was it a good one?" There followed a long thoughtful pause, then came his response, "Well, Gram, I wouldn't call it good. You can't really say a program about natural disasters is good—but it sure was interesting."

21. The Eighties Come Running

Being a woman should never stop you from what
you want.

—author unknown

We entered the eighties a much changed community—and nation. Many were still reeling from the repercussions of the Vietnam War and from the stunning changes in social mores. In Yosemite, life was gearing into a faster pace, but when one took the time to look around, the utter magnificence of the Valley still proved a soothing balm. This held true for visitors as well because travel to the Park was on the upswing and backcountry use at an all-time high.

FEMINISM

Feminism, a movement that arose nationally in the mid-seventies, was by this time making itself felt in the Park. There were more females on the NPS employment roll, a result of the strengthened minority hiring practices. Gradually we even began to see women trained as law enforcement rangers. As their careers advanced, both Anne and Betsy were required to have this law enforcement training for their seasonal jobs. In Anne's day of backcountry rangering she was not required to carry a gun on her person, but a decade later Betsy, a Valley horse patrol ranger, had the whole gun/mace/radio outfit strapped to her side. Each of them, fortunately, possessed the ability to use controlled conversation and common sense in their dealings with the public rather than abrupt confrontation.

Yes, women had entered the park protective division and the park interpretive division, as well as many other facets of the NPS workforce. They began to serve on trail crews, fire crews, maintenance crews, and in all aspects of office jobs. The early eighties brought Dr. Helen Clyatt onto the Yosemite Medical Clinic staff; the early nineties brought B. J. Griffin to the Park as assistant superintendent—both firsts for women in Yosemite.

In my eyes, as part of the woman as homemaker and family nurturer generation, it was the emergence of a whole new socioeconomic system. I found myself championing feminism in the definitive sense of the word. I strongly believed that women had the right to equal education and job opportunities, an equal salary scale for an equal job, equal rights before the law—and I crusaded for the ERA. I greatly admired many of these career women.

Along with my admiration and encouragement of the women in the workforce came the flip side. Questions gnawed at me. What had I done with my life, and how might it have been different had I been given the different choices, literally and traditionally. The question of self-esteem, or lack of, really hit me on our Peruvian Mountain Travel trip in 1985. As was becoming the norm, we were the oldest trekkers in a group of a dozen. This particular trip included several yuppie pairings: men and women in their late thirties, each partner a professional, all urban oriented. My low point came at dinner the first night as the question was passed around, "And what do you do?" "Homemaker" was on a level with nothingness in the early days of feminism. It was difficult for me to even get the word out of my mouth. Later, I thought about my reaction, my seeming lack of the important career skills, and my feeling of low self-esteem when confronted so suddenly that evening with the question. Then I riled at myself for my own easy acceptance of the current opinion that homemaking was a nothing career. The next time I was confronted with the question (by a rather officious academic gentleman at a friend's retirement dinner) I was able to look him in the eye. "I'm a homemaker," said I, "a job that can be one of life's broadest and most creative of professions when one takes the time to do it justice." I added that I also wrote letters (pre E-mail days) and I *listened*. Not too many people have the time to listen these days—to be there for the friends and loved-ones who need a sounding board. The gentleman must have wondered what he'd said to open that can of worms!

I managed to have short seasonal stints of doing-it-all when working for the backcountry division five springtimes in the early eighties. I gave myself the impressive title of "Backcountry Specialist" and filled a vacant slot for the three months preceding the arrival of the summer seasonals. I considered—living in the Park those many years, covering many of the trails personally, and hearing about those I hadn't from a husband who covered them all—I did have a bit of expertise in this area. (I didn't quite have business cards printed with my self-given title thereon, but I thought about it.) Even with no children at home I found it very necessary to hone skills in the management of time. As much as I enjoyed working with Ron Mackie, Laurel Munson, Mike Osborne, Trace DeSandres, and the others, by the time mid-June and the eager seasonals rolled in, I was well ready to get back to my letter writing and listening.

As the eighties brought more women into the workforce in Yosemite, the need for professional childcare became crucial. The Yosemite Child Care Center opened in 1984. The Eade-Osbornes, Lawson-Bottis, and Jim Tuckers were the driving forces behind this accomplishment. The NPS provided a residence adjacent to the schoolyard and financed the renovations needed to meet code requirements. With the support of Dan Jensen, YPCC executive, the Company gave seed money. A staff was hired and soon the venture was open and thriving. Day care became a business, and even more women entered the workplace as the job variety continued to expand.

Another important factor in the go to work trend was the increase in cost of living, including the considerable rent increases in the Park. Two incomes were essential in many instances to make ends meet. It was also becoming the thing to do. A couple of women answered my "Why did you go to work?" with "Because everyone else was working and it was no fun to stay home." Before long "the second income was making the extras possible." My hat is off to the women I still know in the Valley who are balancing job, family and the many extracurricular activities modern families seem to accumulate. My hope is that they still have time to listen—in the way that only women can.

Yes, I admire these women who are out in the various fields of the working world, my daughters and daughters-in-law among them. It certainly brings another dimension into the home. But I find, in this eighth decade of my life, that I envy them not one whit. I know myself well enough to readily admit I could not have done it all. Instead I have reaped the rewards of a way of life tradition and the times dealt to me. As for the future, I think the vote is still out on whether anyone can do it all without compromising something in the process.

SECOND CAREERS

Two of my special Yosemite ladies found cause to enter the working-world in the mid-life stage. Neither was a professional in the résumé sense of the word, but both became valued professionals before retirement. For me, they became symbols of the latent career capabilities present in many of my generation. These two were married to YPCC executives and lived in the Park in the fifties and sixties. We raised children, did good works, and had fun together. We were homemakers. Then came the seventies with changing lives and situations. When the Curry Company per se was eased out, Art and Jan Robinson moved to Mariposa where son Joe attended high school. Eileen and Henry Berrey did the same. In May of 1972, our Chuck had the painful task of meeting us at the San Francisco Airport with the shocking news that Art had suffered a fatal heart attack the previous day. He was only fifty-one, the same age as Charlie, whose birthday we had just toasted on the flight home from Europe. Art was much too young.

Jan Robinson elected to remain in Mariposa, and soon became a valued employee in the County Clerk's office, then later in a local law firm. After a few years she wanted a change of scene so moved to San Diego to add her expertise to the Academic Personnel Department of UC San Diego for a few years. Jan retired in 1987. What admiration I have for this woman with her innate charm, infectious sense of humor, and courage in absorbing and dealing with life's challenges. She is a cherished member of our extended family.

Eileen Berrey also entered a second career soon after the Berreys moved from the Park. After a brief stint at Best's Studio, Eileen joined the National Park Service. The NPS had been that bunch on the other side of the Valley and now it became *her* bunch. Henry was then the business manager of the Yosemite Association (earlier called the Yosemite Natural History Association).[1] The two drove daily up the Merced canyon from their Midpines home. Eileen's first NPS job was in the Pines Campground as fee collector, information giver, and arbiter of camper concerns. She served in the Public Information Office, with its endless queries, and she worked with the Interpretive Division in the Valley Visitor Center. She graced each of these positions with the innate sense of fairness and understanding that so marked her being. She would often be in the Visitor Center answering endless questions when I was at my backcountry permit window answering another variety of endless question. We shared many a chuckle over the foibles of the world-on-vacation.

One of the fringe benefits most enjoyed by Eileen, during those Park Service years, was her association with the younger people with whom she worked. They became her close friends and she mentor to many of them. This affection was much in evidence at Eileen's 1998 funeral in Mariposa's St. Joseph's Church. Well over half the attendees were the ages of her sons or younger. A great sense of love and respect prevailed that day.

I had known Eileen since our arrival in Yosemite in the earliest fifties. I can say I knew her well during both of her careers. The first was that of homemaker and gracious hostess at many of the Company social functions, a lady of dignity and elegance. The second was that of greeter and caretaker of the myriad of Park tourists who crossed her path daily, an often-repetitious yet important job. She managed both with much the same graciousness and intelligence. This was the essence of Eileen Berrey. That both Jan and Eileen are of *my* generation fills me with a deep sense of pride. When the chips were down, they each forged ahead into new careers—careers they graced with the dignity of our generation, the kindness of their very natures, and the humor of the ages.

THE WRENCH OF RENT HIKES

For years, one of the perks of living in Yosemite, miles from traditional services and conveniences, was the very reasonable cost of housing. This attraction began to unravel in 1982. David Stockman, advisor to President Reagan, was looking for ways to ease the national deficit. He decided the National Parks were not contributing their share of monies.[2] The Office of Management and Budget decreed that the cost of government housing must be comparable to prices charged in neighboring communities. That these prices were the inflated rates of tourist towns mattered not to the Washington bureaucrats. Rents skyrocketed—ours more than doubled—for houses that had received the minimal of government maintenance over the previous decade. While the rent increases were not commensurate with the moderate NPS salaries, the attitude of OMB appeared to be "rent is rent and pay is pay, and the two were not related."[3]

Morale in the NPS sector hit an all-time low. A protest action was mounted—and the Yosemite Tenant's Association was formed.[4] Many of us chipped in toward the necessary lawyer fees, and the battle went forward. In a 1988 explanatory letter published in *Ranger: The Journal of the Association of National Park Service Rangers* Jim Snyder wrote "The Yosemite Tenants Association is a tenant organization created by many tenants in and out of the NPS [we would be considered "out"] to achieve fair and equitable treatment for the benefit of the Park when their redress inside the service and department was clearly cut off in favor of overriding policies."[5]

The Tenant's Association brought suit against the government in 1983. Federal Judge Edward Price was appointed to hear the case.

In 1984, Judge Price issued a preliminary injunction temporarily barring collection of adjusted rents, back-dated to May 1, 1983. The case dragged on until 1988 when Judge Price finally decided for the government and dismissed the case. Many felt that justice had not been served. A study, ordered by Congress in response to the housing furor and subsequent judgment, found much of this same housing (throughout the park system) "degrading." Of five thousand employee-housing units inspected, half were found to be in "fair to poor to obsolete condition."[6]

Many employees could no longer afford to live inside the Park and pay the inflated housing costs while gaining no personal equity. Three trends came into play at this juncture: good people left the Park Service for better-paying jobs, NPS employees bought homes in areas surrounding the Park (creating a soon felt loss of community cohesiveness and an increased traffic flow on access roads), and more women went into the workforce to increase the family income.

A YEAR TO REMEMBER

Occasionally a year comes along when, to quote Emily Dickinson, "to live is so startling, it leaves time for little else." Nineteen hundred and eighty-three was just such a year for me. Treasured among my collection of Christmas ornaments is a simple disc-shaped puff of red felt on which the words "I Survived 1983" were lovingly appliquéd by Betsy.

Looking back on this landmark year, the most fascinating aspect to me is that if I were to ask my extended family members to name the remembered "event-of-the-year," each would give a different answer. For Chuck and Dana, it would be the birth of their third child and first son, Trevor, that December. For Anne and Chas it would be their Everest attempt in the fall of the year—after months and months of concentrated conditioning and preparation. For Rob it would be his marriage to Amy Riesman on July 2 in a lovely garden wedding in Pittsfield, New York. For Betsy it would be *her* marriage to Kerry Grande in the garden of the Superintendent's Old House, in September—a warm and loving Don Baldwin ceremony.

Given two chances, Betsy's second-named event would be her agonizing wait at the emergency entrance of the clinic—the wait for an NPS ambulance bringing her parents down from the high country one late July afternoon. I had fallen asleep at the wheel of our pick-up, resulting in a three hundred-foot roll down a steep embankment along the Tioga Road above Yosemite Creek.

Charlie might not want to give lip service to priorities, but I know that for him top spot for 1983 memories goes to his fight to get his compression-fractured back functioning again. His long-anticipated departure for Nepal and the Everest base camp was just a short six weeks after our accident. He worked religiously at all the right back-strengthening exercises, dispensed fatherly concern at Betsy's wedding, and was off to Nepal by September's end—pack on back.

For my ninety-year-old father, the event of 1983 was the unexpected death of his wife, Jody, early in January, leading to upheaval, unhappiness, and eventually his own death late in the year. For my brother Joe and Nancy, who took him into their Fresno home, it was watching his spirit and life ebb away, and handling the accompanying concerns.

For my brother Rob, 1983 saw the traumatic break-up of a lengthy relationship, with all of the lingering loneliness. For granddaughter Heidi, it was coming to California to celebrate her seventh birthday as a junior bridesmaid on Aunt Betsy's wedding day. For two-year-old granddaughter Betsy, it was just coming to the wedding—and to Yosemite for the first time.

For Queen Elizabeth II, I like to think the high point of 1983 was her visit to Yosemite in March. I was thrilled when we were invited to attend the special church service in our little chapel that Sunday. We passed the FBI check, I dug out a proper hat, and off we went— to be seated across the aisle, one row back, from Her Majesty and Prince Phillip. My British blood pumped!

For me, 1983 was all of the above. What a lesson in coping that year became. I think my one letdown in self-management led to our accident. I was exhausted, just out of a cast due to hand ligament surgery, and had bid an emotional farewell to Anne and Chas just two days before. I'd been lying awake at night wondering if we'd ever see them again on the one hand, and planning Betsy's upcoming wedding on the other. And so I finally fell asleep—very poor timing. I came blearily awake as our tires hit the roadside gravel and remember thinking "It's out of my hands now" as I passed out. Seat belts and a higher power saved our lives that day. And I lay in bed that night too—nursing broken ribs, bruises, and stitches—thinking "Bill Germany, if you can't cater this upcoming wedding, it's not going to happen!"[7]

In October came the unexpected death of my dear friend Anne Macaulay (of our Young Lakes trip). She was the first of my close-knit college group to go. Overnight the rest of us felt quite mortal.

When Charlie came home from Nepal later that month, just a few weeks before my dad was to die, I was truly in the depths. He, on the other hand, was on the euphoric high one picks up on those glorious Himalayan treks. The one saving grace was that I had experienced just such a high the preceding year, was prepared for the vast difference in our emotional levels, and managed to put up with him anyway.

BACKCOUNTRY NEMESES

Backcountry use was in high gear in the early eighties. The Wilderness Permit program was in full swing, and the public became educated. Backpackers reserved permits in advance or came prepared with alternative routes should quotas be filled. The growing downside to these adventures into the wilds was the invasion of *Giardia lamblia* into our heretofore pristine mountain streams and lakes. This bug is a parasitic protozoan causing intestinal problems when ingested. It was introduced into the watercourses of the west during the seventies, and can be quite debilitating unless treated. Since the host can be either human or animal, it proliferated in our backcountry. Gone were the days of trusting the purity of the running creeks and rivers. Iodine crystals, Potable Agua tablets, and, later, filter pumps became an integral part of each backpacker's gear.

An equally important item on the gear list was sufficient rope to hang one's food high above the reach of marauding bears. This feat was tricky, and as the decade progressed and bears became worldlier, more hikers came out of the backcountry early—and hungry. The bear boxes and canisters of the nineties were soon on the drawing board.

BITS AND PIECES

In the Valley, during the eighties, the Art Center was established in the old Pohono Studio near the post office. The Vintners' and Chefs' Dinners were initiated at the Ahwahnee during the less crowded winter months. The Peregrine falcon program was instigated to protect that endangered species. Climbing routes on El Capitan would be closed to all comers if a falcon's nest was discovered in the vacinity. Actor Lee Stetson began his increasingly popular John Muir impersonation programs at the Visitor Center, becoming John Muir to a whole generation. Father Rod Craig came to the Valley, became friend to all, and stayed too short a time. The Keay family was our downhill neighbor, and the Ingrams of Yosemite West came into our lives. Rotary International arrived as the Lion's Club dwindled, making one wonder why add a *new* and not support the *old?* October of 1983 brought the 500th meeting of the Conversation Club. Former members gathered with present members for a fitting tribute and a gracious Wawona Hotel dinner served in the solarium. Since Charlie was then in Nepal, I went with Hal and Barbara Morris, up from Santa Cruz.

In 1984, Ansel Adams died. He was honored that summer with the earlier-mentioned gathering of dignitaries and friends in the lovely Parsons Lodge area of Tuolumne Meadows. It was a sparkling high country day, worthy of the gifted photographer and the formal dedication of his Mt. Ansel Adams. Yosemite National Park received its own honor the following year when it was added to the World Heritage List. It joined 187 other similarly honored sites around the world, including nine other U.S. National Parks.

The Wawona Hotel was the scene of another gala in 1984, the fiftieth wedding anniversary of Pat and Avery Sturm. Charlie, Jan

Robinson, and I had the honor of being seated with three outstanding couples—Pat and Avery, Charley and Mary Proctor, and Katherine and Tom Coakley—all of whom had celebrated fifty years of marriage.[8] Pretty impressive statistics! Sitting under those fragrant pine trees on that sloping verdant lawn brought back memories of earlier good times when our family rendezvoused with my brother Joe and wife Nancy Polhemus, up from Fresno with their Deb, Steve and Martha. These were the special occasions that found the youngsters polished and sparkling in anticipation of dinner in that historic hotel dining room. The hotel, so reminiscent of old New England establishments (white façade, covered porches, wicker furniture and all), continued to stand out as a true place of charm and grace throughout our Park years.

In the early eighties a local Park Service committee started a much-enjoyed tradition, still in existence these many years later. The Yosemite Alumni Picnic is held on the lawns of the Wawona Hotel each mid-September. In the very first years it was a gathering of NPS employees and retirees who had served in Yosemite at some point in their careers. This was soon expanded to include anyone who had worked in Yosemite—and we got in on the fun. And fun it was when old friends turned up in droves. The schedule of events included a golf tournament in the morning, followed by a social hour and an excellent mid-afternoon alfresco dinner put on by the Company. Following the dinner, the annual Yosemite Alumni Award was presented to a person or couple in honor of notable community involvement. Early recipients were Carl Sharsmith, Shirley Sargent, Ferdinand Castillo, Avery Sturm, Virginia Adams, and Walt Castle among others. Charlie and I were so honored, along with the Tommy Tuckers, in 1993. We deeply appreciated being selected, and I appreciated the fact that this was an occasion when couples had been honored. This was relatively new thinking. No one deserved inclusion more than Pat Sturm, along with Avery, but it just wasn't done in that manner when he received the award.

The mid-eighties brought the Gormans to the Park, with Mary Ellen soon spearheading the revitalization of the Book Group. A good discussion group evolved with Kay Pitts, Anne Graham, Linda Abbott, Mary Vocelka, and others. Pat and Jack Morehead returned for an unprecedented third round in the Park. Jack was now our superintendent and moved the superintendency back into Park housing. Roger and Nancy Rudolph came back, with two children in tow. Roger served as chief ranger for several years. B.J. Griffin came, our first female assistant superintendent. She was later to return in the nineties as the first Yosemite National Park female superintendent. How very different from the fifties.

The medical clinic underwent another transition. Good Samaritan, a medical management group from Southern California, took over its supervision. No longer were our doctors responsible for the administration facet of the Clinic. The medical staff at this time consisted of Jim Wurgler, Gary Flashner, Mike Schankerman, and Bill Bowie (seasonally). In 1988, the year after we moved to Wawona, Jim and Jody Wurgler also left the Valley. Jim went to head up Good Samaritan's operation in Grand Canyon National Park in Arizona. They were much missed by the Yosemite community.

SCHOOL DAYS

The entity changing the least during our Park tenure was the Yosemite Elementary School with its Kindergarten–eighth grades. Certainly the enrollment numbers vacillated, teachers and principals came and went, and the Parent Group evolved into the Parent Teachers League, but the school remained the nucleus of community activities. By the nineties it could be said to be the one remaining hub of activities for the Yosemite community. Sports programs, the ski program, and scouting involved the school, if only for facility use. Parent volunteers aided in the library, on field trips, and in classrooms. I did a stint in Mrs. Shackelton's primary room early in the eighties, long after our own were beyond college. I thoroughly enjoyed working with the youngsters. The group I came to know are now well beyond college.

Ti Shackelton, like Bona Mae McHenry and Pauline Trabucco before her, *stayed* and became much loved by her small students over the years. Ti first aided at YES in the early seventies when the family returned from duty in Hawaii Volcanoes National Park. When a staff position opened, she took over the first and second grades. At this time, numbers being down, Pauline Trabucco taught a combined Yosemite-El Portal kindergarten in El Portal. When Pauline retired, the Yosemite kinders came home to Ti, and there they remained until Ti's retirement in 1999. The community, together with returning friends and students, gathered on the school grounds that Saturday in June to honor Ti Shackelton with just the kind of gathering she loved. It was an old-timey potluck school picnic enjoyed by kids of all ages. For the Yosemite Elementary School, Ti had proven to be a wonderful "bridge" those last few years, the necessary connection between what had been and what was to come—and a special lady in my book.

To Charlie and me, the first half of the decade brought two more Vermont grandchildren: Betsy Anne in early 1981 and Trevor in late 1983. Our in-law family was completed in the persons of Amy Riesman and Kerry Grande. And the two of us launched into our overseas adventure travels with gusto.

As the eighties progressed, we became acutely aware that our days in the dental office and in the Valley were winding down. We—along with a very few others—were now the elders in the Park. Where had the years gone? Charlie decided that he would retire in 1987, when he reached the age of sixty-five. Again that unique facet of Yosemite life surfaced: One could not reside in the Valley once the job had terminated. Our job was nearly over. We needed to discuss a move.

22. Our Wawona

I've learned that children and grandparents are natural allies.

—*Jackson Brown, Jr.*

Living in the Park for thirty-five years had spoiled us for the return to a metropolis. This we knew as we faced retirement, but the question of where to reestablish proved a dilemma. And then we turned to our ace in the hole: Wawona, the property we had purchased in 1953. We seldom used the Wawona cabin as the children were growing up, lying as it did so close to our Valley home. It was rental property, first for summer tourist trade, under the care of Harold and Norman May, later for long-term employee housing. In those days of low-cost housing shortage in the Park, it was difficult to say no to calls begging for permission to rent the cabin. Though we enlarged and winterized it along the way, the cabin was not what we wanted for a retirement home. Our building consultants helped us make a momentous decision in the spring of 1985: to tear down what was there and start from scratch.

A BIT OF HISTORY

For all of the years we have been associated with the Park, Wawona, its inholders, and its politics have been the bane of the National Park Service's existence. When the Washburn family, long-time innkeepers in what became Wawona, sold their real property (some 2,665 acres, including the hotel buildings) to the U.S. government in 1932,

Section 35 remained as privately owned land.[1] Al Bruce had filed claim to a 160-acre Wawona parcel in 1885 when John Washburn let his claim to this land lapse. The claim was added to the 160 acres Bruce already owned giving him title to a half section of land. The government's acquisition of the remaining Washburn property in 1932 left the privately owned (by the Bruce family and others) 640 acres of Section 35 completely encircled by Yosemite National Park. Section 35 became an inholding in the definitive sense of the word.[2]

In 1950, Rusty Rust and Bill Ellis purchased an acre of Section 35 from Babe Tognazini (of the Bruce family). When the Ellises moved from the Park in 1953, we bought their half-acre as future equity. We were naively unaware of the hassles we were taking on by becoming inholders. We went quietly about finishing the small, rustic cabin Bill Ellis had begun. The first overt move on the part of the NPS to let us know they were not looking kindly on inholders came later that decade. We were informed that Charlie's concession contract would not be renewed if we failed to give the government the option on our land. A locally respected lawyer advised the NPS that this maneuver was deemed unconstitutional, and the matter rested.

In August 1965, then Superintendent Preston released to the press the news of a potential Land Acquisition Policy, which would affect Yosemite inholders.[3] Our ears perked up. The plan to purchase national park inholdings—privately owned land lying within Park boundaries—was an ongoing part of Mission 66. A land acquisition team was at work in Washington to determine the feasibility of the government's continuing to spend the large amount of money required to purchase developed (i.e., property with building thereon) land in Wawona's Section 35. Should the government, instead, concentrate on the purchase of undeveloped lots, with purchase of developed lands made only when the owner approached the government and only if monies were available? A year later, the government was put into the position of having to buy one hundred sixty acres of adjoining Section 36 for $175,000 from a land development company whose first roads were defacing the polished granite of the very visible Wawona Dome.

In the seventies, the National Park Service again began an aggressive land acquisition policy in Section 35—and in other National Parks plagued by inholdings. Property owners were approached by the U.S. government land agents with offers to buy. Some eagerly sold and moved on. Some not so eagerly sold with a leaseback arrangement of ten, fifteen, or twenty years, or the lifetime of owner.[4] Some owners sensed a threat of condemnation in the case of noncompliance. These, too, grudgingly sold out. We quietly hung on.

Into the forefront of the fight stepped Charles Cushman. Cushman was a dynamic, out-spoken Wawona property owner who objected vociferously to the NPS tactics and intent. In 1978, he led in organizing the National Inholders Association (NIA) and took the battle state- and nationwide.[5] California's U.S. Representative Phillip Burton had introduced a bill in the House that year to buy up all private inholdings in the national parks within four years. The NIA garnered enough support to defeat the bill. The pressure eased in Wawona. In the years to follow, however, Cushman went too far right for our taste. Although he began as an environmentalist, he became soured by the Wawona experience. "He became very good at selling anti-green agenda," wrote Margaret Knox in a spring 1993 article for *Wilderness* magazine.

The NPS's stated goal during this aggressive land purchase of the late seventies was to restore Section 35 to wilderness. Those selling outright to the government did so with the sense that the structures would be removed as they were purchased. This happened in relatively few cases. The policy shifted somewhere along the line toward maintaining the acquired buildings for NPS use. Tensions between the NPS and the property owners increased. This era was not one of the National Park Service's shining hours in regard to Wawona community relationships. The Park Service had definitely shifted emphasis from "create wilderness" in Section 35 to "use acquired houses for NPS needs." Our response to this shift was that our property would be better off under our care than as part of the NPS assemblage. Again, we quietly hung on. The U.S. government eventually ran out of acquisition money, the aggression ended, and the Park Service now owned, or had on leaseback, a glut of houses. Many of these acquisitions are not structurally adequate for year round use. It took a considerable financial outlay in the nineties to bring even a few up to the year-round standards of NPS housing.

ON BUILDING A HOME

In the spring of 1985, we decided to put aside "quietly hanging on" and take an active roll in Wawona. As a result, we spent much of the next two years learning the ins and outs of building a house. Another Woessner adventure was under way as we worked many hours each week, sometimes alone, more often with our capable builders Tre Ford, Lee Gallagher, and their crew. There wasn't a fixture, door, surface or knob that Charlie and I didn't handpick at the appropriate outlet in Fresno. We became the ultimate go-fers, and the Friday providers of paychecks and cookies. We worked hard—and we had fun. My specific jobs evolved into sanding boards and painting the inside walls. I spent hours balanced on a ladder. Charlie's expertise came through in measuring and sawing boards, and, later, tackling the electrical wiring. Many of the practical-but-charming features of the house resulted from our being on the spot when the "this way, that way, or how?" decisions were made. It was a positive experience for us both, and one our marriage survived. Once we agreed on the project's direction, it just flowed.

By the end of the summer of 1987, the house had come together nicely. We met the stringent NPS and Mariposa County (now much involved in Wawona planning) rules and regulations. The result was a wonderful house: a large multiuse central room—the great hall— with bedroom wings off to the east and west. Now we only awaited the completion of the NPS community sewer system. By mid-October we were connected, passed all inspections, and moved out of the Valley.

Moved out of the Valley. Five such easy words to write, five such traumatic words to accept. After our thirty-seven years of living in the midst of the comings and goings of so many Park Service and other friends, it was not an easy transition. One of the hardest things to accept was that—as far as NPS officialdom was concerned—the Woessners were no longer a "we." We had become a "they." We were the outsiders. This feature of the transition had not occurred to me until we were in the middle of it. And it hurt.

In the month following our move, Betsy and Kerry completed their move to Hagerman, Idaho, the first step in Kerry's U.S. Fish and Wildlife career and Betsy's final step out of Yosemite. And then we lost our beloved Pat Sturm to cancer. We would never be able to share our new home with her. It was a bleak winter's beginning.

LOOKING AROUND

In the two years spent building our Wawona home, I had taken little time to absorb the make-up of the community around us. In retrospect, I realize we were too involved in the job at hand to notice the comings and goings. So it came as a shock to me to discover that there were not going to be potential friends in many of the houses surrounding us. True, these were privately owned or leaseback cabins[6] but they were short-term rentals, handled through either the Redwoods Corporation or Norman May's Camp Chilnualna. Others were privately owned, sporadically occupied in the summer months, and stood forlornly empty much of the year. For the number of houses in Wawona's Section 35, the number of permanent residents was disappointingly low. We had, it seems, traded one type of resort area for another.

The make-up of the permanent population in Wawona, well under a hundred, is a conglomerate mix. It is composed of NPS personnel; Company employees, many of them seasonal; a few self-employed or employed outside the Park persons; and the group of retirees we joined.

The Wawona area, in the NPS sense, is headquarters for the southern end of the Park. It has a ranger office, maintenance facilities and a fire control division. A segment of the permanent population of Wawona is comprised of needed NPS personnel, although there is a growing trend to own a home outside the Park and commute to the work place. Conversely, a few Wawona residents commute to NPS jobs in the Valley.

The Company's seasonal operations of the Wawona Hotel and the Badger Pass ski area bring younger, more transient employees into the Wawona residential scene. There are a few people who are self-employed or commute to work outside the Park. Among the former are the owner/proprietor of the Pine Tree Market, the manager/owners of the Redwoods operation and Camp Chilnualna, and the Wawona Elementary School personnel.

Added to these numbers are the two- to three-dozen retirees like us, with another like contingent coming for the summer season. Many of the permanent resident retirees have owned their cabins for years, enjoyed them seasonally with their families, then permanently established in Wawona when retirement came.

We soon discovered many former patients of Charlie's and were heartily welcomed into our new community. Among the welcomers were the Yosts, Flowers, Bassetts, McKinnys, Mays and LaCroixs. We soon met the Stuckys, Pauline Eaton, the Sischos, and DeLorias. We were not golfers, but they accepted us anyway. We renewed acquaintance with Lurline Atardo, the Lobergs from earlier Valley days, and the Krauses from Betsy's ski racing days.

Then, with his retirement from the post office in 1990, Rusty and Jane Rust joined us on our hillside. The joy was clouded, however, by the knowledge that Rusty had been diagnosed with colon cancer. His retirement party that winter was an outpouring of love from both locals and the many who returned from near and far, our four children among them

Rusty died in January 1992. That day the Park lost one of its greatest admirers—and the Yosemite community, one of its most dedicated workers. Jane continues to live in Wawona, and was our close friend and neighbor for many more years. Her home became the gathering place and haven for several generations of family.

SLEEPY HOLLOW

Not long after our move to Wawona, I was cheerily greeted outside the post office with "Welcome to Sleepy Hollow." And so it was—until an article appeared in *Sunset Magazine* extolling the virtues of the southern end of Yosemite National Park and telling the world of its treasured quiet spots. About the same time large hotel/motel complexes began to spring up in the Fish Camp and Oakhurst areas, and bus use mushroomed. We noted little decrease in private vehicle use, however. The Mariposa Grove of Big Trees became the area's prime attraction. When the grove road was snow-free and open, its small parking lot filled immediately, as did the miniscule parking area at the Park's entrance station on Highway 41. The Wawona parking lots—designated or makeshift—absorbed the rest of the cars. Their passengers happily took advantage of the new, free shuttle buses to the grove.

Sleepy Hollow it was no longer. We soon resorted to habits gleaned from Valley summers when one's post office or store trip revolved around tourist hours. Our special river swimming holes became inundated with people who didn't seem to mind stepping over and around bodies to reach the crowded pools. The glorious southern end of the Park had indeed been discovered.

LOOKING BACK

We kept our Valley connections over the next decade, and watched friends move on to other positions, other places, or into retirement. The biggest exodus came with the transfer of the concession contract from Music Corporation of America to Delaware North, a company based in Buffalo, New York, in late 1993. The Yosemite Park and Curry Company name was used no longer. The Yosemite Concessions Services had taken over.

When we moved from the Valley, Jack Morehead was still at the helm of the local NPS. Jack was succeeded by Mike Finley; B. J. Griffin, the Park's first woman superintendent; and Stan Albright in the years of our Wawona tenure. By attrition our contact with Valley Park Service personnel dwindled and we missed this connection.

The Good Samaritan group opted not to rebid on the medical concession contract sometime toward the mid-nineties. A medical group from Modesto picked up the contract. By this time we had turned to Fresno and Oakhurst for our medical needs. Gradually our Valley ties loosened.

LOOKING FORWARD

Charlie and I appreciated that Wawona made an easy home base for our expanding travels. To come and go proved quite uncomplicated. No house sitter needed, simply turn off the water heater, lock the doors, leave "hold the mail" and "stop the paper" instructions, and off we went.

Wawona also proved to be a welcoming place for grandchildren—and we all shared some glorious days. As the Valley had been the Yosemite touchstone for our four, so Wawona became the Park touchstone for our six younger grandchildren, all born after we left the Valley. From Colorado came Emily and Catie Woessner, from Jackson Hole came Jacob and Collin Grande, and over the mountains from Carson City came Anna and Charlie Macquarie. Heidi, Betsy, and Trevor Woessner, who were old enough to have enjoyed Valley visits, came from distant Vermont whenever they could. All loved hanging out by the river and sliding down the slippery, stream-covered granite boulders at the "school pool." They relished the hikes and tram rides through the Big Trees, perhaps followed by a quick dip in the hotel pool. There was a myriad of things to do up at Swinging Bridge, from paddling around as a tot, to sliding down the wet granite on an inner tube or perhaps jumping off the swaying bridge when daring-do struck as a pre-teen.

This was the legacy of Wawona for the Woessner grandchildren. There were outings to Glacier Point, hikes to Taft Point, excursions to sample Valley beaches, even a Tenaya picnic on occasion. Then it was home to Wawona and a joint-effort dinner. With these treasured events, Yosemite became their Park too. Charlie and I felt twice blessed to be able to provide for our grandchildren much that had been the history of their parents. In many ways our twelve Wawona years were unlike our Valley years, but they became a comfortable final chapter to our precious Park years.

In the later nineties the pull to be near family, to have needed amenities closer at hand, to lessen the load of snow shoveling and log-splitting, and perhaps simply the lure of a new adventure culminated in bringing our Wawona—and Park—years to a close. We moved over the Sierra to Carson City, Nevada—and Anne's family—in October of 1998.

23. Life with an Adventurer

You cannot discover new oceans unless you have the courage
to lose sight of the shore.
                                    —*Adapted from Andre Gide*

I came to this marriage, and to Yosemite, from a conservative, me-
thodical family. If we did one thing a week above and beyond the
routine, it was a big week. I joined with one who had been raised in
much the same school but had long since kicked over the traces. One
of Charlie's first pronouncements, upon our settling in, was that this
was not to be the kind of household where "the Drano was put down
the drain every Tuesday." I knew exactly what he meant. If we
wanted to do something—and the job didn't need him—that was
the day to get out and go. Later-learned lessons included not letting
the weather get in the way of an outing and not waiting around all
day for the occasional person who vaguely said he might drop by.

I discovered, however, that one doesn't jump from being a Timid
Tilly into the role of true adventurer overnight. It was difficult to put
aside my innate distrust of the unknown. But slowly, very slowly,
with Charlie's urging, the reticence lessened. My sense of adventure
grew. Practically speaking, I knew the adventures were going to be
had in any case, and I decided I was not going to be left out. We
began with a lot of picnicking, camping, and exploring in the Park,
then branched out to the east side of the Sierra. Adding babies and
small children to the entourage did not make us home-bound,
though it did slow me down a bit.

I worked hard to hone my adventure skills in the early years, while our children seemed to be born with adventure in their blood. Each was a trooper. My own adventure-growth went on hold during their earliest childhood years. After all, how many times would an eager-to-get-out couple push a stroller up the horse trail to the top of Vernal Falls in the springtime? Exactly once! Charlie had no trouble finding hiking/backpacking comrades in those days—and eventually his own boys earned the right to be included. I know my daughters and daughters-in-law a generation later would not put up with being left at home with little ones quite as willingly as I, but that was simply the way it was done in those days, no apologies to the feminists.

As the kids grew we ventured further afield, covering the parks of Yellowstone, Teton, Rocky Mountain, our beloved red rock country of Arches and Canyonlands, Bryce, Zion, and Grand Canyon. Having friends in many of these parks over the years added zest to the fun of exploring of them. We were often the beneficiaries of some quite special grand tours. Affection for these western parks grew strong in the hearts of the whole family, and is sifting down to the third generation as their horizons expand.

A unique trip was announced in our *Sierra Club Bulletin* for Easter week 1962. It was the club's first-ever camping trip on the Big Island in Hawaii. We signed up, parked two-year-old Betsy with the Conners in Alameda, and off the five of us flew. We joined our friends the McKeans along the way, landed in Hilo, were welcomed with leis, assigned to our transport vehicles and were soon on our way. We camped in Hawaii Volcanoes National Park, on the slopes of Mauna Kea, and on pristine beaches. We had some quite important Sierra Clubbers with us in the persons of Stuart Kimball, Lewis Clark, and the Ed Wayburns, delightful people all. The group proved a good mixture of types and ages, and great fun for the kids. Several people climbed Mauna Kea; all enjoyed the beaches. Our last night was spent in the campground at lovely Hapuna Beach, quite near the future site of Rockefeller's Mauna Kea Beach Resort. We were deluged with rain that last evening. People—and the ubiquitous cockroaches—quickly took refuge under nearby shelters. We brought home some wet, musty camping gear on the plane the next day, and I have always wondered how many Hawaiian cockroaches entered sacrosanct California in those same damp sleeping bags.

THE GRAND

I had my next true adventure ten years later. This one went down in the annals of family history as "the greening of Mom." I was invited to join Kathy Betts (then in the Tetons), Connie Metherell (coming from Cedar City, Utah), and Nancy Maynard (still living in Yosemite) for a raft trip running the Colorado River through the magnificent Grand Canyon. The trip was under the auspices of Grand Canyon Expeditions, river guide Ron Smith's outfit based in Kanab, Utah. Our group consisted of thirteen paying customers and three boatmen, divided between two motorized pontoon rafts. After putting in at Lee's Ferry below Glen Canyon Dam, we were ten awe-inspiring days on the river, going all the way to Lake Mead. We reveled in being just ourselves—no one's wife, no one's mother, no one's cook. This sense of freedom, added to the grandeur of the canyon, the thrill of running its rapids, and the evolving camaraderie created a heady, never to be forgotten experience. The adventure also proved to be the greening of another: a bouncy, solo young lady on leave from a Chicago nine-to-five desk job. Her plan was to get off the river at Phantom Ranch, vacation over. When the time came, however, she was so immersed in the canyon's spell that she called her boss from the wilderness phone at Phantom and told him she was taking an extra week. If the job wasn't still hers on return, "shove it!" And on she went with us, to the very end of the line at Lake Mead. I gave Charlie the birthday present of just such a trip some years later, and went back myself. Strong is the pull of this Colorado River and its path through the ages.

SO MUCH TO SEE

The years busily moved along, the travels continued, with the Valley, then Wawona, as a great home base. Charlie and I had neither the time nor means to get into adventuring in other countries, on other continents until our four were out of college—and then we didn't stop. The banner kick-off year for us was 1980. We took another group tour, to New Zealand, which culminated in the spectacular trek of the famed Milford Track. That magnificent hike, the noteworthy New Zealand ice cream, and the camaraderie of the group made the trip a huge success, and whetted our appetite for more.

The following summer I went back to trip over my family roots in Britain with Shirley Conner and her sister Natalie Hamilton. Natalie had the use of a car, and we made the most of it—from the cliffs of Dover to the Highlands of Scotland. Among the many highlights on that trip was meeting son-in-law Chas's parents, Charlie and Elisabeth Macquarie.

To round out the busy year, we joined my brother Joe and wife Nancy for our first trip to Oaxaca, Mexico that November. Their Deborah, married to a Oaxacanio, still lives in the lovely, old colonial city. She and Enrique proved superior guides. It was on this trip that we had the joy of discovering Puerto Escondido, a sleepy village with pristine beaches, on the southwestern coast. We also experienced the mystical place in the mountains of Chiapas that is San Cristobal de Las Casas. I can still hear the cadence of many sandled feet as they passed beneath our hotel window early on a fog-shrouded morning. It was market day in San Cristobal and heavy loads were on the backs of those heading for the town square.

AN ENCHANTING WORLD

Toward the end of 1981, when the travel urge again tugged, Charlie casually asked if I would like to go on a cruise. I think my mouth fell open—I *know* my mind registered disbelief. I really thought he'd flipped out, this man who hates dressing up, to say nothing of being confined to the deck of a ship (after long stints at sea during WWII). I countered with, "You've got to be kidding. Are you prepared for costume parties and Captain's dinners?" Thinking fast, I added "How about some kind of an adventure trip?"

I have come to the conclusion that true adventurers share a common "What the hell, let's see what's around the next bend. Might miss something great if we stop now" attitude. Charlie, now into his eighth decade, is still of this persuasion. Had he lived during the mid-eighteen hundreds, he would have led his wagon train west across the prairies and through the passes. I never was able to conjure up that kind of fearlessness, but I gave it a good try. Living in Yosemite spurred me on. It nurtured the desire to see far-flung places and provided the setting in which to train for these ventures. And train I did for our next venture: Nepal. We were just emerging from winter, and few trails were snow-free. I wore a rut between our house and Curry Village, my daily hike. I climbed to Columbia Point several times. We managed to do the Hite Cove trail just once too often, leaving me to wonder if they would even let me into Nepal with oozing poison oak covering one arm. Repetitious and dull as these walks may sound, the efforts paid off handsomely when we got on the ancient up and down trails in Nepal.

So there we were, in the spring of 1982, launched on the trek of my lifetime: the spectacular Kali Gandaki Gorge in Nepal. This deep river gorge lies between the soaring, snow-clad peaks of the Annapurnas and Dhaulagiri. "*Om mani padme hum*: Blessed is the jewel born in the lotus." It was a journey to the unknown, an encounter with a beautiful country and people, a memory to last forever. That Anne was there, successfully scaling her own Ama Dablam, made it an even more cherished journey. We trekked nearly one hundred and fifty miles in eighteen days, and the three all-important trek necessities—comfortable hiking boots, a cozy sleeping bag and congenial travel mates—performed above and beyond. The tinkling bells, announcing an oncoming donkey train in that car-less country, still ring in my memory. The wafting fragrance of huge daphne bushes and the grandeur of the rhododendron trees were breathtaking. My calves can still feel the steep climb of the stone-staired trails carved long before the invention of the switchback. In Nepal, one seems to go up—to come down. Always present were the snow-capped majesties that surrounded us and spurred us on, and the lovely, smiling faces of the children in every village we passed. It was a glorious adventure. Namaste, Nepal.

I had great hopes of returning the following year to accompany Charlie on the trek to the Everest base camp where Anne and Chas would be climbing with the American Men and Women on Everest group. However, to my great disappointment, earlier-noted family commitments and crises deemed otherwise.

In spite of the worry number I managed to do on myself before each adventure, I loved them. I didn't expect accommodations to be grand, I didn't mind a good tramp each day, and I enjoyed experimenting with the different foods. The tales of various plumbing facilities, or lack of, could fill a separate chapter—and provide many a chuckle. I marveled at how clean one could feel after the use of a single pan of warm washing water delivered to the tent each evening, and I hummed a few bars of Kris Kristofferson as each morning I donned my "cleanest dirty shirt." We reveled in the camaraderie of the evenings—the coming together—be it in a dining tent (Nepal and Peru), around a campfire (Africa and Alaska), or on the deck of a small ship (the Galápagos and Turkey). I was hooked—on the world, as well as on Yosemite.

CLIMBING TO THE CLOUDS, DIPPING IN THE SEA

In April 1985, just before we delved seriously into our Wawona project, we went south, to trek the ancient Inca Trail to Machu Picchu in the high Andes of Peru. The *feeling* of this trip, from the very beginning, lacked the welcoming spirit and security we had encountered in Nepal. Since all American planes were banned from Peru at the time, we flew into Guayaquil, Equador, changed to a Peruvian airline, and flew on to Lima. At both the Guayaquil and Lima Airports we encountered patrolling military. Innocents that we were, we found it a bit disconcerting. It was at this time the Shining Path guerilla forces were gathering a sizeable following in the Andean mountain villages. Inflation was rampant, and the natives were suffering. Many were moving into Lima, to makeshift huts, attempting to eke out a living by selling odds and ends on the street corners. Smiles were rare among the populace; faces and backs were old at twenty.

Amid the seeming turmoil, our group came together in the Lima hotel and we flew on to Cuzco. Lying as it does at an 11,000-foot elevation in the Andes, Cuzco was our acclimation spot. After a chew on the prescribed coca leaves to allay altitude headaches, we felt fine. We remained in Cuzco for a couple of days, exploring at will. The nearby Incan ruins were intriguing: How had the ancient people transported these giant boulders? How had they been able to so perfectly fit the huge building blocks together? We heard a fascinating legend telling of the ancients' ability to soften the rock, mold it, and then return it to the solid state—to withstand the ages.

Then one morning we were on our way to Machu Picchu. We met our porters at the trailhead, added our gear to their loads, and were soon on the trail. We were four nights on this trek but, unlike our experience with the Sherpas of Nepal, rapport was never established with our Quechuan porters. They were not surly, but theirs were the stoic, non-smiling Indian countenances, and they were intent on doing the job. We wound our way up over steep, high passes, again climbed ancient stone stairways, and marveled, between gasps for air, at the views. We explored the smaller Incan ruins encountered along the way. My favorite, Winay-Wayna, was still in the beginning stages of excavation. There lay the outline of huge stone structures, still completely enmeshed in climbing, green vines. Mysterious and enchanting. We approached Machu Picchu from above, literally rounding a corner to find it lying along its own ridge beneath us. The train tourists had gathered for their late afternoon departure and were soon away. Except for the few who shared the small hotel, we had the magnificence to ourselves that evening and until train time the next morning. We explored in wondrous solitude and communed with the ancient artisans.

It was while on this Peruvian trip that I became aware of the similarities in much of the flora the world over. We hiked through a myriad of blooms on this trek: scotch broom, salvia, cosmos, fibrous begonias, and the many kinds of orchids. Never mind that they were differently named, or that their colors didn't always jibe with our familiar ones, they were definitely family-connected. I also became quite aware, soon thereafter, that I am not a jungle person. Our Machu Picchu adventure was followed by a hot, steamy, itchy two-night interlude in a game refuge on an Amazon tributary before we flew back to Lima—and I hated it. I was too-soon ready to be off to the Galápagos, bug bites and all. It has been my experience the world over that bugs absolutely love me.

The Galápagos is bird-lover country as well as a place to get right down to the evolution of things. It is now an Ecuadorian National Park—with strict rules—and it is well cared for. Other than one land-dwelling area, visitors to the islands must live aboard the ships, sailing or motor, small or large. The number of people allowed on any one island at a time is very closely regulated. The Ecuadorians have done a fine control job. We saw many birds, including the Magnificent Frigate bird, the silly Blue-footed Boobies, several varieties of Darwin's finches, and the lovely Vermillion Flycatcher. We saw marine and land iguanas, and the delicate Sally-lightfoot crabs. The famous Galápagos tortoises we viewed only in captivity as the island where they roam freely, Isabella, was closed by fire. Ten of us lived for a week on our small craft, with its capable, friendly crew of three, and basked in looking at the world around us and in being lazy. We visited many islands, and snorkeled with the seals, penguins, and some friendly sharks. In turn, we introduced our Ecuadorian crew to the mysteries of an Easter egg hunt. It was a perfect way to unwind from the rigors of Peru.

ON SAFARI, WITH CAMERA AND CURIOSITY

By late 1988, we were well settled into our Wawona digs when the wanderlust surfaced again. It wasn't difficult to pick our next destination: East Africa. After poring over the catalogue from Overseas Adventure Travel of Cambridge, Massachusetts, we opted for the Serengeti Tented Safari, a two-week trip centered entirely in Tanzania. This camera safari included the Rift Valley Maasai country; the Serengeti National Park, with its endless plains and migratory paths;

the Olduvai Gorge, scene of Leakey archeological discoveries; Lake Manyara National Park; and what turned out to be the high point of the trip: the Ngorongoro Crater.

The journey to Arusha via Amsterdam and Dar-Es-Salaam proved to be the longest getting-somewhere project in our travels thus far. Flying over the vastness that is Africa can make one feel very insignificant and far from home. Finally, we arrived and were taken in hand by our capable guides. We were divided into two groups of fourteen, each group assigned to a crew of four natives and one yellow truck. Off we went early the next morning. Half of our group of fourteen was an extended family from Brazil, which added further to the exotic flavor of the trip. Along with African animal and native lore, we learned much about life among the upper class in Brazil.

Our yellow truck was large—and powerful. It had comfortable bench-like seats and canvas siding that could be rolled down in inclement weather. Everything needed to survive for two weeks was loaded into its proper compartment on the vehicle: duffels, tents, food, preparation equipment, tables, chairs, and a huge water tank to be refilled along the way when clean water sources could be found. This was a true camping safari. Only once were we shown how to put up our tent: Then we were on our own.

It was a bit rugged in places, but our complete self-sufficiency made possible camps in the more rewarding animal-sighting areas. We were fortunate in that we saw all the animals we had hoped to see. Among them were leopards, white and black rhinos, lazy hippos, and lions in abundance. We sighted speedy cheetahs, and many loveable, gangling giraffes. We saw saggy-baggy elephants in their regal splendor, elephants of all sizes.

Nineteen hundred and eighty-nine was one of the last years camping was allowed on the floor of Ngorongoro Crater. Now safaris stay on the rim, day-trip down into the Crater—and miss a lot. It was an eerie feeling to lie snug in one's tent knowing that a herd of water buffalo could be bedded down among the trees not two hundred yards away. And it was breathtaking to behold an ancient matriarchal elephant come lumbering through the nearby trees. We saw the best of it—but at no time did we wander away from a camp or vehicle. The *wildness* of these animals was fully understood and at all times highly respected.

Our crew was a happy, outgoing bunch, each from a different ethnic tribe. Our leader, Francois, was a tall, handsome Watusi. His family had been evicted from Rwanda and settled in Burundi where Francois had been educated in a French Catholic school. He spoke musical English. The cook, Nick, was of the Chagga tribe. His helper, Tomas, tall and straight, was a Maasai. Juma, our jovial driver, lived in Arusha and was a member of still another tribe. These were the people who made us aware of the importance of "tribe." In Africa, one's ethnic group, not the nation, is the core of one's loyalty. We think often about these insights in light of the African uprisings, bloodshed, and ethnic purging of recent years.

I returned from that trip—a trip on which we'd experienced basic existence and coping—very aware of how much we have in our country and, conversely, how much of the world's population has so little. Have we complicated our lives with too many things? Is more really better? I passed through a perplexing reentry into my own world upon return from this particular journey. It has been recently brought to my attention that our kind of safari is seldom offered any more. Today's travelers, more affluent and less adventuresome, will pay more money, expect more thrills, and get more frills—to the loss of simply being there.

HEADING DOWN UNDER

Australia for its sights and its history as one of the other British penal/indentured servant colonies had long been a place I wanted to see. We also wanted to explore the renowned Great Barrier Reef. We were disappointed in neither. Our trip in 1992 introduced us to my Wessel/Bent cousins; to their lovely Sydney, a sparkling city on a bay much like San Francisco, and to Sydney's world famous, soaring Opera House, a delight to the eye. The trip took us to the newly built Capitol City of Canberra, with its sobering War Museum; to ski-country Australia, where many of our Badger Pass instructors had taught skiing during our summers; to the dignity of Melbourne; and to the fun of Cairns. We sailed, we snorkeled, we explored—and we ate. It was a mellow adventure among a comfortable people. We found their independence, informality and joie de vivre, plus the ability to work hard, quite reminiscent of their counterparts in the American west.

FORAYS AND FRIENDS IN THE FAR NORTH

Charlie had always felt the need to get to Alaska—the last frontier. For me, the forty-ninth state was not even close to the top of my want-to-see list. Oh my, was I wrong. By July of 1994, Charlie had studied, planned, and outfitted us for a trip to the far north. Off we went in our faithful Toyota 4x4 pickup that was to be our home-away-from-home for the next six weeks, equipment loaded inside and bicycles on the back. We and the Toyota ferried up the Inland Passage from Bellingham, Washington, stopping to explore towns along the way as time allowed. A four-day stopover in picturesque Juneau gave us two nights in Glacier Bay, and our first overall, then close-up, view of the magnificent mountains and glaciers. We toured the bay to see glaciers "calving" and whales breaching, to become spellbound. In the lodge dining room one morning, Charles Kurault was quietly having a solitary breakfast in back of us. One cannot fail to recognize that voice—even in the mundane act of ordering of breakfast. A couple of years later we happened onto a cassette narrating his Alaskan adventure—in that same distinctive voice—and we compared journeys.

Our arrival in Skagway meant the end of our water journey, and the Toyota took over. We drove up over White Pass, then dropped down into Atlin, British Columbia to stay three interesting days with Cindy and Wayne Merry, friends from earlier Yosemite days. I was particularly struck by the myriad of hanging flower baskets in Atlin—the glorious rebirth of color after the long, white winter. I also grew to love the vibrant fireweed of Alaska, with its variant pink to brilliant purple shades. It was everywhere.

On we went to historic Whitehorse on the banks of the Yukon River—the gold rush highway of earlier days. We drove the long, gravel miles into McCarthy and the Kennicott copper mine in the heart of Wrangell-St. Elias National Park, and let our imaginations run rampant in these old mining towns. I celebrated my birthday with a picnic on a wildflower-covered hillside overlooking the town of Valdez. Gorgeous mountains, glaciers, and bays. Then on to Seward and Homer, where we found friends in the persons of Tod and Ahna Sharp. Tod is the son of our long-time NPS friends Bob and Betty Sharp and had schooled and skied with ours in Yosemite.

In Anchorage, we had a short visit with Steve Shackelton (another second generation NPS connection), then on to Talkeetna. This stop was a must, since it is historically the jumping off spot, by air, for the climbers of Denali—and so it had been for Anne and Chas in 1978. In Denali National Park, we spent two treasured days at the North Face Lodge on the far side of the park, seemingly right under Denali. We were blest with superb views, perfect weather, plentiful caribou, a few Dall sheep, even a grizzly, and, again some Yosemite-connected friends: Frank Bonaventura, as ever, driving a tour bus, dispensing the best of narratives, and exuding enthusiasm, and Donna and Tom Habecker, now Denali North District Ranger for the NPS.

After a short stop in Fairbanks, the time came to again head south. We decided to connect with the less-traveled Cassiar Highway. Among the highlights of the long drive was a side trip on another long, gravel road into Eagle, an early mining town right on the banks of the Yukon. When the National Park Service created the myriad of new Alaskan Parks in the early eighties, this area became Yukon Charley National Preserve—and Park Service employees became anathema. In self-defense, civilian clothes became the uniform. This was the setting for John McPhee's epic *Coming into the Country.* On to Dawson, further up the Yukon, with its dirt streets, board sidewalks and weathered old buildings. When we finally found writer Robert Service's cabin, a crusty old character seated in an ancient rocking chair was reading from Service's works. *The Crema-tion of Sam McGee* never sounded more authentic.

We reconnected with the Cassiar Highway, and the long drive south on another gravel road began in earnest. After reentering the U.S. in Montana, we slowly wended our way home, reflecting deeply upon this eye-opening adventure, the many Yosemite connections we had found, the time of true togetherness. We echoed these thoughts:

> Wilderness is more than a word—more than an area of land. It is a spirit of our inner self. It adds vitality to our life and provides sanctuary from the problems of a complex society. (Author unknown)

INTO BYZANTIUM

Our trip to Turkey in 1996 was a lesson in ancient history. We were transported to the intrigues and mosques of Byzantium/Constantinople/now Istanbul, to the tales of Troy, and to the marble streets of Ephesus where we walked in the footsteps of Antony and Cleopatra. Absorbing Asia Minor, the crossroads of the world with its written history dating back to the fifth century B.C., takes a real mind adjustment for one from a country having a mere blip of recorded history. Our travel mates were Mary and Ned Barker, who had been on the 1983 Everest support expedition with Charlie. Our guide was Enver (Greg) Lucas who had worked in Yosemite in the seventies and been Charlie's dental patient. We were ten days on a gulet, the lovely polished-wood motor/sailing boat of the Turks. Our group numbered eleven, plus Enver and a crew of three, and we explored the intriguing south coast of Turkey from Kusadasi to Antalya.

We saw ancient Lycian rock tombs carved into cliffsides; we explored seaside villages; we sailed by—and over—ancient ruins, snorkeling through some of them. We parted heavy foliage to visit coastal ruins and climbed high trails to view others. At the end of one such endeavor, we found the intriguing Termessos, or Eagle's Nest, a relatively unexcavated gem on a high, breathtaking hilltop. This was one of two Lycian cities that Alexander the Great failed to capture in his siege of the Persian Empire.

We were also exposed to modern Turkey, with all of its turmoil and hopes. Like the United States, it contains many ethnic groups, but is basically a Muslim country wanting—and striving—to be part of the western democratic world. We came home with a deeper understanding and heightened respect for yet another land. Gule, Gule: go happily Turkey.

IN RETROSPECT

Without my years of living and growing in Yosemite, without the mate who challenged life, himself, and me, I would not have fallen into these adventures. These trips were the frosting on my cake. As I write of the near-fifty years in our Park's history that I was privileged to personally live and know, of its inevitable changes, of the wonderful people with whom I crossed paths, and of the extraordinary beauty that is Yosemite National Park, I am aware that my whole journey has been the adventure of a lifetime. How fortunate I am that it walked into my life that spring day in 1950.

Epilogue

The rise of the Merced River and the flooding of Yosemite Valley, that New Year's Day in 1997, hastened the decline of the Valley community. The story of that decline, the political ramifications, and the hardships inflicted on good people will be another's tale to tell. My story is presented in tribute to the community I was privileged to know.

NOTES

CHAPTER 1
1. This rolled-up carpet had been waiting for delivery and was in the YPCC warehouse during the November flood.
2. Author's note: Charlie Hill was responsible for my Charlie's name change to "Chuck" before I got there to object. Hill thought there were already enough Charlies in the Park. This, however, is my story so I will call him by the name I know.
3. Named for our Assistant Superintendent John Wosky, the arbiter in matters of house appearance.
4. Later moved to the Pioneer Village in Wawona.
5. The Tecoya area later became a part of the Yosemite Village.

CHAPTER 2
1. Pat Phillips Kessler subsequently went far in her nursing career. She became active in various nursing organizations and served on the University of California Board of Regents representing the UCSF campus in the mid-nineties.
2. The Training Center was established to train incoming Park rangers. More on this in Chapter 5.
3. Pre-1950 medical information from: *The Mariposa Sentinel*, Mariposa County Historical Society, Volume XXV, numbers 3, 4, and 5, 1983 YNP Research Library Archives.
4. Dr. Bob Riechers passed away in his Sunriver, Oregon home in March of 1999. We all felt the loss.

CHAPTER 3
1. *Yosemite Sentinel* article: "The Church in the Valley" by Steve Harrison, YNP Research Library Archives.
2. Klister: a gooey pine tar/wax mixture used on the base of cross-country skis to aid in ascents. Climbing-skins were narrow strips of fur-like material strapped onto the bottom of skis for the same purpose. Fishscale skis had a permanent base for cross-country skis which became popular in the seventies.
3. John Preston Correspondence, January 18, 1956 YNP Research Library Archives.
4. A less harried description of the elegant Bracebridge Christmas Dinner, held yearly at the Ahwahnee Hotel, will be offered in the chapter Christmas in Yosemite.

CHAPTER 4
1. From a letter written to Ralph Anderson of the NPS in 1951 YNP Research Library Archives.
2. *Yosemite and Its Innkeepers* by Shirley Sargent, Flying Spur Press, 1975.
3. *Nature Study*, vol. 42, Oct. 1988 YNP Research Library Archives.
4. Pre-1951 information from: *Ansel Adams—A Biography* by Mary Street Allendar, Henry Holt & Co. Inc., 1996 and Anne Adams Helm's *Descendents of David Best....* Self-published, 1995 YNP Research Library Archives.
5. Pre-1951 information from *Yosemite Sentinel* articles YNP Research Library Archives.

6. *Battling for the National Parks* by George B. Hartzog, Jr., Moyer Bell Limited, 1988.

CHAPTER 5

1. *Parks, Politics and the People* by Conrad Wirth, University of Oklahoma Press: Norman, 1980.
2. *Yosemite National Park—Final Prospectus Mission 66*, 917.3 YNP Research Library Archives.
3. Nancy was the daughter of Park engineer Les and Nelle Moe, sister of Maynard and Allen. The Moes lived across the loop from us and were among the first to welcome Charlie into the community. Nancy later married Bob Eckart, son of Elsie Oehlmann.

CHAPTER 6

1. *An Island in Yosemite* by George Harlan, Self-Published, YNP Research Library Archives.
2. Other trail crew foremen included Wes Bolton, Jack Knierieman, Jose Lopez and Tim Ludington.
3. *The History of the Sierra Club* by Michael P. Cohen, Sierra Club Books, SF, 1988.
4. *Letters and Images 1916-1984* by Ansel Adams, Little, Brown and Co., 1988.
5. John Preston Correspondence 1956, 1957, 1958 YNP Research Library.
6. *Tioga Road*—A Yosemite National Park History Association publication, 1961.

CHAPTER 7

1. The three who spearheaded the operation when I was first involved were Elsie Oehlmann, Muriel Ouimet and Mary Proctor. Later, Jan Robinson and Eileen Berrey joined in the purchasing project.
2. *The Ahwahnee—Yosemite's Classic Hotel* by Shirley Sargent, Yosemite Park and Curry Company, 1977.
3. A close friend of my parents, Algernon Angell, sang with the group for many years. Unfortunately, he retired prior to our arrival in the Park. In ensuing years, and until his death at ninety-five, he would call us with Christmas wishes each December and we would reminisce about the Bracebridge festivities. Al's voice and spirit were long felt in our holiday household.

CHAPTER 8

1. Chuck took exception to my writing this, saying he found downing a quick sandwich to get back out on the hill sooner much more to his liking.
2. *Parks, Politics and the People* by Conrad L. Wirth, University of Oklahoma Press, 1980.
3. *Battling for the National Parks* by George B. Hartzog Jr., Moyer Bell, Ltd., 1988.
4. In his autobiography, Hartzog expressed his opinion that the firefall was "as appropriate to the majesty of Yosemite Valley as horns on a rabbit." One wonders how many firefalls he observed, from where, and with whom.
5. *Macaulay Firefall* article, *Sierra Sun Star* edition 3/16/72, YNP Research Library Archives.
6. My brother Robert Polhemus called the firefall from Curry the summer he worked there. It was a considerable claim to fame on his part. He didn't have quite the stentorian voice of David Curry but he gave it all he had as he

bellowed out, "Hello, Glacier." Then to the answering "Hello, Camp Curry" he blasted, "Let the fire fall."

7. When our Rob and Cindy Hadley graduated from the eighth grade in 1969, the Hadleys gave the after-graduation party in their home. Many of the graduates, even some of the parents, had never been in the superintendent's house. It was a gracious and enjoyable evening.

CHAPTER 10

1. *Camp 4—Recollections of a Yosemite Rockclimber* by Steve Roper, The Mountaineers, 1994.

2. A siege climb is one laying fixed ropes up a climb enabling the climber to return to the base of the cliff at any time, to resume climbing at will. These climbers did not have to bivouac on the route's face and could retreat during inclement weather.

3. Press Clipping File, YNP Research Library Archives.

4. *Wilderness Search and Rescue* by Tim Setnika, Appalachian Mountain Club, Boston, 1980.

5. It is interesting to note, these years later, how many in this early climbing group went on to successful business ventures evolving from the sport, be it climbing equipment, clothing, photography or writing.

6. When Anne was in Katmandu, Nepal, in 1982, she was honored to get Maurice Herzog's autograph.

CHAPTER 12

1. *Edward Taylor Parsons Memorial Lodge,* article by Elizabeth S. O'Neill, Tuolumne Meadows Historian, YNP Research Library Archives.

2. *Yosemite and Its Innkeepers* by Shirley Sargent, Flying Spur Press, 1975.

3. Jerry Mernin followed in his NPS father's footsteps, going on to have a long and productive NPS career, his in Yellowstone National Park.

4. The Yosemite Fund has contributed generously to the bear-proof box installation program.

CHAPTER 13

1. Rob later worked for Dillon Gillies at the Ram Restaurant in Sun Valley, Idaho during his stop-out year from UC Davis.

2. Early history gleaned from Martha Miller's self-written biographical notes. Later history came from her résumé and from my recollections.

CHAPTER 14

1. *History of Winter Sports in Yosemite* by Mary Curry Tresidder, 1963. Reprinted in the *Yosemite Sentinel* in November, 1974, YNP Research Library Archives.

2. Personal input from Wayne Merry to author.

CHAPTER 16

1. Frazil ice comes from an interesting phenomenon: in high water, spray from the fall freezes on its way to earth. The woods near us were often full of these white, frothy ice crystals along the stream banks in the spring.

2. This is the name given by our children to the stone bench commemorating the site of John Muir's cabin on the bank of Yosemite Creek.

3. When we first arrived in the Valley the ice rink was the Camp Curry parking area, carefully layered with water, which was frozen by the winter chill. Later a mechanical freezing unit and pipes were obtained from Squaw Valley after the 1960 Olympics and installed behind the Curry Village garages.

4. Also known as the Red Footbridge or Superintendent's Bridge (near the Superintendent's meadow house).

5. Baseball leagues weren't a factor in our kids' growing up. They hadn't entered the Valley scene yet.

CHAPTER 17

1. *A Report on the Hippie Problem and Related Phenomena* by Russell Cahill and Darryl Steele, June 28, 1967, YNP Research Library Archives.

2. Statement of James O'Toole in *1970 Information on Memorial Day, July 4th and Labor Day Weekends*, YNP Research Library Archives, NPS Division of Visitor Protection.

3. *1970 Information on Memorial Day, July 4th, and Labor Day Weekends*, YNP Research Library, NPS Division of Visitor Protection.

4. Ibid.

5. Ibid.

6. Ibid.

7. Russell K. Olsen, YNP Collections File 3415 July 4, 1970 Misc., YNP Research Library Archives.

8. *Riot Echo…* by Ron Taylor, *Fresno Bee* 5/16/71, YNP Research Library Archives.

CHAPTER 18

1. This is the group responsible for law enforcement in and on national park properties in Washington, DC.

2. This type of bridge is used by the military. It is a portable bridge consisting of prefabricated steel sections.

3. Vince Johnson, then just a nuisance to his older brother and the Woessner boys was, however, the one who came back. He now lives in the Valley with wife Carol and their two offspring, working in a law enforcement capacity for the NPS. Coincidentally, Carol works with "our Jeannette" in the dental office for Charlie's successor Dale Soria.

4. 1971 Press clipping file, YNP Research Archives.

5. San Jose *Mercury News*, 8/6/72, H. A. Worthington interview. Press clipping file, YNP Research Library Archives.

6. This was before the instigation of the Wilderness Permit program.

7. Superintendent Reports, YNP Research Library Archives.

8. *Take Down Flag, Feed Horses* by Bill Everhart, University of Illinois Press, 1998.

9. Ibid.

10. *Yosemite and Its Innkeepers* by Shirley Sargent, Flying Spur Press, 1975.

11. *Take Over Threat at Yosemite Park, Business Week* magazine, 6/3/72, 979 447 Y-16 #23, YNP Research Library Archives.

12. *Yosemite: Outdoor Classroom*, Merced *Sun Star*, 12/23/71, YNP Research Library Archives.

13. *A Short History (1971-1996), Upon the 25th Anniversary of the Y.I.* A draft by Donald Rees, Papers of the Y.I., YNP Research Library Archives.

14. This opening of Park doors to an outside educational program was a major

departure from traditional Park policy. Once this policy had been breached, the Yosemite Natural History Association (later called Yosemite Association) stepped up its seminar program, and the Ansel Adams winter photography workshops began.

15. Among this group were Stacey Studebaker, Bob Hansen (now Executive Secretary of the Yosemite Fund), Vince Kehoe, Art Baggett, Marilyn Muse, B.J. Pollan, Vicki Jo Lawsen, Barb Eastman, and Howard Weamer.

16. OSHA: Occupational Safety and Health Administration.

17. Statements of Director Gary Everhardt at a Congressional Hearing on Concessionaire and Planning Activities in YNP, 7/28/75, YNP Research Library Archives.

18. *New York Times* article, 9/6/82, YNP Research Library Archives.

CHAPTER 19

1. *Sierra Club—Southern Sierra* article, 8/9/76, YNP Research Library archives.

2. Forty-eight workshops were set up around the state and 60,000 workbooks were sent out.

3. To many, the desecration of the pristine west end of the Valley by the addition of a large, paved parking area will never be acceptable. "Taft Toe" became the rallying cry. The battle continues on into the new century.

4. This substitution had been made by the new company, was deplored by locals in general, historians in particular, and Shirley Sargeant actively.

5. *Telling Tales From the Sierra*, by Kay Mills, *Los Angeles Times*, 9/15/85, YNP Research Library Archives.

6. *Santa Barbara News-Press* article, 5/29/83, and *Fact Sheet, Julia F. Parker* 921.2, YNP Research Library Archives.

7. *Fresno Bee* article, 1960, Press-clipping collection, YNP Research Library Archives.

8. Conversation with Craig Bates, YNP Museum Curator.

9. *San Francisco Chronicle* article, 8/77, Press-clipping collection, YNP Research Library Archives.

10. *The Great Yosemite Gold Rush* by Galen Rowell. *Audubon Magazine*, 9/77, YNP Research Library Archives.

11. Author aside: No one came to live in Yosemite because of the housing, a fact that has not changed.

12. Into this category I put the Hardys, Grahams, Abbotts and the Goertzens, also the Gehens, Bannons, Meyers and Quigleys. Then came the Welches, Bill Johnstons, Jensens and Pomeroos.

CHAPTER 20

1. Conversation with Bob Roney, then a member of the Badger fire crew, now NPS Senior Interpreter.

2. *The Evolution of NPS Fire Policy,* Jan W. van Wagtendonk, Ph.D. Presented before an International Symposium on *Fire and the Environment: Eco and Cultural Perspectives,* Knoxville, Tennessee, March 1980. Ref/#634-928 N 762, YNP Research Library Archives.

3. *Prescribed Burning,* Harold H. Biswell, Ph.D., U.S. Press, 1989.

4. van Wagtendonk, Jan W., USDI NPS 1988.

5. This flood was touted in the newspapers as being "the one of greatest damage and loss."

6. *The Ground Shook and the Sky Fell,* Jim Snyder, article in *Yosemite—a Journal for Members of the Yosemite Association,* Fall 1996, Vol. 58, No. 4.

CHAPTER 21

1. On Henry Berrey's retirement in the eighties, Steve Medley took the helm of the Y.A., with the title, eventually, of president.

2. *Take Down Flag, Feed Horses* by William Everhart, University of Oklahoma Press, 1998.

3. Ibid.

4. Our neighbor, Jay Johnson, chaired this group, with the active help of Walt Castle, Jim Snyder, Ron Mackie, Chris Becker, Bill Wendt and many others.

5. *Ranger,* Volume IV, #1, Winter 1988, YNP Research Library Archives.

6. *Take Down Flag, Feed Horses* by William Everhart, University of Oklahoma Press, 1998.

7. Bill Germany: long-time YPC employee. In food service management in 1983. Well, he did and the wedding was. Thanks, Bill.

8. Tom Coakley came to Mariposa in the late '50s to assume the Superior Court Judgeship. He and Katherine had been great friends of my parents in the Bay Area, and became important in our lives as well.

CHAPTER 22

1. *Yosemite's Historic Wawona* by Shirley Sargent, Flying Spur Press, 1979.

2. For further historical Wawona information see *Stage to Yosemite* by Anne Reynolds and Albert Gordon, Big Tree Books, 1994.

3. Press Memo 8/18/65 from the office of John Preston, YNP Research Library Archives.

4. In the case of a leaseback, the government purchased the property from the original owner, paying property value at that time. The government then leased the property back to the original owner at a fixed rental fee and for a specific time.

5. *The Lone Ranger* by Jill Hamburg, *California Magazine,* November 1990, YNP Research Library Archives.

6. Traditionally houses in Wawona were referred to as "cabins."

INDEX